performing
the sacred

Engaging Culture

WILLIAM A. DYRNESS
AND ROBERT K. JOHNSTON,
SERIES EDITORS

The Engaging Culture series is designed to help Christians respond with theological discernment to our contemporary culture. Each volume explores particular cultural expressions, seeking to discover God's presence in the world and to involve readers in sympathetic dialogue and active discipleship. These books encourage neither an uninformed rejection nor an uncritical embrace of culture, but active engagement informed by theological reflection.

performing
the sacred

theology and theatre in dialogue

todd e. johnson
& dale savidge

foreword by robert smyth

Baker Academic

a division of Baker Publishing Group
Grand Rapids, Michigan

From Todd:

To the memory of my parents, Glenn Johnson and Helen Johnson, who taught me by their performance of the Christian faith how to behave and act as a disciple and schooled me in faith, hope, and love.

From Dale:

To my wife, Tammy, and my children, Tim, Trish, and Olivia, who have had a part in everything I have ever done of any value.

© 2009 by Todd E. Johnson and Dale Savidge

Published by Baker Academic
a division of Baker Publishing Group
P.O. Box 6287, Grand Rapids, MI 49516-6287
www.bakeracademic.com

Printed in the United States of America

Library of Congress Cataloging-in-Publication Data
Johnson, Todd Eric, 1960–
    Performing the sacred : theology and theatre in dialogue / Todd E. Johnson and Dale
Savidge ; foreword by Robert Smyth.
       p.   cm. (Engaging culture)
    Includes bibliographical references and index.
    ISBN 978-0-8010-2952-3 (pbk.)
    1. Theater—Religious aspects—Christianity. 2. Performing arts—Religious aspects—Christianity. I. Savidge, Dale, 1956– II. Title.
PN2049.J65 2009
264'.72—dc22
                                             2009007647

contents

foreword

I spend much of my life in a black box.

It is a magical place to be. Every few weeks there is a gathering. Someone will bring a Word, someone a Sound, someone Light, another Movement. There is a cascade of collaboration. Something new, something for the moment, is being born.

And then we hold our breath. For this thing is never complete until the audience arrives. And the conversation begins again.

That's the rhythm of my life.

So, it's encouraging when someone writes a good book about it. About the things you care about.

What you are holding is not another "how-to" book, or "let's all do Christian Art" pamphlet; rather, it is a fascinating exploration of the theological dynamics that make the theatre such a vibrant art form. An intriguing look at how the theatre often parallels the quests and questions of theology.

At its center are three lights that keep returning to illuminate the work—incarnation, community, and presence.

Incarnation—the story breathed to life, the word made flesh.

Community—the gathering of live artists, live audience.

Presence—the sense of the holy, the taste of grace. From its beginnings theatre has existed to invoke or examine the transcendent.

At the heart of the theatre is always a story. For people of faith it is also The Story. The Story that lays a foundation of meaning for all other stories.

Because you're reading this I would assume you're interested in the confluence of faith and the larger culture, in ideas and art, in the refreshing impact of stories well told. That you are either a practitioner or an interested participant in the art form.

If you are a theatre artist it will remind you of the rich gift you share: a playground to explore both the hard questions and the immense joys of the human experience; to chart this unique place between angel and animal, the mix of real body and keen spiritual awareness.

If you are an audience member, it will open your eyes wider to the wonders and discoveries to be found in good theatre. Wet your appetite to find more.

It helps too, that both of the authors are invigorated by their faith and really love the theatre. Their excitement is palpable. For Dale and Todd this is a conversation, the sharing of an exploration together.

It's a joy to tag along.

Enjoy the journey.

Robert Smyth
Lamb's Players Theatre
San Diego, California

introduction

Todd and Dale Go to the Theatre

The preliminary work on this book began in June 2005 during a week we spent together in Chicago. That week, Chicago's Lookingglass Theatre Company premiered *Hillbilly Antigone*, a musical reworking of the Sophoclean tragedy. It utilized early country music and melodramatic stage conventions to relocate the ancient conflict between personal conscience and the rule of the state to the Appalachian Mountains and the Hatfield-McCoy feuds. We had the pleasure of attending this show together and reflecting on it over pizza later that night. It's always better to experience theatre with a friend than alone. Theatre is meant to be an experience in community, the community between actors and their audience as well as the community of audience members. Good theatre should be digested after the fact, discussed and reexperienced through conversation and reflection. Doing this is one way of obeying the admonition to "guard the heart": one doesn't avoid difficult subject matter but rather reflects and critiques it after the fact; and it never hurts to have a deep-dish pizza to lubricate the process.

Hillbilly was great fun, a great way to spend a couple of hours—in a beautiful theatre full of enthusiastic people experiencing a quality presentation marked with professionalism from conception to execution. We were reminded, again, how much the theatre experience differs from television or film. It matters greatly that you are in a room with other people, aware of the artists and the audience, fully alive together in both space and time, experiencing something together.

Purists might take exception to the liberties taken with Sophocles' plot in *Hillbilly Antigone*. Others might react to Appalachian stereotypes.[1] *Antigone* is a monumental play, and the time-period relocation forces a reduction in the stature of the story and theme of the original. Nevertheless, Looking-glass Theatre created an entertaining and engaging experience. Generically it was a musical, with a comedic quality not unlike the film *O Brother, Where Art Thou?* another dramatic work derived from Greek mythology. A trio of bluegrass musicians took the role of a Greek chorus. The play read contemporary cultural themes into the Antigone story. Mountain religion (Creon was a Pentecostal preacher in the mountain community) and politics (Creon was played with the inflections of President George W. Bush) intermingled. *Hillbilly Antigone*, while not a perfect theatrical piece, provides a launching pad for introducing the important themes of our book.

Theatre has the ability to communicate multiple streams of content (political, social, religious, personal) on multiple levels (intellectual, emotional, kinesthetic). A multilayered theatre piece such as *Hillbilly Antigone* is challenging and thus richly rewarding. Audience members filter their experience in the theatre through their own political, religious, social, and personal worldviews. We responded, as Christians, to the use of a church as the setting for Pastor Creon's conflict with Antigone. We caught the subtle irony regarding Christianity but also the truth that religious people have been guilty of using religion as a weapon against individuals.

We were reminded again how pleasurable theatre is and also how very significant an experience in the theatre can be. Theatre audiences aren't lulled into being passive receptors; they are awakened and stimulated, made aware of their presence among the actors and other members of the audience. They are confronted with story, character, language, and ideas that engage the emotions and intellect together. Not just the content of the performance (the script, story, etc.) but the total experience can have a profound impact on audiences; for this reason theatre has endured for centuries and continues to thrive even with competition from its electronic offspring. Theatre, as interactive experience, connects with a deep human need for community and for interaction with other humans.

Theatre and Theology in Dialogue

This book began as a dialogue between theologian Todd Johnson and theatre artist Dale Savidge. As we grew in our friendship and as our conversations progressed, we realized that the dialogue wasn't just between us personally; it was between our disciplines. Not only do we have ideas to exchange as friends, but theology and theatre can also learn a great deal from each other.

In addition to speaking the language of our respective disciplines, we are conversant in each other's worlds. While in seminary in Chicago, Todd studied acting and worked as an actor in local theatre there. While an undergraduate, Dale studied theology and only took up theatre later, in graduate school. So part of the pleasure of our conversation is that we can understand and appreciate each other's worlds. We met during a two-year investigation into the role of theatre in contemporary worship, in a program called the Theatre in Worship Initiative, which was directed by Christians in Theatre Arts and funded in part by the Calvin Institute for Christian Worship.

Our starting point is that theatre has theological content: not just the content of the performance but as an art form, theatre uniquely reflects the *imago Dei*, the image of God imbued into humanity. We view theology as a way of knowing about God and as a way of knowing God as disciples and as God's children, and it is our premise that theology can be understood through the lens of theatre and that theatre can be understood through the lens of theology. We take into account the many, varied manifestations of theatre in culture, from script-based performances to improvisation to drama in worship. Neither theatre nor theology is static; both are dynamic, changing, living entities.

The theatre event, of all the arts, uniquely embodies the central tenets of the Christian faith. The fact that live human beings embody the characters of a play speaks of the *incarnate* nature of God in Christ. The fact that the actors perform for a live audience highlights the *communal* nature of theatre and reflects the Trinity: Father, Son, and Holy Spirit in relationship. The fact that the relationship between audience and performer allows for interaction and influence between the two speaks of the *presence* of God transforming the world through nature and grace. We will investigate these three categories and apply them to theatre throughout this book.

Theatre happens in the "here and now." By contrast, narrative forms (novels and stories) happen in the "there and then." Theatre is often a re-presentation of the past, but its essential character is in the present (temporally), and it is physically present to the audience (spatially). Christianity certainly involves the past; the history of our faith is rich with meaning for us. And the Christian faith is lived in the present and in the presence of God. As we progress through this book, we will find many such parallels between theology and theatre.

Theatre and the Christian church haven't always seen themselves as compatible—and that's the first of many understatements in our book. History is replete with examples of suspicion and outright hostility on both sides. Particularly in the West, Christianity has had difficulty with an art so closely tied to the human body. Theatre, for its part, has reacted by retreating from Christianity. We'll explore this antagonism and also examine some encouraging instances of church-theatre collaboration in the twenty-first century.

Some Definitions

Theatre is a branch of the performing arts; as such it is referred to as one of the interpretative (as opposed to creative) arts. Live theatre is a hybrid art form combining the literary arts (scripts) with the plastic arts (physical realities in space and time). We prefer to use the category of narrative art rather than literary art, since theatre may have a narrative without having a script, as in improvisation.[2]

The word "theatre" derives from the Greek *theatron*, which is literally "seeing place." Theatre generally refers to the performance or production aspects of the art. "Drama" derives from the Greek *dromenon*, which is literally "a thing done." It refers to the genre of literature that is written in dialogue (or monologue), is intended for public performance, and is driven by the imitation of an action. A drama is a script that is incomplete until performed in a theatrical production. We use the terms "drama" and "theatre" in these senses throughout this book.

The mode of performance in theatre is "mimesis." In a theatrical performance, the actor who imitates, or takes on another character, is no longer speaking/acting as himself or herself. This is a critical distinction. Jesus told stories, and quite dramatic stories, but we have no indication he ever enacted them. He chose not to assume the role of the characters in his stories, their physical and vocal mannerisms, but rather to speak as himself. Did he use inflections or gestures to heighten the imaginative context of a parable? Possibly, though we have no way of knowing since there is no record of how he spoke, only of what he spoke. But in a theatrical performance we are in the presence of mimesis, the imitation of another reality, and the personality of the actor is subordinated to or subsumed in the character being portrayed.

Further, theatre presupposes a physical reality, the physical presence of actor and audience. We cannot divorce ourselves from our bodies and still remain human. Theatre cannot happen without living bodies sharing time and space together. Theatre, unlike film and television, creates a space for humans to interact in person, in real time, with a circular communication from stage to audience and back to stage. It creates, either for a night or for a season of plays, a community.

Christianity is perhaps harder to define. It is a religion, a way of life, a commitment, a relationship. We use the word "Christian" as a noun, not as an adjective. Christians are people who have entered into a relationship with Christ and have made a commitment to be his disciples. The earliest Christian creed is "Jesus Christ is Lord," and Christians affirm this belief with integrity. Christians believe certain things: that God is triune; that God was revealed in the incarnation, death, and resurrection of Jesus Christ; and that God remains present in this world through the Holy Spirit.

Many kinds of Christians participate in the theatrical community. We do not presuppose any particular type of Christian, by either denomination, worship style, or other expression of Christian belief. Rather, we define Christianity writ large. We are concerned with the inner hub of the faith. Some things in this book will not resonate with all Christians, and we omit some elements of faith-theatre interaction that are peculiar to particular groups of Christians. Our goal is to provide a resource that all Christian disciples will find beneficial; building on the center, we hope that Christians in all corners of Christ's church will find this book useful.

Theatre and Christianity: Intersecting and Integrating

Christianity and theatre have frequently intersected in history. In our own time, Christians are involved in theatre at every level: as academics; as theatre professionals; in ministry; as participants in touring or resident repertory companies, missions, or community theatre, and so on. Ours is a time of harmony between theatre and church, at least to the extent that the church enthusiastically uses theatre for its own ends. However, like much that is produced by the Christian subculture, theatre in church is often drastically different from "the theatre" as a mainstream cultural institution. We will examine how the church handles theatre and how the theatre reflects on the Christian faith.

We speak of theatre and Christianity intersecting, interacting, and integrating. Sometimes a theatrical piece includes all three. Sometimes they intersect; often they collide! Sometimes the theatre integrates Christianity or Christians as subject matter. Christianity is a dominant cultural force in America and in Western culture, and as a cultural activity, the theatre connects with Christianity quite frequently.

The theatre deals with issues of faith, and of Christian faith, far more often and far more seriously than do film or television. A quick search of theatre reviews on the *New York Times* Web site or a glance at the last several issues of *American Theatre* magazine will reveal numerous professional productions of works that engage spirituality and Christianity. Some are attacks on the Christian faith; most are explorations—honest explorations—of faith. This is in contrast to the frequent stereotypical representations of Christians in the electronic media. One need only remember the film *Saved* to see what an easy target conservative Christians make and how superficially a film-maker can present Christianity.

In the winter of 2008, as we completed this book, we could refer to dozens of reviews of theatrical performances that treat the faith, in this decade alone. There is Robert Wilson's *Temptation of Saint Anthony*, a multifaceted adaptation of Gustave Flaubert's novel of the same name, which was part of the Brooklyn Academy of Music Next Wave Festival in the fall of 2004. That same season saw the appearance of Val Kilmer in *The Ten Commandments* in Los Angeles. In the spring of 2005, *Doubt, a Parable* opened at the Manhattan Theatre Club with Cherry Jones and Brian F. O'Byrne taking the stage in a John Patrick Shanley piece "written with an uncanny blend of compassion and detachment."[3] David Rambo's *God's Man in Texas* is frequently produced across the United States, and Tracy Lett's *Man from Nebraska*, a play that continues to be presented in prestigious regional theatres, not only dramatizes its central character's crisis of faith but also suggests a positive resolution to that crisis. Throughout the book we offer many other examples of how the theatre is tackling issues of faith and Christianity.

"Ritual" is another term that occurs frequently in our study. Rituals are predefined patterns of behavior appropriate for given people in given circumstances. For example, one would eat differently at McDonalds than one would at a five-star restaurant. Patterns of dress and behavior are different, though the ritual of eating the meal is similar. A "rite" is a type of ritual performed in a specific time and place, by specific people, and in which the type of behavior is clearly and intentionally different from ordinary behavior. A rite can usually be named: a wedding, a baptism, a funeral.[4] Ritual is the appropriate use of signs, words, and gestures in specific situations. You kiss your aunt; you don't kiss a stranger on the street, even though you might say "hello" to both of them. Theatre uses sign, word, and gesture to tell a story; it is a specific rite, a rite of storytelling, a rite of entertainment. Through signs, words, and gestures, we tell a story by becoming a story.

The Context for This Book

Performing the Sacred is not the first book to address the relationship between theatre and faith. Previous treatments have taken either historical or practical approaches. Some begin with the relationship between theatre and religion in ancient Greece or Egypt, follow that thread to medieval Europe and the Church's use of theatre to illustrate biblical stories, on to various antitheatrical attitudes among the Reformers and the Puritans, into the twentieth century and the new medievalism of the contemporary church and the embrace of theatre as one way among many to connect with culturally savvy congregants. History is a good teacher. It is also a humbling teacher, because there really is "nothing new under the sun." Any application of theatre in worship today is derived, consciously or not, from something tried by the church in earlier years.

Practical books about theatre and Christianity sometimes take a "how to" approach, which is often nothing more than adding Christian language to chapters found in any theatre appreciation text. Techniques for directing or lighting are pretty much the same whether they are used in a church, a community theatre, or a school. Certainly there are ethical/moral dimensions to the actor-director relationship that the Christian faith can illuminate. Often these are accepted in mainstream theatre practice because they work, not because they derive from an authoritative text, such as the Bible. Other practical books identify various applications of theatre to the practice of Christianity. Some create taxonomies of religious drama; others lay out methods for using theatre in worship. You can peruse the bibliography for examples of these books.

Most of these historical and practical books treat the relationship between Christianity and theatre on a superficial level. Rarely do they probe below the surface. We should not be surprised. It is a characteristic of contemporary (early twenty-first-century) Western Christians to be utilitarian and pragmatic—indeed, this is a characteristic of the culture in which we live and to which we minister. No argument is necessary; evidence of our infatuation with quick solutions and shortcuts abounds. People can live their entire lives on the fast track, never taking time to reflect on what it means to live. People can live their Christian faith in the same way, quickly and efficiently, but deaf and blind to the movement of the Spirit around them.

Be Still, and Know That I Am God

Theatre is an art form that, even when performed at a crisp pace, allows for reflection and contemplation. It slows down life. It isn't a loud assault on the senses.[5] This may explain why many theatre artists are also baseball fans, a sport said to compress twenty minutes of excitement into three hours of playing time. The ability to sit still and be quiet for theatre (and to a greater degree for grand opera) is militated against by a culture that rewards speed and volubility. Baseball games now feature inter-inning extravaganzas and pulsing rock music to keep the fans from becoming restless. Likewise, rock music tributes are some of the most popular shows on Broadway, season after season.

Case in point: the recent Broadway production of *Faith Healer*, by Brian Friel, is a two-hour-plus series of four, thirty-five-minute monologues. None of the three characters speaks to the others; they talk directly to the audience for thirty-five minutes at a time. The original cast—Ralph Fiennes, Cherry Jones, and Ian McDiarmid—was spectacular, but the required stillness was, even for a theatre lover, an exercise in discipline. The play will likely never, in its current form, be made into a movie. The experience of theatre, like the experience of God, invites stillness and quietness.

Near the end of Thornton Wilder's *Our Town*, Emily Webb, the young girl at the center of the story, asks: "Do any human beings ever realize life while they live it?—every, every minute?" The Stage Manager answers immediately, "No," and then pauses before he continues: "The saints and poets, maybe—they do some."[6] Emily has died; she has been allowed to revisit a day in her life and is now returning to the grave. From her new perspective she recognizes the significance of life, and she longs for the living to see it with her. Art and religion are the activities that give humans that perspective: "saints and poets" provide the path. When theatre and Christianity intersect, the potential for spiritual insight coupled with Truth is formidable.

The distinction of this book is its attempt to view the theatre experience in light of Christian theology and to examine the central tenets of Christian theology through the lens of the theatre. We suggest a symbiotic connection between theatre and Christianity: they are not just similar; rather they share major commonalities at the core of their existences. The essential elements of theatre and the essential elements of Christianity—incarnation, community, and presence—are congruent. We confirm these similarities throughout this book, and at the end we explore the significance of this fact.

This book is written for people who make theatre (actors, directors, designers, ministers, liturgists, etc.) and for people who experience theatre (audiences and congregations). It is also an appeal to Christians who are not artists or audiences to return to this ancient art that so closely models the Christian faith. It is an appeal to Christians who aren't artists to benefit from the contemplative life of the artist, to slow down, lower the volume, and experience what life and faith consist of below the surface. It is not a call to the life of an ascetic, one withdrawn from the life of the senses; the purpose of contemplation and reflection is to strengthen us for a productive life in society and culture. Theatre as an endeavor and an experience teaches us vital attributes of the Christian faith and what it means to be fully human, fully alive and present, and created in the image of God, who is always present.

Hillbilly Antigone 2005

Earlier we commented on the multiple levels on which theatre affects an audience: political, social, religious, personal. *Hillbilly Antigone* worked on all these levels. The politics of dictatorial power mingled with the politics of mountain families and with authoritarianism in primitive religious sects. Creon was cast as a power-hungry megalomaniac at every level of life in the village. As audience members, we not only observed these various communities on stage (the families, the village); we became our own community (the audience—mingling at intermission), and we entered into a relationship with the actors, forming a community in the theatre. There was a sense that we were contributing, that the performance was relying on our attention and reaction, that how we received it *mattered*. We were in community at every level.

This production combined a historically significant piece of literature from fifth-century-BCE Greece with a familiar American cultural context, that of early twentieth-century Appalachia, staged with conventions derived from nineteenth-century melodrama and experienced by an audience removed in space and time from all three of those cultures. And yet it worked! We had both seen the film *O Brother, Where Art Thou?* and the similarities with *Hillbilly Antigone* were immediately apparent. So were the differences. We were within a few feet of living human characters, with guns and knives so close we could have been threatened by them. The sound of the gunshots had a physical presence, and the violence and affection between the characters was palpable. There was a distinct and appropriate absence of special effects or realistic spectacle. The show was homespun and earthy, not virtual or prepackaged. It incarnated the story. We were present to the story, and the storytellers were present to us.

Good theatre addresses issues of ultimate concern: life and death, relationships, family, survival. There is a sense that what is happening matters, that our lives depend on it and we'd better pay attention. This was certainly the case with *Hillbilly Antigone*. The show was enacted with certain rituals front and center: the staging of church, the routines associated with Pentecostal worship, a funeral service, primitive snake handling and strychnine drinking, and so on. There were also the familiar rituals of family: meals, courtship, birth, and death. By enacting these rituals in our presence, in the community established with the audience, the actors drew us into the story empathetically and kinesthetically, as well as intellectually and emotionally.

We have begun a conversation, and now we invite you into our conversation. You'll "hear" us speak separately (Todd wrote chapters 2 and 3, and Dale wrote chapters 1, 4, and 5), and you'll "hear" us dialogue in the conclusion. Enjoy the conversation: agree, disagree, but by all means please join in. It is our hope that people of faith and people of the theatre will engage in a rich and fruitful dialogue—because we really do have something to learn from each other.

a survey
of christianity
and theatre
in history

Dale Savidge

At no time in history was the relationship between theatre and Christianity warmer than during the medieval period in Europe. By the fourteenth century, nearly every European country had experienced some form of religious drama, such as the mystery cycles in England or the plays of Hrosvitha in Germany. The *auto sacramentales* in Spain, one-act religious plays dealing with the celebration of the Eucharist, came later, during the Spanish golden age, and were as popular in their time as musical theatre is today. Pedro Calderón de la Barca, an ordained Catholic priest and one of the greatest Spanish playwrights of all time, penned one of these *autos* in 1649, *The Great Theater of the World*. In this remarkable mix of biblical and allegorical drama, God, identified as the "Author," begins by calling the World to perform "the Play of Life."

> Author: Now, therefore, World, order thy stage and the settings place, and gather together appropriate properties. I will then appoint rehearsals, and thou—from first to last—shall be the Great World's Theater, and Man the cast.[1]

What follows is a drama about life and the drama of life. Various characters are called forth; they are assigned their roles and given their appropriate costumes and stage properties. Each one acts according to his role: the rich man, a king, a peasant, a beggar, and a child. Wisdom and Beauty also make an appearance. The comingling of allegory and realistic dialogue (as when the beggar and the peasant complain about their lot in life and in the play) causes us to see our own lives as part of a great cosmic drama, under the directorial control of the Creator.

> Author: It matters not what part a man doth play in Life's great Drama. What he must do is play the best he can the part that's given him. And when the play is over, Beggar and King shall once again be equals, and shall be judged as equals.[2]

God, the Author, calls this play "Do Good, for God is Good," and that moral is reinforced throughout the drama. The setting is two globes: God is seated on "the throne of glory" in one; the other, where the characters play their roles, has two doors: a cradle where they enter and a coffin where they exit. God authors and directs the play and also sits as the audience for its enactment. God says, "This play I have devised for my enjoyment."[3] At the end Beauty and the Peasant are invited to "the Table's mystery ineffable," and God calls all creation to "low kneel before this sacred Bread" and "praise God's holy majesty, the Author of the World."[4] When we recall that the *auto sacramentales* were performed during the Feast of Corpus Christi (the annual celebration of the Eucharist as the body and blood of Christ), we see clearly the close relationship between theatre and theology in them. As we shall see, historically and theologically, the connections between sacraments and theatre run deep.

The Great Theater of the World is one of many historical examples of how the art of theatre, and the institution of theatre, have intersected with Christian faith. As we look back at this interaction, we should consider that our reflections will be conditioned by who we are and what we believe, by our worldview; it's impossible to be totally objective in reading history. In this short study, we look through the lens of the Christian faith (in particular three theological categories: incarnation, community, and presence) to examine the interaction of theatre and Christianity.

Examining theatre history presents many challenges, not the least of which is the gathering of evidence. Theatre is an ephemeral art that is experienced in a specific and unrepeatable time and place. You may experience a second performance of Calderón de la Barca's play, for example, but although the play text may be unchanged, the performance will be different by virtue of the change of cast, director, designers, and so on. Even if the second performance is by the same company, the actors will make alterations in their performance because the audience is different. Such is the dynamic nature of theatre; such also is the dynamic nature of life.

The artifacts of theatre history include play texts; remains of theatre buildings; eyewitness accounts of actors, scenery, costumes, and other visual elements; and firsthand descriptions of plays in performance. Theatre that intersects with the Christian faith does not often use the technical elements of theatre any differently than secular theatre does. It follows that many studies of theatre history and the church are rooted in the dramas, the texts, of representative periods.[5]

A chronological approach is the most popular method of arranging theatre history. Such an approach, based on Enlightenment historiography, assumes there are major historical divisions in the progression of the theatre. These divisions may be centuries, countries, reigns, art movements, genres, and so on.[6] It presumes a forward movement, from unsophisticated to polished, from primitive to refined. For example, theatre history begins in primitive Egyptian and Greek ritual and matures into the literary masterworks of classical Greek civilization. After the dark period of the Middle Ages, theatre reaches a golden age in the Renaissance with the plays of Shakespeare and his contemporaries. As the world becomes more sophisticated, so too drama evolves in complexity. At the same time, theatrical production borrows from the Industrial Revolution to become the multifaceted creature it is today. Needless to say, this method has come in for vigorous, and deserved, critique in the last few decades. Is the highly complex and technological experience we associate with professional/commercial theatre better than the ancient rituals of preliterate Greece or the traditional theatre of Asian countries?

Alternative methodologies, including revisionist historiography (feminist, ethnic, political, etc.) and structural/semiotic approaches, offer other ways of reading theatre history. Richard Southern regards primitive and refined examples of theatre as chronologically simultaneous and critically on a par with each other.[7] He views the ritual/theatre of remote tribes that continues well into this century as a "phase" of theatre distinct from technologically sophisticated theatre—Broadway, for example. One is not an improvement on the other; the primitive is not striving for the sophisticated. Rather they differ in kind. Southern then distills theatre in any of the seven phases into the two elements necessary for *any* theatrical event: the actor and the audience. The "essence" of theatre is thus a player and someone to experience the performance; a story for the player to tell is also assumed. Everything else (a formal script, scenery, costume, etc.) is a welcome but not essential accoutrement of the interaction of actor and audience.

It is important to recognize the reduction of theatre to these essentials, if for no other reason than to counter the tyranny of the text (to borrow a phrase from Antonin Artaud). The study of theatre history is not only the study of dramatic genres; limiting theatre (performance) to drama (text) blinds us to many lively and important examples of theatre, including some in the Old Testament and others during the Middle Ages. It also guides the exploration of the *origins* of theatre, a subject that has significance for our conversation. It has become commonplace in theatre history texts to locate the roots of theatre in ritual, and from that to extrapolate theories of theatre that focus on the two common elements of religion and theatre: narrative and ritual. In this historical survey we focus on ritual as a source of theatre and as a phenomenon sharing similarities with theatrical performance.

In our reading of theatre history, we need to consider both text-based theatre and those performances that may not have a text. That is, some theatre issues primarily from story and drama; other theatre foregrounds the performance and makes the text just one of many components in the theatrical experience (mime, dance, etc.). It's tempting for Christians, as people of the *Logos*, to value text-based theatre over other types of performance, but we want to avoid that bias in our survey. We see some theatre emerging from the need to tell stories, and we see some emerging from what Aristotle called the mimetic instinct, the tendency for humans to imitate and role-play.

The Ritual Origins of Theatre in the Ancient World

The Birth of Theatre in Primitive Ritual

The relationship between theatre and ritual is complex; it differs according to cultural norms and periods. For example, when you attend a performance of a realistic play from the modern period, you may not sense any ritual in it. The characters are like people from the real world, acting and speaking realistically in the context of the conflict that the author has created. But if you were to attend a performance of Chinese theatre, such as the Peking Opera, you would grasp its connection to the traditions and religion of the Chinese, and you'd have a strong sense that what you were experiencing was not just a play but a ritual. The presence of singing and dancing, elevated beyond the conversational use of the voice and the body, together with the environment and the story, would mark the experience as something other than theatre, even though it would be using the resources of theatre.

In this chapter we explore the relationship between ritual and theatre from a historical perspective. There is widespread acceptance that the first great age of formal theatre, the fifth century BCE in Greece, derived from the ritual worship of Greek gods, especially the god Dionysus. Some scholars believe this connection is textual, that Greek drama developed from dithyrambs, choral odes to the gods. The English word "tragedy" comes from the Greek *tragoida*, which is literally translated "goat song." (The Greeks sacrificed goats in their worship of Dionysus.) Others see a connection with shamanistic rituals performed by a person under the control of spiritual forces; this theory emphasizes the performance more than the texts being performed. The theatre buildings used by fifth-century Greek playwrights were descendents of temples dedicated to the gods. Yet other scholars view theatre and ritual as two manifestations of performance. Some performance tended toward "entertainment" (theatrical performance), and some tended toward "efficacy" (ritual with an intended outcome), but both ritual and theatre were performative activities.[8]

The Cambridge School of Anthropology (CSA) was articulated around 1912–14 by a group of English anthropologists, using archaeological and literary evidence. This school suggested that both the genre of tragedy (the literature of the stage) and the medium of theatre (the performance of that literature) had their roots in religious myth and ritual. (In 1927 A. W. Pickard-Cambridge called much of the CSA scholarship into question. He found no evidence of preexistent rituals that might have led to theatre or of extant Greek tragedies that manifested ritual roots.)[9] The CSA theory posited that ritual developed into drama as the magical element of the ritual weakened in the face of declining belief, as the mimetic element grew and the participants were divided between performers and spectators, and as myths were replaced by heroic sagas. Historians of theatre have noticed a similar movement from sacred to secular in the medieval theatre.

The CSA theory suggested an *ur*-ritual (or primordial ritual) centered on the birth-death-rebirth of a god. This basic alternation of death and life is found in myths across cultures and centuries: death as a necessary prelude to life. This pattern is clearly an archetype for many religious ceremonies. Aristotle's *Poetics* names two sources of tragedy: the aforementioned dithyramb and the *satyrikon* (a joyful paean to the rebirth of the god). This ritual structure also has a seasonal context: death in winter followed by rebirth in spring, growth in summer, and decay in fall leading to another death. It isn't hard to see how our own use of theatre in church follows a similar pattern; Christmas (birth) and Easter (death and rebirth) are prime occasions for dramatic celebrations.

Other theorists drew attention to the performance medium rather than the texts. William Ridgeway cited examples of ritual performances from Burma, China, Japan, and Africa and recognized in them "the doctrine that the actor was originally a medium."[10] Ernest T. Kirby developed his shamanist theory of acting by focusing on the performative act. Underlying this approach to the origin and essence of theatre as a medium of performance is Aristotle's observation that imitation is an activity intuitive to humans. People, even and especially as children, tend to imitate and role-play in life. This inherent tendency supposedly led to the use of the mimetic (i.e., theatrical) in religion and later in art. In her chapter titled "The Primitive Theater," Margot Berthold traces "the roots of shamanism as a particular psychological 'technique' of early hunting cultures" through thousands of years in human history.[11] According to Berthold, shamans are religious leaders who are believed capable of entering a trancelike state and channeling spirits from other worlds into the presence of the participants.

Shamans are, of course, not actors; what they purport to do is very real to them and to those gathered in their presence. Whether one can trace the origins of theatre to shamanistic ritual or not (and it is impossible to prove either with the available evidence), we do not treat theatre as an act of incarnating spiritual forces, be they holy or unholy, in the presence of communicants gathered for the express purpose of experiencing a magical/spiritual event. Still, there is a transcendent quality in the act of mimesis that creates an encounter with something beyond simple human interaction.

Eli Rozik critiques ritual theory by asking why it continues to attract both scholars and practitioners of the theatre: "In my view, the only answer is that it is a matter of a metaphorical aura that, for romantic reasons, people wish to attribute to theatre. This metaphorical aura is supposed to lend theatre a numinous quality that not only does it not always radiate, but that perhaps less than anything else defines its nature."[12] He rightly cautions against a sentimental embrace of the ritual origins of theatre.

Christians legitimately look for traces of the spiritual in every human activity. But theatre and religion are not identical pursuits. Without doubt, some theatre touches on religious concerns, some theatre creates a ritualized environment, and for a believer in a religion the act of creating or experiencing theatre may be a religious experience. It is also true that religious ritual may be theatrical; however, it is always performative. But to equate the medium of theatre with the practice of a religion is reductive and confusing. Christians need not approach theatre as religion in order to value it as artists or audience members.

We will see later in this chapter that the shaman theory of theatrical origins has also evolved into a position on the essence of theatre in the work of Artaud and his successors. When we take up the twentieth century and the work of several avant-garde directors, we will see this theory in practice.

Theatre in the Bible: Old and New Testaments

It is a surprise and a mystery why books on the relationship of the Christian faith and the theatre fail to begin with or even touch on activities of the ancient Israelites that were either theatrical or actually theatre.[13] Although there is no evidence that Old Testament Jews built theatres, one need not have a theatre building to have theatre. Evidence of dramatic structure can be found in at least three biblical books, and there are further examples of theatrical performances among the prophets. We will look at biblical evidence of theatre as an adjective as well as a noun: activities that are theatrical in nature as well as theatre per se.

In his *Religious Drama: Ends and Means*, Harold Ehrensperger makes only passing reference to the ancient Israelites, referring to them as one of the "nontheatrical races."[14] Other drama-ministry handbooks do not mention them at all.[15] It is not surprising that theatre history written by secularists makes dismissive, if any, reference to the theatrical traditions of the Israelites. A recent article in the *Quodlibet Journal* notes the apparent absence of drama/theatre references in the Old Testament;[16] the author reached this conclusion by perusing the *Hodder Dictionary of Bible Themes*. We need to go beyond simple word searches to probe this topic. Robert Webber offers an excellent survey of the theatrical nature of Hebrew worship in which the relationship of the worshipers to God was not merely stated but was also acted out.[17]

Theatre studies divide the discipline many ways, but one metadivision is "formal dramatics" versus "informal dramatics." The former refers to the act of rehearsing a piece of theatre, usually a play script, for presentation to an invited audience; that is, a product is prepared and delivered. The latter, often called creative or educational dramatics, refers to the process of role-playing (either with a play script or in improvised situations) with no intention of presenting the work to an invited audience; the participants are both actors and audience.

Some striking examples of informal dramatics can be found in the history books of the Old Testament. Some of the people in these narratives role-play in order to deceive. For example, notice David's mad behavior in 1 Samuel 21 (which is eerily similar to Hamlet's "antic disposition") and Joab's instruction to the wise woman in 2 Samuel 14. In 1 Kings 20, the prophet of God takes on the role of a wounded man in order to bring a message from God to the king. But these incidents may be taken as simply role-playing or even deception in life, not as examples of creative dramatics.

A clearer incident, which does take us into the realm of educational or informal dramatics, is the meeting between Elisha and the king of Israel in 2 Kings 13. Here the prophet has a message to deliver: "you will strike Syria *only* three times" (v. 19b). But instead of simply delivering this message verbally, beginning in verse 15 the prophet instructs the king to play out the message, to enact the word that God was bringing to him. With great detail the author records how Elisha directs the king to shoot an arrow, even going so far as to place his hands on the king's hands. He then instructs the king to strike the arrows on the ground, and after the king does so three times, the message is delivered. This is known in Hebrew culture and language as an *ot*, an important manner in which Hebrews communicated. It involved using the whole body and enacting the message as well as speaking it.

It is a short step from this story to the creative use of role-playing in religious education classes, where students are asked to act out the Scriptures in place of an instructor reading and teaching them through a lecture. In Jeremiah 13, God uses creative dramatics to teach the prophet. The message is delivered verbally in verse 8, but over a period of "many days" God takes Jeremiah through a series of actions with a linen loincloth that vividly signify the message to be delivered. Later in the book, in chapter 19, Jeremiah is instructed to illustrate a message of judgment with the breaking of a prop, a potter's earthen flask, in the sight of his audience. In Jeremiah 24, two baskets of figs become enacted symbols of God's dealing with his people and his enemies. In chapter 27, "bonds and yokes" are used in much the same manner.

We shouldn't overlook the significance of God using the medium of interactive role-playing to communicate with people. This is the same God who created humanity in God's own image, an image that must surely encompass the inclination to create. Made in the image of the Creator, we are creative. Further, one manifestation of this impulse to create is the use of mimetic activity, acting, as a means of communication outside a formal structured presentation to an audience. Creative dramatics have been extended beyond education to psychodrama, drama therapy, and counseling sessions.[18]

The Old Testament also records examples of formal dramatics, theatre prepared for presentation to an audience. Historians tend to overlook ancient Israelite theatre because the Jews didn't build permanent structures for the presentation of plays. We have noted that the theatres of the ancient Greeks in the ninth through sixth centuries BCE were primarily arenas for religious rituals in honor of the god Dionysus. It is possible that the tabernacle and later the temple housed performances of Old Testament stories in much the same way that the medieval church welcomed liturgical dramas in the tenth and eleventh centuries CE. The New Testament Greek word for "tabernacle" is *skena*, which is etymologically related to the classical Greek word *skene*, the scene house of the ancient Greek theatre. The *skene* was originally a tent or booth. Both words carry the connotation of a dwelling place, in particular a place where a god would dwell with humans. Hence, in John 1, Jesus is declared to have "tabernacled" (*eskanosen*—literally "pitch a tent") among us. It is a central tenet of the Christian faith that God, who is a spirit utterly "other" than creation, chose to dwell in the created world through the incarnation of the Son in time and now through the indwelling of the Spirit in the hearts of Christians.

Recent studies have theorized that the stories collected in the Bible, recorded for us as historical narratives, may originally have been performed in Hebrew worship. This argument is supported by the fact that the culture of the ancient Israelites, at least until the time of Joshua, was built on an oral tradition (note that in Josh. 1:8 he is told to adhere to "this book of the law" [NRSV]—the first instance in the Bible of a person being instructed to follow a book; previously God's servants waited to hear his voice audibly). Such performances may have employed storytelling, with a single speaker maintaining his own personality while relaying the story through voice and gesture. Or they may have involved an ensemble of actors imitating the characters of the stories in a performance encased in the worship rituals.

Suggesting that the biblical account was acted does not in any way diminish the historical veracity of its content. Whether the Jews heard the story of Moses and the burning bush read by a speaker or watched it acted out by an ensemble of priests would not have changed their acceptance of it as a historical event that occurred in a real time and place. In "Drama and the Sacred: Recovering the Dramatic Tradition in Scripture and Worship," theologian Tom Boogaart suggests several reasons for believing that the stories of the Old Testament were originally enacted in Hebrew worship. He interprets the structure of the stories, with their division into scenes and an Aristotelian "beginning, middle, end" sequence, as indicative of their dramatic quality. The centrality of conflict, an essential element of drama, also points to their inherent theatricality. Boogaart and Jeff Barker, a playwright and director, have put this thesis to the test in a series of performances of Old Testament stories called *And God Said*.[19]

That the stories of the Bible are dramatic and lend themselves to the stage has long been understood and capitalized on by theatre artists. On stage and on film, the great conflict that follows the fall from grace in Genesis 3 is at the root of all dramatic material. It might even be argued that if human beings existed in the absence of sin, at peace with creation and one another, there would be no drama. But the presence of dramatic quality does not constitute proof positive that the Hebrews staged these stories as theatrical events, and the absence of archaeological evidence of at least a stage (in physical ruins or in the biblical record of the tabernacle and the temple) means that this theory is not provable.

Still, Christians should celebrate, embrace, and experiment with the dramatic material found in their Scriptures. Apart from the narratives in the historical books of the Bible, scholars often point to the book of Job as an example of biblical drama; it is, after all, a Wisdom book, not a historical book. The story is structured much like a Greek tragedy (or rather, Greek tragedies are structured much like the story of Job, a story that predates them by several centuries). There is an opening scene of conflict, or agon, followed by the middle chapters in which a chorus (Job's three friends) explores the nature of his suffering, and a resolution in the final chapters by the intervention of God. The Greeks would have called this divine intervention a deus ex machina, or a contrived ending, but Christians recognize it as the right of a sovereign God to shape the destiny of God's people. Job is a Hebrew apologetic, a lament; it parallels tragedy but wasn't written as a tragedy. Its purpose was to illustrate that speech to God supersedes speech about God: prayer trumps theology. Further exploration of this dramatic book might pursue these questions: Does Job suffer justly or unjustly? What is the role of irony in the story? How does his pathos, his passion, reveal the role of God in the world of Job? The student of this great story who has also studied the Greek theatre of the fifth century BCE will find many obvious parallels in the book of Job.

The translators of the New International Version of the Bible approached the Song of Songs, a poem describing the beauty and pleasure of physical love, as a drama. The verses are laid out in dialogue form, with speakers assigned, thus making it suitable for performance. Several dramatic adaptations of the Song of Songs, for example, *The Greatest Song*, by Calvin Seerveld, have exploited the theatricality of this book. *The Dramatized Old Testament* is a two-volume collection of NIV texts arranged for performance. It was originally published as *The Dramatized Bible* in England and used in many Anglican churches.[20] In his preface the editor, Michael Perry, writes:

> We like to think that further encouragement is given to the exercise of dramatizing the Bible for worship by one special discovery. It does appear that the Hebrew people in temple worship used drama to rehearse the acts of God in their history—notably the crossing of the Red Sea and their deliverance from the slavery of Egypt. Such dramatic presentations were not entertainment—though they would have been marvelously entertaining. And they were far more than visual aids—though Hebrew faith did require each generation to recall before the next, God's saving interventions, so that his mercy and his demands would not be forgotten. The Hebrew dramas had a teaching role, and they were acts of worship too—precedents of our own "anamnesis," that is, the calling to mind of the saving work of Christ in the drama we term, ac-

cording to our Christian tradition, the Lord's Supper, the Holy Communion/ the Eucharist, the Mass.[21]

In Perry's comments both the apologetic need ("special encouragement") and the leap to performance are evident. He goes on to find in certain psalms, especially number 118, further evidence of biblical performances.

Earlier in this section, we discussed examples of informal dramatics among the prophets Jeremiah, Elisha, Ezekiel, and others. In some of these same books, we can find instances of formal, theatrical presentations. These are not strictly text-based performances, and this is another distinction to bear in mind as we look for evidence of highly structured theatre among the ancient Israelites. Not only do we find informal dramatics, role-playing not intended for formal performance, but we also find theatre unaccompanied by a script or even words. This is mime, and the word itself derives from the Greek word that describes the method of telling a story through the use of mimesis, or imitation. It is certainly a step removed from storytelling in that the actor (from the Greek word *hupokrite*, lit. "answerer" or "mask wearer") takes on another character—he or she wears a mask figuratively if not literally.

The clearest example of mimetic performance in the prophetic literature is found in Ezekiel 4. The speaker in this chapter is God, who becomes both author and director of the performance that the prophet will be called upon to enact (anticipating the Author in Calderón de la Barca's *Great Theater of the World*). In verses 4 through 8, we can see the planning for this theatrical performance:

You also, son of man, take a clay tablet and lay it before you, and portray on it a city, Jerusalem. Lay siege against it, build a siege wall against it, and heap up a mound against it; set camps against it also, and place battering rams against it all around. Moreover take for yourself an iron plate, and set it *as* an iron wall between you and the city. [This is the scenic background for the performance.] Set your face against it, and it shall be besieged, and you shall lay siege against it. This *will be* a sign to the house of Israel. [Ezekiel's performance utilized a multiplicity of theatrical signs; today the study of such signs is called semiotics.]

Lie also on your left side, and lay the iniquity of the house of Israel upon it. *According* to the number of the days that you lie on it, you shall bear their iniquity. For I have laid on you the years of their iniquity, according to the number of the days, three hundred and ninety days; so you shall bear the iniquity of the house of Israel. And when you have completed them, lie again on your right side; then you shall bear the iniquity of the house of Judah forty days. I have laid on you a day for each year. [This is the stage movement, or blocking, for the performance.]

Therefore you shall set your face toward the siege of Jerusalem; your arm *shall be* uncovered, and you shall prophesy against it. And surely I will restrain you so that you cannot turn from one side to another till you have ended the days of your siege. [These are further references to blocking and to costume.] (Ezek. 4:1–8)

Nowhere is any text given to the prophet to speak; his actions will say all that is necessary. God's control of this performance extended even to telling the actor what to eat. Ezekiel 5 and 12 contain other mimetic performances by this prophet, but chapter 4 is a clear demonstration that the ancient Israelites were acquainted with theatrical performance; they had texts in their tradition that were formatted in dialogue and others that may have been performed in their worship.

I have also spoken by the prophets, and I have multiplied visions, and used similitudes, by the ministry of the prophets. (Hosea 12:10 KJV)

This is a most striking statement by the God of the prophets. It reveals God's chosen methods for prophetic communication, and included among them are "similitudes." The Hebrew word here is *Damah*, which is translated "to be like." It is also translated "compare" and is connected to the New Testament "parable." A parable is a story "laid beside" a truth. The prophets foreshadow the use of parables in the New Testament by these mimetic performances, which God not only used but inspired and directed.

In the New Testament there is an example of the informal dramatics used by the prophets (Acts 21:10–11), and the Lord's use of parables is often cited in support of Christian participation in theatre. The mere presence of story, however, doesn't indicate theatrical performance; nowhere are we told that Jesus acted out the parables that he told. Furthermore, it is stated that he turned to parables only after the multitudes refused his message and his messianic claims (Matt. 13:13). Our modern penchant for simplifying truth, for illustrating it and making it palatable to those who have no inclination to receive it, is not illustrated in the parabolic ministry of Christ. Indeed, should we seek biblical methods as patterns for our own, we might be inclined to stage more theatre like that of Ezekiel and Jeremiah.

There is no record, in Scripture or tradition, of Jesus having attended or acknowledged the theatre of his day, if there was theatre to be seen in Palestine in the first century CE. Rome certainly constructed theatre buildings, but Roman drama paled in comparison to the Greek drama. It is not at all clear that the plays of Seneca, considered to be the greatest tragedian of the Roman Empire, were even staged during his lifetime. If this was true in Rome, the capital of the empire, it was more so in the far-flung provinces under Roman occupation. It is no surprise that we have no record of Jesus's attitude toward the theatre of the Roman Empire.

The only reference Jesus makes to anything theatrical is when he calls the Pharisees "hypocrites," a word derived from the Greek *hupokrite*. As noted earlier, this translates literally into "mask wearer"; it has come to denote a person who tries to pass as someone other than who he or she is. Jesus applies the term pejoratively to religious leaders who wore masks of piety, covering their true characters in order to deceive the populous. Nowhere does Christ mention actors, the relationship of his followers to theatrical entertainment, or the role of drama in his kingdom. We should not be surprised, however, since he gives no direct commands in regard to many other cultural activities (literature, the arts, music, politics, etc.).

We do have one striking example of Jesus acting. In Luke 24, we have the account of his resurrection appearance on the road to Emmaus. Cleopas and another disciple were on the road when they were approached by Jesus. They engaged in conversation for a while, and at some point Jesus "acted as though He were going farther" (Luke 24:28 NASB). This dissimulation caused the disciples to invite Jesus to dinner, where they recognized him as he was breaking the bread. Jesus could have revealed himself or just followed them to dinner, but he chose to act as if he were continuing down the road in order to draw them to himself.

There are many more evidences of theatre and drama in the Bible to explore; we hope we've opened the door for you to see the possibilities. Further exploration might provide you an apologetic for working in the theatre, if you need one, or it might awaken your imagination to ways you can involve theatre in the expression of your faith.

Philosophical Attitudes toward Theatre within and without the Church

As Christians interested in positive church-theatre relations, we must confront the fact that the church has often opposed the theatre. *The Antitheatrical Prejudice*, by Jonas Barish, is a comprehensive study of historical animosity to the theatrical arts. Much of this lengthy treatise is devoted to Christianity's opposition to theatre. If all philosophy is a footnote to Plato, it may be said that all antitheatrical prejudice flows from objections the Greek philosopher raised in *The Republic* in the fourth century BCE. We begin this section with a survey of Plato's objections to the theatre.

The mimetic arts (and for Plato this would include poetry in general) are first regarded as inferior to philosophy because they are an inferior reflection of and at a distance from reality and truth. Further, they make a primary appeal to the emotions, sensory perceptions, and the like, which are assumed to be inferior to the rational, intellectual capacity in humans. Not only are the imitative arts inferior, they are also deceptive; poets and actors don't just pretend, they lie. In this Plato can be seen as admitting, not in so many words but by implication, the power of the mimetic arts and in particular the theatre. If the written word has potency, the written word spoken by an actor has even more power to influence.

Pejorative uses of theatrical terminology are numerous: we tell children not to "act up" or "make a scene"; something overwrought is "melodramatic"; and we would not want to be seen "making a spectacle" of ourselves.[22] Imitating another character in life, as in hypocrisy (remember *hupokrite*) or some psychological disorders, is projected onto the art of acting another character on stage. This confusion is an underlying cause of many Christian objections to the theatre.

For Plato imitation is not only deceptive it is also "formative." That is, actors risk becoming what they imitate on stage. The early church fathers extended this concern to the audience; *attending* theatrical displays was dangerous because audiences tend to imitate what they experience for pleasure. One can easily make the connection to arguments against television, film, and video games today. The connection of theatre to pagan rites simply added urgency to antitheatrical polemics. Tertullian drew the connection between theatre and Roman *ludi* very clearly. He called theatre a "trick of art" and not "real." His fiery *de Spectaculus* (*On the Spectacles*, CE 197–202) portrayed the theatre as a demonic plot to alienate people from God. To be fair, Tertullian (a North African theologian) was probably unfamiliar with any legitimate theatre; he was responding to theatrical spectacles common in the Roman world (gladiatorial contests, *naumaticae*, etc.), which were gathering points for lascivious persons. What is significant about Tertullian's work is that he extends the argument of Plato that the theatre attracts audiences by exciting the emotions (an anthropological complaint) and finds the forces of evil at work instead (a spiritual complaint). He cites Psalm 1 in support of his position.

What both Plato and Tertullian fail to acknowledge is the existence of the fictive, of playacting, apart from real life. The world of the stage is not real life. Tertullian fumes against actors who shave their beards, add to their height with *cothurni* (high-heeled shoes worn by actors), and wear masks or jewelry, condemning these practices as subverting the work of the Creator. "The Author of truth hates all the false; He regards as adultery all that is unreal. Condemning, therefore, as He does hypocrisy in every form, He never will approve any putting on of voice, or sex, or age; He never will approve pretended loves, and wraths, and groans, and tears."[23]

Not only is this a violation of human nature, Tertullian argues, but it is also a violation of God's sovereignty as Creator. Of course, actors don't present themselves on stage as themselves. Their modifications of voice and body are fictional, intended to create another character, not to mislead people about their own character.

Plato would ban the artist from his ideal state for still another reason: vicariously experiencing passions in the theatre short-circuits compassionate response to those same experiences in real life. If one is titillated by pity and fear in the drama, one's ability to sense and respond to one's neighbors with pity and fear in reality is deadened. Another church father, Augustine, takes up this argument in his *Confessions* and in *The City of God*. Augustine believed that emotional stimulation in the theatre was "an insidious form of self indulgence; it relieves us of the need to act, and so feeds our passivity and narcissism."[24]

Augustine, unlike Tertullian, took a practical approach to his criticism of the theatre. He dismissed it not on ontological grounds but because he saw it affecting the health of the church in his day. He also distinguished the works of dramatic poets (the texts of the theatre) from the performances in theatre buildings. As a result, animosity toward the theatre from the Middle Ages onward tended to be directed not toward writers but toward actors. Denis Diderot suggested actors were able to assume so many different characters only because they lacked character themselves.[25] Plato's complaint that actors are liars led to the complaint that actors are immoral. The use and display of the body was seen as an occupational hazard; as Protestant Christianity adopted a Platonic distrust of the material world, this argument gained ground and potency.

Augustine apprehended the distinction between fiction and reality by distinguishing the motives behind acting and life. In life if one dissembles it is evidence of the intention to deceive; in the theatre the motive behind mimesis is to give pleasure.[26] It is essential to maintain this distinction. Augustine extends the distinction to both plays and actors, reclaiming the "truth" of mimetic creation for theatre as a genre and as a medium. We shall see in the following section why this was important (after Plato) and why it is significant that a church father would be the one to carry on the philosophy of Aristotle in regard to theatre.

Aristotle, in his *Poetics*, first sets poetry (and the mimetic arts in general) apart from philosophy, education, and politics by stating that the purpose of poetry is aesthetic. Art brings pleasure, first and only; if it teaches, that is incidental to its character. Our English word "pleasure" is perhaps too debased now to adequately convey the elevated nature of this response. Aristotle does not dismiss the moral content of art because morality is a necessary contributor to the aesthetic experience. His point is that artists are not to pursue education, moral or otherwise, but rather to create out of their own ethical and moral sensibility a work of art that brings pleasure to the reader/audience. This pleasure involves *catharsis*, or a purgation of unhealthy emotions (pity and fear) through the audiences' vicarious experience of the suffering of the tragic hero. It is in the pleasurable experience that the audience is instructed, matured, and prodded.

The Roman critic Horace, in his *Ars Poetica*, melds Aristotle's "to please" with Plato's "to teach" and dictates that art should pursue both aims. In the next section we'll see how the medieval drama accomplishes teaching by illustration in the texts while pleasure/catharsis are relegated to the medium and experience of theatre. Much later the French critic Marmontel commented that plays reconcile us to the criminal, not the crime.[27] So we may derive pleasure from an actor's portrayal of a criminal without being taught that the crime is morally acceptable.

We conclude this section by looking at the fruit of the antitheatrical positions we've been surveying. The Puritans could be expected to be most vocal on this point, and they did not disappoint. William Prynne's *Histriomastix*, a one-thousand-page rant against the evils of the theatre, condemns this venue as a destination for vice and the evils of actors as characterless purveyors of vice (women on the stage is an especially egregious offense). It was issued in 1633, just preceding the civil war in England, the overthrow of the monarchy, and the shuttering of the theatres in London in 1642. It was not the first Puritan attack: a "generation of slowly intensifying pamphlet warfare" preceded and laid the ground for Prynne and his brothers to launch their vehement attacks.[28] Theatre was lumped together with a host of evils: gambling, sports, effeminacy, dancing, long hair, and so on.

Much of the Puritan objection can be traced to the apparent uselessness of theatre. Pleasure was no longer a proper end of human activity. The connection between church and theatre in the Middle Ages having been severed, theatre was set adrift from utilitarian aims. Aristotle's concept of catharsis (the purgation of pity and fear through the vicarious experience of them) and Horace's insistence on the dual aims of instruction and pleasure ("to teach" and "to please") did not figure in this narrow vision of life.

A Puritan sensibility continued in some corners of Protestant Christianity as evidenced in *Christians and the Theater*, written in 1876 by J. M. Buckley. The author paints with a wide brush, encompassing many amusements in his portrait of the evils of the stage. Consider just one example: "Few things are more unfavorable to the practice of religion than the practice of Theatergoing, and . . . nothing is more potent in causing men to relinquish a strictly religious life than the spirit and associations of the Theater."[29]

Plato and Tertullian are present in Buckley's assumptions that the theatre is sensual (emotional) and that vice on stage is attractive and will lure the young onto its path. Such generalizations characterize historic Christian attacks on the theatre as a medium and as an institution. In the final section of this chapter, we return to some twentieth-century manifestations of Christian antitheatricalism. Between the time of our early North African friends, Tertullian and Augustine, and that of the Puritans, an embrace of the theatre by the church occurred, to which we now turn.

The "Rebirth" of Theatre in the Middle Ages

The theory of the rebirth of theatre in the Middle Ages is as commonplace as the theory of the birth of theatre in ancient rituals.[30] This second application of ritual to theatre assumes (1) that theatre had died and so needed to be reborn, and (2) that the resurrection of theatre as an art and an institution came about because of the encouragement of the medieval church. This application of ritual theory holds great appeal for Christians and is repeated frequently as an apologetic for the use of theatre in church and as a vocation. We see again the twin strands of theatre emerging from narrative (the stories of the Bible) and ritual (the liturgies of the church).

The assertion that the theatre had died in the years between CE 500 and 900 (the beginnings of Christendom) is disputable. Oscar G. Brockett's *History of the Theatre* identifies four theatrical activities that continued during these years: Roman mimes, Teutonic minstrelsy, popular festivals and pagan rites, and Christian ceremonies; these all carried vestiges of the great theatre of the ancient world,[31] and each retained its connection to religious observance. These nontextual theatrical activities are an important part of understanding theatre history. They are still manifest in our contemporary culture, even in our churches.

The theatre in the medieval church did not emerge ex nihilo. "As time went by, the rites of the Christian church also became more elaborate, and liturgical drama was ultimately to emerge out of these elaborations—and within the church itself—during the tenth century. This final step, however, was merely a culmination of innovations that can be traced back into preceding centuries."[32] The Church appropriated elements of the surrounding culture, and this included popular forms of theatre. In the church they were wedded to sacred texts and liturgies.

Tropes are dramatic interpolations inserted into a church service.[33] They were an outgrowth of antiphonal chanting by choirs; the choric voices were reduced to individual voices. The earliest and most often cited, the *Quem*

Queritis, dates from about CE 923 to 934 and was sung at the Easter vigil, the first liturgy celebrating the resurrection each year.

> Quem quaeritis in sepulchro, O Christicolae?
> Jesum Nazarenum crucifixum, O coelicolae.
>
> Whom do you seek in the sepulcher, O followers of Christ?
> Jesus of Nazareth who was crucified, O celestial ones.

The movement from narrative to dialogue is obvious, and liturgical directives from the period bear out the fact that the lines were divided between priests. We aren't sure whether the priests who spoke these lines imitated the characters in the story or simply read the lines. Later tropes are longer and more elaborate, continuing into the early fourteenth century, but how they were performed is unclear. We have presented the words typographically in dialogue form, but we don't know if the performance had moved from narrative or storytelling to mimetic representation. There is evidence that the priests altered the space in which the tropes were presented, and that they altered their vestments in minor ways to suggest characters. Whether or not the tropes were performed mimetically, this is at least a very clear step in the direction of theatre.

Another issue is whether the congregants were treated as audience or participants. In the Good Friday liturgy, which is the oldest liturgy still in use in the Roman Catholic tradition, the passion from John's Gospel is read, and the people take the role of crowds calling for the Lord's crucifixion. This is certainly theatrical, but it is not theatre since there is no audience. It is liturgical; everyone is a participant. This practice was later amended with the insertion of the congregation chanting the "hosannas" on Palm Sunday. The line between theatre and liturgy in this case is a fine but important one. The congregation participates in an offering to God; it is not an audience with worship offered for or to it.

In the tenth century, Ethelwold, bishop of Winchester, recorded instructions for the performance of a trope in a Benedictine monastery:

> While the third lesson is being chanted, let four brethren vest themselves. Let one of these, vested in an alb, enter as though to take part in the service, and let him approach the sepulcher without attracting attention and sit there quietly with a palm in his hand. While the third respond is chanted, let the remaining three follow, and let them all, vested in copes, bearing in their hands thuribles with incense, and stepping delicately as those who seek something, approach the sepulcher. These things are done in imitation of

the angel sitting in the monument, and the women with spices coming to anoint the body of Jesus.[34]

These instructions imply that a modicum of impersonation was expected, in movement if not also in voice. One can easily follow the thread from this rudimentary interpolation in a liturgical service to the seasonal pageants still popular in churches today. One development of this simple beginning, the Oberammergau Passion Play, was first staged in 1633 and continues to be presented by the small village of Oberammergau, Germany, every ten years to the present. In America several passion plays are included as members of the Institute of Outdoor Drama.[35]

Few people realize that much of medieval Christian worship was public and stational, moving from one place to another within a city. Initially practiced in Jerusalem, where people retraced the last hours of our Lord, this devotion later became the stations of the cross within a single church, apart from the actual location. These were tremendously popular and emotional experiences. These practices also raise the issue of the relationship between theatre and worship. The use of stained glass imagery as a visual means to teach in an illiterate world and St. Francis's creation of the crèche to tell the story of the nativity also point to the use of theatre in religious education. Medieval drama and much medieval art were also processional in nature, more interested in narrative movement than the unification of space.[36] For this reason the drama was performed on open platforms or wagons rather than picture-framed proscenium stages.

In his *Studies in the English Mystery Plays*, Charles Davidson takes an unusual approach to this topic. Instead of crediting the rebirth of drama to utilitarian promptings (drama can teach or illustrate), he adopts Aristotle's instinctual mimesis theory: liturgical drama arose from the natural desire to imitate, the same source for the dramas of ancient Greece. He contends that the Western world was searching for "thoughts worthy of dramatic expression. The early Greeks found such in the worship of Dionysus; the inheritors of their worn-out civilization felt in the profoundest sense a dynamic idea in the Christian faith. We have, then, to seek the sources of the new drama in the Christian ideals."[37]

Davidson believes that the earliest church dramas have an artistic, aesthetic basis rather than a purely functional one. The distinction is not merely academic. If Christians look back to the drama of the early Middle Ages, they will see either a purely utilitarian use of the medium of theatre for the expression of their faith or a freedom to explore the stories of their faith through the medium of theatre, using the God-given inclination to imitate.

The use of theatre to tell the Christian story in the medieval Church is understandable, but it is surprising given the numerous church diatribes against the theatre, which began with the early church fathers and continued even after the advent of liturgical drama in the tenth century. Benjamin Hunningher addresses this discrepancy in *The Origin of the Theater*. He delves into romanticist historiography, which was bent on locating the origins of modern theatre in the church and "also as the single and total source of an entirely independent dramatic art."[38] In the late nineteenth century, the publication of Sir James Frazier's *Golden Bough* became "another analogy to strengthen the theory of the ecclesiastical origin of drama."[39] Hunningher brings these twin theories together:

> What has escaped most people, however, is that the word "religion" has completely different meanings in the mouth of the ethnologist and in the mouth of the faithful. Can a connection be made between something that springs from the conjuring rites of a totemistic community and the prayers and hymns to the Saviour uttered by a Christian congregation? Has the frenzy of the fertility dances in the primitive and ancient world anything in common with the joy of those redeemed from the cycle of life and death and reborn to a Higher Life? Have, then, analogies with primitive cults and Greek religion any value for the thesis that Christianity gave form to a dramatic art?[40]

Hunningher's answer is a definitive "no." He mixes arguments against the ritual origin of theatre with the ritual essence of theatre when he concludes: "Can a religion which looks through life and above it longing for fulfillment of the Kingdom of Heaven, can a church which 'has almost replaced good and evil by the bodily and non-bodily' spontaneously and willingly resurrect an art which exists by the grace of earthly life and may not pass on its boundaries?"[41] The question is, of course, rhetorical.

That the medieval Church integrated theatre, whether for illustration or instinctively, is beyond question. This fact, together with ongoing performances of folk plays and court revels, generated new and lively theatre in Western European countries from the tenth to the fifteenth centuries. Here we are necessarily summarizing and generalizing a progression quite vast in terms of time and geography.

Much has already been said about the "rebirth" of theatre as a genre of literature and as a performance medium during the Middle Ages in Europe. By the fifteenth century a robust body of work was in evidence in nearly every European country, from cycles of plays based on the Bible to morality plays to folk dramas. Because of the pervasive influence of the Church, in no period in the history of Christianity or the theatre was a closer relationship between the two more in evidence than in the Middle Ages.

In the discussion of ritual theory, we suggested that theatre arose in the church for two reasons: as a natural outgrowth of religious ritual and due to the inherent human tendency toward mimesis. The first takes into consideration the interest of priests to illustrate, by way of liturgical drama, the truths of the Scripture. The second takes into consideration the ongoing tradition of popular entertainment that toured the rural areas uninterrupted throughout this period.

The liturgical drama performed by the priests in the sanctuary, spoken in Latin and usually accompanied by music, soon gave way to dramatic adaptations of biblical stories. These "mystery" plays were performed outside the doors of the church and were staged by citizens of the towns sponsoring them. The English word "mystery" derives, circa 1375, from *misterium*, which in turn derives from the Latin *ministerium*, "service, occupation, office, ministry," influenced in form by *mysterium*. The plays were ministries (not strictly in a religious sense, but also in a communal sense) of the medieval guilds. There is also a connection to the Greek *mysterion*, a "secret rite or doctrine," from *mystes*, "one who has been initiated," from *myein*, "to close, shut," perhaps referring to the lips (in secrecy) or to the eyes (only initiates were allowed to see the sacred rites). *Mysterion* is the Greek word used in the Septuagint for the "secret counsel of God" and translated by Tertullian into Latin as *sacramentum*. The plays were also dramatic enactments of biblical doctrine and tradition. This brief etymology indicates the close connection of these plays to the social structure (guilds and towns) as well as the religious structure of the age and indirectly connects theatre with sacrament.

The mystery plays developed after transubstantiation was formally declared a doctrine by the Church in 1215. They were conceived as plays, not ritual elements in a church service, which emphasized the humanity and earthly ministry of Christ. Characters in these plays are more lifelike than their liturgical predecessors, and the language used is the vernacular of the country in which they were conceived rather than the official Latin of the Mass. They were called Corpus Christi plays, owing both to their origins in that feast day celebration (instituted in 1264) and to their attention to the physical reality of the gospel story.[42] They were also called "cycle" plays, not just because the short plays were performed in a cycle but also because they embody "a doctrinal pattern of Fall, Redemption and Judgment. This pattern happens to bear a marked resemblance to that prescribed by Aristotle for Greek dramatists with its sharply defined beginning, middle and end."[43] We will return to the mystery plays in chapter 3.

Mystery plays gave way in time to "miracle plays" (dramas based on the lives of saints) and later to morality plays (dramas intended to communicate moral choices through typological characters). The latter, didactic plays typified by the anonymous *Everyman* (ca. 1500), were widely used in and outside the church throughout the liturgical calendar year and were especially adaptable to groups of touring actors. The theatre, which had been confined to the church building in the liturgical drama, then moved into the town center with the mystery and miracle plays, now went on the road with the morality plays. In so doing, it reconnected with the strains of theatre that Oscar Brockett identifies as continuing throughout the early medieval period.

The writer of Ecclesiastes said, "There is nothing new under the sun." With a little effort one can find these three broad categories of medieval drama (liturgical, mystery, and morality) widely used in the Christian community today. In some services, typically those still connected to a historic liturgy, the style of Latin music-drama still pervades, in either tropes or chanted/sung oratorios or cantatas. Often these are only slightly "theatrical" in terms of presentation (nonmimetic) and staging (suggestive costume and scenery). In other churches, perhaps those straddling the traditional to contemporary continuum, mystery-like plays, based on the Bible but humanizing them with humor and associating them with important dates in the calendar (typically Christmas and Easter), are the primary application of theatre in worship. These pageants, like their medieval counterparts, are elaborately staged spectacles. No expense is spared to realistically portray the period, country, and characters. Machinery is employed to fly angels and carry Jesus to heaven; lighting and fog machines simulate the flames of hell and the empty tomb. Other churches, especially those eschewing historical connections in liturgy, architecture, and anything else that smacks of the traditional, borrow freely from the surrounding culture to make morality-play statements of their worldview and belief systems. Slice-of-life sketches or imitations of pop-culture drama, usually drawn from television and movies, are tweaked to carry a moral and/or introduce a question that will be addressed in the sermon.

The medieval theatre, whether one sees it birthed in the ritual of the church or carried on in an unbroken mimetic tradition from the Romans, or both, was richly varied and is the precedent for many of the ways that twenty-first-century Christians use the theatre in their worship.

The Relationship between Church, Ritual, and Theatre in the Modern World

Many authors have described the relationship between Christianity and the theatre as a love-hate, back-and-forth, hot-and-cold affair. In 1956 the bishop of Chichester, presiding over the International Conference on Religious Drama sponsored by the Religious Drama Society of Great Britain, viewed the relationship of theatre and church with unbridled optimism. What led to that optimism was the appearance on the English stage of the plays of Christopher Fry and T. S. Eliot. It seemed that at last the mainstream theatre was accepting drama with a distinctively Christian flavor.

The evidences of harmony between church and theatre are sometimes literary (as in the plays of Eliot, the drama of the Middle Ages, and the preponderance of short plays in the contemporary church), sometimes theoretical (the apologetics of Augustine, theories of poetry applied to drama), and sometimes practical (the popularity of mystery plays in England and the money spent on pageants in twenty-first-century America).

Theatre and the Contemporary Church

Around the turn of the twentieth century, several cultural conditions existed in which church-theatre relations could thaw and even warm. This background is explicated in Peter Senkbeil's dissertation, "Faith in Theatre." Senkbeil notes the rise of amateur theatre, especially outside New York and in the little theatre movement, which made the practice of theatre more accessible to Americans in general. As Protestant churches turned their attention to social and cultural concerns, the arts and theatre became a platform for religious aims. Of course, this was countered by fundamentalists, and theatre came in for criticism along with other social gospel initiatives.[44] But as the influence of fundamentalism waned, theatre has become not just a welcome adjunct to worship but in some circles a requirement. Apologetic handbooks for drama ministry are quick to note this development.[45]

It is interesting to note the recurrent word "today" in these enthusiastic reports. The evangelical Western church of the twenty-first century is fixated on contemporaneity. In 2008, as we write this book, the use of live drama in church services has begun to wane, having been overtaken by filmed drama. This is no doubt partly due to the availability of inexpensive camera and editing equipment, but it is also motivated by the desire to be relevant and contemporary. The boundaries of "contemporary" are always shifting, and many churches shift their use of the arts accordingly.

The subject of church-theatre relations in the modern period demands far more consideration than the scope of this chapter permits. We encourage you to note the references cited for further reading. Documentation of this period is far more extensive than that of the previous periods discussed, and details vary widely by decade, denomination, and country. Because this book is published in the Western Hemisphere and is directed to Christians working there, specifically in English-speaking countries, we emphasize primarily developments in the United Kingdom and North America.

Toward the end of the nineteenth century, English poets began to dabble in playwriting. Their verse dramas were not often produced, and in fact many were not written to be produced at all, but at the turn of the century these dramatic efforts increased and became a full-fledged revival of verse drama. Coincident with this verse-drama revival was renewed interest in the dramatic arts by the Church of England. One director, E. Martin Browne, stood at the genesis of both movements.

In 1930 Browne returned to England from a teaching stint at the Carnegie Institute of Technology and was asked by Bishop George Bell to take the reins of the fledgling Religious Drama Society of Great Britain. Four years later he collaborated with T. S. Eliot on the poet's first drama, *The Rock*. Bishop Bell saw this production and issued an invitation to Eliot to write the 1935 Canterbury Festival play; his masterpiece *Murder in the Cathedral* was the result. The author originally titled the play "Fear in the Way," but Browne proposed a detective-story approach, and the suggested title stuck. Though the play was produced professionally in Eliot's lifetime and continues to enjoy frequent productions in England and America, Eliot considered it weighed down by liturgical and poetic underpinnings. He soon turned to more subtle fare, such as *The Cocktail Party*.

Throughout the development of twentieth-century verse and religious drama, there remained an assumption that the portrayal of religious themes in drama must make use of poetic diction. Prose was considered too pedestrian and rooted in sensory experience for the numinous quality of plays that treat spiritual subjects. This movement was literary and generic, and not at all in synch with the rediscovery of ritual performance by Artaud and his successors. Other poets with Christian leanings, such as Gordon Bottomley, Anne Ridler, Norman Nicholson, Ronald Duncan, and Charles Williams, took their turn at playwriting with little commercial success. Eliot and Browne were eager to take their work to the commercial theatre, and the shift to drawing-room comedy with subdued poetic and religious intentions was designed to bring them attention from the mainstream (i.e., London) theatre. They succeeded, and from 1939 to 1958 Browne directed a series of Eliot's plays, each less poetic and less religious.

Christopher Fry is another Christian who made his mark on the development of religious drama in England. Eliot came to drama as an established poet; Fry came to drama as a director and actor. Browne introduced him to the Religious Drama Society in 1937, after he had directed the premiere of George Bernard Shaw's *Village Wooing* at the Tunbridge Wells Repertory Theatre. He soon wrote *The Boy with a Cart*, a didactic piece, and then a play based on Moses in Egypt, *The Firstborn* (1945). Though not as well known as his later, less "religious" work (such as *A Sleep of Prisoners* or *The Lady's Not for Burning*), this play is far more than a recounting of the biblical facts. Fry launches the audience into the struggle of Moses to understand the workings of God in the captivity, and the play exemplifies the author's continual "exploring for the truth of the human creature."[46] His plays read like the medieval cycle dramas, which merged the sacred and secular dimensions in a seamless pattern.

Once these playwrights had successfully offered their Christian worldviews on the commercial stage, interest in the theatre among Christians began to accelerate.[47] Like the liturgical drama of the Middle Ages, this involvement did not appear out of a vacuum, but it certainly became more noticeable. Browne was invited to teach in America again, this time at Union Theological Seminary. Other schools introduced courses in religious drama, and now it is the rare evangelical liberal arts college that does not have a theatre department, and many offer undergraduate degrees in theatre. Two evangelical universities (Regent University in Virginia Beach, Virginia, and Baylor University in Waco, Texas) offer graduate degrees in theatre.

Enthusiasm for verse drama waned in the 1950s as kitchen-sink realism and postwar social drama took hold. Eliot and Fry lost their luster among commercial producers; with the exception of the occasional musical (*Godspell*, for example) or medieval adaptation (*The Mysteries* in England), Christianity was not given theatrical treatment by such a large group of writers. Concurrently, the church began once again to open its doors to theatre, on condition that the theatre would serve the purposes of the church. In 1958 Robert Steele wrote, "As persons get a bigger bang out of preparing the next church play, they withdraw more from the world."[48]

In 1970 the Nazarene Publishing House released Carl S. McClain's *Morals and the Movies*. McClain writes:

> Sultry love scenes and the portrayal of animal passion required of the actors and actresses in their frequent rehearsals, the constant round of fast living with its cocktail parties, deteriorate their morals so that movie colonies . . . are proverbial for their immorality and loose living. . . . At a theater or movie house one is influenced not only by what transpires on the stage or the screen. . . . I submit that a frequenter of the theater or movie house cannot at the same time be a spiritual force for good, a vital Christian leader or Sunday School teacher.[49]

The Nazarenes included cautions against the theatre in church manuals.[50] Other denominations (including the Presbyterian and the Methodist) issued similar warnings. By the late twentieth century, however, few Christian denominations were issuing warnings against the theatre; rather, many if not most had embraced it as a useful tool in evangelism. The exceptions are found in Christian denominations with primitive worship models such as the noninstrumental Church of Christ; these churches do not permit musical instruments in their services, and they often extend this restrictive understanding of the New Testament church to the use of other arts—drama among them.

Aside from a reluctance to embrace theatre in the context of worship, some Christian denominations still carry reservations about the pursuit of theatre as a career. In the context of history this should not be surprising. Since the time of the early church fathers, actors have been viewed with suspicion if not with animosity. Economic conditions contribute to this attitude ("How will you find work with that BA in theatre degree?"), and the celebrity culture creates a false impression of the working life of the actor: constant parties and fast living. But there is also a deeply rooted Platonism at work in those Christians who view the body and the senses as things to be subjugated to the intellect, and therefore any profession that relies on daily use of the sensual apparatus should be called into question. We return to this issue in the section dealing with the Christian theatre artist in chapter 4.

In the 1970s Christian artists organized themselves into first touring and then later resident faith-based theatre companies in York, England (Riding Lights Theatre), Houston, Texas (The A.D. Players), San Diego, California (The Lamb's Players), Seattle, Washington (Taproot Theatre Company), and Pittsburgh, Pennsylvania (Saltworks Theatre Company), to name a few. Other groups were organized on a more explicitly ministry-based model, and various solo and small ensemble performing groups have carried on the minstrel tradition of the Middle Ages up to the present time.

The Embrace of Ritual by Avant-garde Theatre Artists

Another major evidence or application of the ritual theory of origins/essence, one that takes the connection out of the theory and into the practice of theatre, occurred in the twentieth century. A group of theorists, directors, and actors, disenchanted with what they viewed as the superficial theatre of realism, began to experiment with ritual as a means of reviving the "deadly theatre" (Peter Brook's term in *The Empty Space*). At the vanguard was the French theorist Antonin Artaud (1896–1948). Artaud wanted a theatre that broached the unconscious, spiritual forces underlying sensory existence; his approach to theatre, which he called "theatre of cruelty," utilized techniques later seen as deriving from ritual. He was a visionary and would not in his own lifetime realize the success of these ideas. But his theories would form the basis for innovative and controversial theatre practice in the work of Jerzy Grotowski, Peter Brook, and Richard Schechner.

Artaud's questioning of traditional theatrical values permeated every discipline of theatre. Dramaturgy, directing, and designing were reevaluated in light of Artaud's theories. A body of plays emerged that took Artaudian theories in a variety of practical directions. These avant-garde dramas, while greatly varied in style and subject matter, shared a common interest in the mythic and ritualistic. There was a common attempt in them to permeate the level of superficial reality and approach a realm of either "unconsciousness" or "super-consciousness." Along with this new body of drama came theorizing and criticism by playwrights and philosophers. But the drama also made new demands on production and especially on acting techniques. The psychological approach to acting pioneered by Konstantin Stanislavsky and codified by his disciples was no longer adequate to guide the actor of the avant-garde. The postmodern theatre refocused on acting technique and hearkened back to some of the approaches of actors before Stanislavsky. There was a renewed emphasis on vocal and bodily training, but to different ends: not the psychological and photographic depiction of real characters but the unleashing of spiritual forces through voice and body.

In *The Theatrical Event*, David Cole discusses a ritualistic approach to theatre and the role of the actor in ritualism. Cole gives the "transcendental principle" of Artaud more specific coordinates with the introduction of the *illud tempus* concept, which he borrows from the field of comparative religion. The *illud tempus*, or "time of origins," has two significant features: "that of being a universe of eternally subsisting relations" and "the potential to be present," both of which are shared by the theatrical event.[51] It is the job of the actor, Cole argues, to "actualize this potential" by re-presenting the *illud tempus*—the world of archetypal myths. Cole cites Mircea Eliade and Carl Jung in support of his theory that the *illud tempus* is made present again in two ways: ritual and dreams. Thus, if the actor is going to perform this mythic world, "the first step must be: exploration of [his] own mind in search of those 'intrapsychic factors' which correspond to its events and personages."[52] Every script, then, represents an embodiment of some archetypal myth, which the actor must discover through a process of self-exploration.

The manifestation of this *illud tempus* in the theatre-ritual is the work of the actor, and this he accomplishes in the same manner as the leaders of primitive rituals: shamans and hungans. This approach to acting theory is presentational as opposed to re-presentational, which was exactly Artaud's point of view. The shaman is a "psychic voyager to the world of the gods," and the hungan is a human "whose presence becomes, through possession, a god's presence."[53] Further, Cole argues that "for the actor, shamanism and hunganism are not alternative modes of encountering the (script) *illud tempu'*, but rather the two successive phases of his encounter with it." Cole goes on to explain: "In the manner of a shaman, he opens a 'way out' toward the *illud tempus*, and then, in the manner of a hungan, he himself becomes the 'way back' of the *illud tempus* toward us. I call this reversal in which the actor goes from shaman to hungan—from masterful explorer to mastered vehicle—the 'rounding.' The rounding is the defining characteristic of theatrical performance. It is in the moment of the rounding that the theatre, as an event, is born."[54]

In Cole's ritualistic context, it is interesting to reexamine Artaud's comments on the actor as priest. Artaud vehemently rejected the concept of theatre as re-presenting an action. He believed that the mise-en-scène should be creative and not merely a "repetition of a present." But he also contended that the theatre of cruelty should be hieratic, or priestly, a theatre that mediates between the sacred and the profane. Jacques Derrida, a postmodernist philosopher, excludes, first and foremost, all "nonsacred" theatre from the Artaudian heritage. "A new epiphany of the supernatural and the divine must occur within cruelty."[55] Andre Serban believes that Artaud was unable to control this "power," which it is the responsibility of the actor-priest to unleash. He uses the analogy of voodoo:

> where there is a feeling of free forces of evil at work, and in which everyone goes into a state that is quite dangerous. One senses that something physical may be happening that might be quite painful, and it's always unseen, unknown. There are people—called priests, priestesses of some sort—who always watch in such ceremonies, who are there to stop, to guide, to control, when the energy of the trances is released to such an extent that one feels "I'm going to lose myself." In that sense, if one really looks at Artaud, one understands what theatre energy can bring about and what we are dealing with, which is something absolutely extraordinary—just as powerful and mysterious as the feeling of falling in love, which is immense and so strong that one can't comprehend it. To control such a force in the theatre one must spend years learning how to deal with it, how to understand it. That's why it requires experimental work—to understand what the power and responsibilities of the actor are, and what is available to him. This area is absolutely untouched now in the Western theatre.[56]

Here again the actor is understood as a mediator between audience-participants and "the higher bodies." For Serban, as for Artaud, such a ritualistic-theatrical experience heightens one's awareness of life.

Artaud credits much of his theorizing in this area to an experience he had with Balinese dance-ritual. He sees in this ritual the "hallucinatory perspective appropriate to every theatrical character."[57] Christopher Innes describes the ritual as "apparently inducing a change in the participants that is not merely symbolical but actual." The Balinese actors actually enter a state of trance and prove invulnerable to self-inflicted stab wounds. It is this trance "which is the justification for the performances."[58] This ritual-drama parallels Artaud's concept of the liberated unconscious. The psychological effectiveness of the primitive ritual trance-state made it a "natural model for the avant garde." Innes sees in these primitive rituals "self-induced trances in which the physical and spiritual worlds are assumed to interpenetrate."[59] The actor-priest uses ritual as a "technique to influence a supernatural power."[60] This process involves a self-exposure and self-sacrifice in public by the actor. Jerzy Grotowski contends that an actor must train his body to be "an obedient instrument capable of performing a spiritual act."[61] The concept of the "holy actor" is central to Grotowski's theories and practice. He describes the actor's art in religious terms, as "offering himself" and "sacrificing" for the audience; of "atoning" and in this way achieving a "secular holiness." He states very forcefully: "The actor must act in a state of trance."[62] In language borrowed from the field of shamanism, Grotowski describes the actor's technique of self-penetration as a "journey" and claims for the actor the power to perform "magical acts."[63]

The concept of actor-priest is organically linked to Artaud's call for a new theatre language. The actor's work becomes sacerdotal and must necessarily rely on hieroglyphs in its communicative efforts with, not to, the audience. Not only language but stage setting, properties, and costumes take on a new significance as religious symbols, much like those employed in high-church liturgies. It is an attempt to incarnate spiritual realities through surrendering the conscious use of the voice and body to spiritual forces.

The theatre of the avant-garde is inherently religious, sacred, holy—but not theocentric. It is centered on the presence of a higher power or consciousness—but not an identifiable "god," and certainly not the God of the Bible. The primary agent of this holy theatre is not the playwright or the director but the actor-priest. A ritual may or may not have a religious component, though most examples of formal ritual are connected to the worship of immaterial forces. Victor Turner defines ritual as "prescribed formal behavior for occasions not given over to technological routine, having reference to beliefs in invisible beings or powers regarded as the first and final causes of all effects."[64] We will give attention to Turner's work, partly because he blends a fascination with theatre into his anthropological study of ritual and partly because his theatrical collaborator, Richard Schechner, observed his "acceptance of traditional Christian values."[65] His two major works on ritual and theatre are instructive; they reflect the impact of ritual theory on contemporary practitioners (such as Peter Brook and Jerzy Grotowski), and they have impacted the work of a leading exponent of ritual performance theory (Richard Schechner).

As an anthropologist, Turner was interested in "coherent communities" such as African villages and primitive tribes. This fertile ground for ritual expression is not dissimilar to the community often found in local churches—especially with regard to the shared history (biblical and ecclesiastical) and the regular gatherings (even nonliturgical churches have a default liturgy). Out of these communities, tribes, or villages, mimetic "performances"—rituals—often arise. More often than not, they are associated with a desire on the part of the community to have some effect on their gods, be they the forces of nature, the cycle of the seasons, or a collective belief system. Turner called these performances "magic mirrors," rituals intended to affect some change by mirroring mimetically the phenomena. Thus, to ensure a successful hunt the participants may act out the hunt with a successful ending.

Hamlet refers to his play, in which he attempts to "catch the conscience of the king," as a "mirror to nature." Theatre is regularly referred to as a mirror in which the audience sees itself on stage. Aristotle believed the experience of an enacted tragedy would bring about a catharsis, a purgation, of unhealthy emotions. As pointed out before, the connection of ritual and myth to the cycle of death and rebirth found in primitive cultures is parallel to the preponderance of theatre in church during the seasons of Christmas and Easter.

According to Turner, the etymology of two words, "performance" and "entertain," holds clues to the ritual underpinnings of all theatrical activity. The word "performance" derives from the French *parfournir*, meaning "to complete" or "to carry out thoroughly," as in an experience that is completed in its representation on the stage. "In the carrying out . . . something new may be generated . . . hitherto unprecedented insights and even new symbols and meanings."[66] "Entertain" comes from the French *entretenir*, which means "to hold apart" or "to hold between." "That is, it can be construed as the making of liminality, the betwixt and between stage."[67] Both of these terms, when considered etymologically, carry far more weight than mere amusement or divertissement. They suggest that a theatrical event is, in both origin and essence, capable of bringing the audience into a place of "willing suspension of disbelief" (to quote Coleridge) where the threshold (*limin*) between "secular living and sacred living" is reached.[68]

The Protestant/Puritan objection to ritual as empty formality is not true of this kind of experience; now we have entered the realm of what Peter Brook calls "Holy Theatre": immediate, living, vital, and inescapable. The content of the play may be religious, even Christian, or it may not. The theatre may be an elaborate auditorium, but probably not. It may be the product of a professional company after rigorous rehearsals and preparation, or it may be experienced in the improvisations of an untrained (i.e., primitive) but wholly committed ensemble acting on their mimetic instincts.

Turner notes that in many societies one role of ritual is "to probe a community's weaknesses, call its leaders to account, desacralize its most cherished values and beliefs, portray its characteristic conflicts and suggest remedies for them, and generally take stock of its current situation in the known world."[69] Christians can read the role of a prophet into that description, and when we turn our attention to theatre in the Old Testament, we will discover clear examples of theatre (as a medium) in the books of the prophets.

However, before the close relationship between ritual and theatre is accepted wholesale, significant differences must be acknowledged. Turner articulates them: ritual is typically obligatory and does not always distinguish between the performer and the spectators; it implies membership in a group, and those members work at it (it is interesting to note that Turner locates "religious drama" in this category). By contrast, theatre is a leisure pursuit, optional to the audience (which is distinguished from the performers); it is a commodity that can be purchased and sadly is often priced out of the range of many people for whom it could be a vital experience.

Conclusion

What motivates scholars and artists to discover ritual links, essential similarities, and even to posit an ontological bridge between theatre and religion? Christians may try to find justification for their involvement in theatre via these ritual associations. Twenty-first-century Christianity sees itself as a cultural underdog; exploiting a supposed link with ritual/religion/myth buys it a place at the table. Actors, once denied a place at the communion table, are now championed as priests in the Holy Theatre. Perhaps it is a result of distilling a complex phenomenon that brings together many disparate art forms into a core of actor-audience communication; such a simplification might lead one astray. Perhaps it is indicative of the thirst in our culture for spirituality, for a connection to forces above and beyond us.

Theatre may indeed approach the realm of ritual, where something more than representation of character and story occurs in the room shared by actors and their audience. To say otherwise would be to ignore the wind-like moving of the Holy Spirit. Actors who are Christians may experience such filling of the Spirit that they are transported in their role, giving way to behavior entirely under the control of the Holy Spirit in a manner consistent with the Word. Audiences may experience an epiphany at a play, whether that play is consciously "Christian" or not; God is not limited by our conscious preparation (as artists or audiences). God's Spirit enters our lives in the most surprising of places—even in the theatre.

When, as Christians, we enter the realm of Holy Theatre, we enter fully cognizant of whom we are surrendering ourselves to: the Holy Spirit. We do not open ourselves to the control of any spiritual forces, because we believe that not all spirits are of God and that they must be tested (1 John 4:1). We see and embrace the relationship between theatre and ritual; theatre is more than amusement, more than a diversion from work. Theatre is a way for us to incarnate our stories, to live with one another in community, and to experience the presence of our fellows and of God. Theatre is a powerful medium.

the theology
of the theatrical
process

Todd E. Johnson

Job Opportunity

The sound of the music was so loud it shook the 1980 Oldsmobile Delta
88 as it played. I looked carefully at the man pounding the dash in time to
the heavy-metal tune blasting from the car's stereo. Teddy was an angular
man in his early thirties with an air of self-importance. Teddy's frame, taut
and razor thin, leaned into life in a way that implied his actions and their
implications carried far more weight than they actually did. I was in the
backseat of the Olds on this beautiful autumn evening as we drove around
the north side of Chicago from dusk to the early hours of the night. I was
not alone in the backseat. I was there, hip to hip, with three others. And
this was to be a ride none of us would ever forget.

The car and the ride were part of the Bailiwick Theatre's play *Job Opportunity*. The play took place principally in the front seat of the Delta 88, and
the paying audience was never larger than four. The cast was no larger than
the audience, but the stage was the expanse of the north side of Sandberg's
"City of Big Shoulders." This is an exceptional and even eccentric play, but
its unique qualities highlight elements of live theatre in general.

The play began with our meeting the actor who played Teddy. He gave us very simple instructions: Once we entered the car and the doors were shut, we were not to open the doors of the car. We were not to touch or otherwise interfere with the actors. We might respond to the play (laugh, gasp, cry, etc.), but we were not to converse with the actors. We entered the car, Teddy put a cassette in the tape player, and we headed out onto the streets of Chicago. The song's chorus foreshadowed what was ahead: "We will break the law." The song was interrupted by cell-phone conversations that provided background on the characters and introduced the story line.

As Teddy spoke with friends on the phone, he explained that he was on his way to pick up Carl to do "that thing." It was clear that Teddy had made plans for Carl but had not given him many details. After a few minutes, we pulled over to pick up Carl, a shorter, thicker, younger man than Teddy. He was holding a pair of work gloves in his hands. It became obvious after only a few moments of their interchange that Carl, though a college graduate, was considered by Teddy, a high school graduate, to be intellectually inferior—or at least not as streetwise. When questioned why he had brought the gloves, Carl replied that he thought they we going to help someone move and was surprised that Teddy didn't have a truck. Teddy began to explain that it wasn't that kind of job.

As an audience, we watched this morality play unfold peering over the shoulders of the actors an arm's length away. It was at first a self-conscious experience. Sitting four abreast in the backseat of a car is not the most comfortable setting. Certainly it was neither one of the luxurious seats at the Goodman nor even the close but accommodating seats at the Steppenwolf. We viewed the actors' faces through a set of rearview mirrors, which provided sight lines enabling us to see them without drawing too much attention to the mirrors. But they brought attention to us, as we easily made eye contact with the actors through the mirrors. Then there were initial questions of safety; we were driving in fairly heavy traffic, not wearing seatbelts, with a driver who was at least partly distracted. This sense of self-awareness was heightened when we would pull over to have Teddy or Carl interact with one of the other actors in the play who were planted on the streets of Chicago. After all, I lived on Chicago's north side; how would I respond if someone saw me in the car?[1] Mostly it made me aware of how integral the audience was to the performance of this play.

As the story unfolded, we learned that Teddy and Carl knew each other from a local watering hole. It seems that a common acquaintance had asked them to pick up a package and deliver it about a mile away. For their efforts they would be rewarded with five hundred dollars, which they could split. Immediately Carl became suspicious about the nature of their work.

He became even more suspicious when Teddy pulled over to pick up the parcel. Carl's discomfort was palpable while he fidgeted waiting for Teddy's return. Teddy returned from his street-corner pick-up with a gym bag and an agreement that they would deliver it without opening it. Carl was incredulous. How could Teddy make such an arrangement? Who knew what they would be transporting? Carl and Teddy began running through a series of arguments about the merits of this enterprise, mostly divided over the possibility of doing something illegal versus the potential of easy money.

By this time the four of us in the backseat had forgotten that this was a play and we were an audience. The actors' timing seemed to naturally incorporate our responses in a casual and spontaneous manner. We literally had been taken on a journey by this play and over time had come to suspend judgment to the point that we lost sight of the fact that this encounter was a fiction. Teddy and Carl, their pasts, their values, and their relationship had become real. They had created a story and were now inviting us into it on the streets of Chicago.

The play reached one climax after another. Teddy delivered the bag even though Carl refused to get out of the car. They drove a short way and parked in an abandoned lot under the elevated train tracks. When they opened the envelope containing their pay, they discovered not hundreds of dollars but thousands. Teddy was insistent; they must keep the money, and they must share it. The two got into an argument, and Carl began to run away. Teddy chased him, and the heated conversation moved from inside the car to outside on the lot, the sounds of their voices echoing off the nearby buildings and filling the Chicago night.

Teddy finally convinced Carl to get back into the car so he could take him home. When the car pulled up in front of Carl's apartment building, the person for whom they had made the delivery was waiting. He approached the car and addressed Teddy and Carl through Carl's window. He interrogated them. Did they get the money? Was Carl with them the whole time? Why didn't Carl come with them when making the delivery? Did Carl get any of the money?

Finally the truth was told. Teddy had bet that Carl wouldn't take the money, a five-hundred-dollar bet. Carl left the car, saying that he and his friendship weren't for sale, but that his friend had sold him out. The actors walked out in front of the car's headlights and took a bow, breaking the hypnotic spell they had cast and ending the play. Though an unusual venue for a play—an Olds Delta 88—it was classic theatre. A story with interesting twists and turns was told. Characters were created with whom one developed emotional connections. And for the duration of the play, the distinction between illusion and reality was suspended.

Theatre and Theology in Dialogue

At first blush, it might seem a bit odd to ask theological questions of an experience like *Job Opportunity*, or any play for that matter. As we have seen, the history of theatre and the church has been uneven at best. Much theatre today has little to do with religion explicitly. Certainly there was no intentional theological content in *Job Opportunity*, though one could draw analogous biblical and theological themes from the story and its characters. Still, what does theology have to do with theatre, or, vice versa, what does theatre have to do with theology?

Interestingly enough, significant works have explored the relationship between theatre and theology, or how the art form of theatre can serve theologians as a paradigm for their task of reflecting on God and the Christian life of faith. The use of theatre as an image to describe God and God's saving acts is not new. Karl Barth (following John Calvin) described the universe God created as *Theatrum Gloria Dei*, envisioning "the created Cosmos . . . [as the] theatre of the great acts of God in grace and salvation."[2] In this case, theatre becomes an analogy by which to understand human history in relationship to its author. For Barth, creation is the theatre of God's covenant, especially evidenced in the theatricality of the role played by Jesus, God incarnate.[3]

The relationship between theology and theatre has been explored in greater detail by Barth's Swiss Catholic colleague Hans Urs von Balthasar in his five-volume opus *Theo-Drama*.[4] In this multivolume work of systematic theology, Balthasar uses drama as a paradigm to understand the theological task of the Christian faith. Balthasar's theological project involves using drama as an analogue for describing God's incarnate action in the world. This moves theology from the realm of speculation to the realm of action and interaction. In particular it connects the dramatic role played by Christ in the saving event of the "paschal mystery" (his dying and rising) to the role played by the baptized in their dying to self and living united in Christ.[5]

Balthasar's work has stimulated further exploration in this area from other theological perspectives. Two theologians who have continued Balthasar's work are Kevin Vanhoozer and Shannon Craigo-Snell.[6] Vanhoozer's work builds on a perceived parallel relationship between dramatic interpretation and the enacted interpretation of the Scriptures, focusing on both the hearing and the doing of the Word. Just as the dramatic script is written to be enacted, so too the Scriptures were written to be interpreted in life. Vanhoozer uses theatre to interpret the theological task within the life of a Christian. On the positive side, Vanhoozer moves from the givenness of the Scriptures to the living of the Christian life. Vanhoozer's work is not as strong in the particularities, such as his one-to-one allegorical correspondence between faith and theatre, and the proposed dynamic equivalents of doctrine and direction, church and theatre company, Bible as script, God as playwright, Holy Spirit as director, and Christian as performer.[7]

Shannon Craigo-Snell furthers the exploration of the relationship between text (script) and performance. Craigo-Snell enters this conversation through the work of Nicholas Wolterstorff, who suggests that the text is incomplete until realized in its performance. Although this may be true for a dramatic script or a musical score, it is an inadvisable analogy for the Scriptures' relationship to the life of a disciple. What Craigo-Snell ingeniously inserts into the text-performance dyad is the process of rehearsal. Through the process of rehearsal, one truly comes to understand the meaning of the text. It is in the doing of the text that one comes to know, not in the knowing of the text that one comes to do. Therefore, the Christian life is one in which we are constantly exploring the meaning of God's revelation through our lived application of the Scriptures to the particularity of our lives.

Ivan Khovacs summarizes Craigo-Snell's work in the following passage:

> Taking the performance rehearsal for our metaphor sheds some light on the temporal location of the Christian between Scripture and the eschatological performance yet to come. To say that our Christian situation is an ongoing rehearsal that anticipates performance at the resurrection has nothing to do with the attitude that "this world is not my home, I'm only passing through" as the revival hymn goes: it has everything to do with recognition that what we do here and now defines the shape of eschatological performance. It is also highly valuing of time and space as our cosmic stage, as well as of the incarnate means we are given to act in it. Finally the embodied performance interpretation called for by the biblical play, far from involving us in abstractions of meaning from the story, "leads to and is continued in an embodied performance: the event of worship and life."[8]

Through Craigo-Snell's work, one can see that the artistic process of theatre, not the theatrical performance alone, is the appropriate analogue for Christian theology and its relationship to the life of faith.

The use of theatre to understand and evaluate Christian theology is a fruitful and fascinating endeavor. The approach taken in this chapter is not to ask just what theatre has to do with theology, but also to ask what theology has to do with theatre. In other words, what does theatre mean theologically, and how does it do so? What theological categories can be used to evaluate the theatrical event, and how might we appreciate the art and craft of theatre, relative to the other arts, from the perspective of Christian theology? How does theatre as an art form (among all the other arts) uniquely reflect the *imago Dei*? This area of theological exploration is noticeably absent in the current conversations between theology and theatre.

While it has been suggested that all art is a performance at some level,[9] we believe that theatre is such a powerful art form because its performative quality embodies three central theological categories that define the nature of human and divine interaction: incarnation, community, and presence. Although other art forms can embody one or two of these qualities, theatre is unique among the arts in its ability to reflect the *imago Dei* in all three ways. In this chapter we explore these three theological categories and how the artistic process of theatre communicates all three of these themes in ways that speak to both the nature of human existence and the divine image and likeness imprinted into humankind, making it such a simple but uniquely engaging art form.

Theatre as a Human and Divine Enterprise: *Incarnation*

The theological category of incarnation is one of the most central—and most controversial—concepts in the history of the church. Saying that God is an incarnate God implies that God can, has, and will dwell within creation. It certainly is the key issue in understanding the relationship between Jesus and God, and all that is implied by the earliest Christian creed, "Jesus Christ is Lord" (Phil. 2:11). The question for the second generation of Christians was how they (who were mostly Hellenists) could understand a God who existed outside time and space and never changed, yet took on human form.

At the center of this issue was the prologue to the Gospel of John, which boldly proclaims, "the Word became flesh and lived among us" (John 1:14 NRSV). The term "Word," a literal translation of the Greek term *logos*, was not a value-neutral term chosen by the author of John's Gospel. *Logos* defined the "word" or "reason" of the divine in pre-Christian Greek philosophy. *Logos* was akin to the Hebrew concept of Wisdom, which was with God and communicated God.[10] This serves as a reminder that the Hebrew God was not a God who was far off, but a God who dwelt with the people of God.[11] But given a Platonic dualism that saw a clear distinction between the realm of God and the realm of creation, the belief that a divine presence could become human was difficult to fathom.

The intersection of the human and the divine in the person Jesus led to the controversies that would ultimately define what we know as "orthodoxy."[12] Just because the orthodox understanding of Christology can be simply stated, "Jesus was fully human and fully divine," does not mean it can be simply understood, nor does it mean that it will be uniformly interpreted. Certainly one of the central theological issues over the past century has been the variety of interpretations of Christology. The relationship between the Jesus of history and the Christ of faith has been an issue Christians have wrestled with since the Enlightenment. And neither modernity nor postmodernity has made those questions less controversial or less reflected upon by theologians. In particular, the contemporary labels of Christology—"from above," where the preexistent Son takes human form, or "from below," where the human Jesus is adopted or deified by God and made divine—continue to perpetuate the controversy.[13]

This issue is like a theological boomerang that never goes away because it is so vital to understanding the nature of the Christian God. That God chose to enter into the limits of our reality in such a way as to be (in some sense) limited by it defines the extravagance of God's love. That is the foundation of John 3:16 and Philippians 2:5–11: the wonder of God's self-giving, self-sacrificing love. God now experiences firsthand the limits of time, space, finitude, and so on. The belief in an incarnate God is belief in a God who has the potential to redeem creation from the inside out. It is a God who offers an alternative vision for the future and places the present moment into the sweep of a narrative that begins with creation and ends with God's reclamation of all heaven and earth. An incarnate God is a God of creation and history; an incarnate God is a God of story.

If for a moment one can suspend the numerous controversies over the doctrine of the incarnation and focus on the concept that Jesus as the incarnate Christ became a human person par excellence and defines what should be the ultimate human experience of life, then incarnation becomes a means of evaluating what is truly human and therefore a model to appraise theatre in relationship to the other arts. The fact that theatre is a performance art means that it is restricted by the limits of time and space. Certain art forms have an inherent ability to transcend time and space. Monet's *Water-Lily Pond* is a painting of the artist's own garden.[14] Although the garden itself changes, the painting is static. However closely it emulates the actual garden, it cannot re-create the changing of the light caused by the sun's rising or setting, the ripples created by wind on the waters, and the swaying of the plants in the same breeze. Unlike a photograph, the process of capturing this image is not instantaneous but occurs over a period of time. Monet can paint or repaint this scene until he has exactly the picture he sees in his mind's eye on the canvas. Once it is finished, it has a quality of timelessness to it. Depending on how well it is preserved, it will look much the same for generations, unlike the garden itself, which is always changing.

Performance art is different. A live musical performance is unique in its singularity. This contrasts with a musical recording, which captures the performance once for all time and has a timeless quality to it. A live performance involves variables that make each performance one of a kind. From changes in the way a piece is played to differences in the musicians, audience, and setting, a performance is unique and bound by space and time.

The relationship between film and theatre is similar to that between recorded music and live performance. Though film and theatre have many similarities, the performative quality of live theatre sets it apart from film. If I were to describe a scene in Mel Brooks's film *The Producers*, I could refer you to a specific scene and note something in particular that Zero Mostel did or an interesting way a scene was shot, and we would have a common reference. But if I were making a reference to the recent theatrical revival of Brooks's movie on Broadway and beyond, we would not have that same referent. Even if we saw the same play on the same night, our view of the stage would offer each of us a unique perspective, and we would each choose where to focus our attention.

Further, though rehearsal is part of the production of both a play and a film, the fact that each performance of a scene in a play is at least somewhat unique makes a play different from a movie. In the making of a film, a scene may be shot many times and from many different camera angles. The film-maker then edits, cutting and splicing the video recordings and arranging them in the sequence that tells the story the way she or he sees fit. Imperfections, undesired interpretations, unwanted shots are removed, at best saved for the "extras" chapter on a DVD or a later "director's cut" edition.

Theatre, though rehearsed, is still ultimately an exercise in spontaneity. At any moment something unexpected may happen. The actors must constantly interact with one another, with the story, and with the audience. And with each performance the play is new and living and timely. Even if the actors could perform a play the exact same way twice, the audience—even the exact same audience—would be different. A performance of *Hamlet* in New York City on September 10, 2001, would be an entirely different experience from a performance of the play two days later because of what the actors and audience would bring to the experience.

Live theatre, then, of all the arts, may best approximate the incarnational character of our God because of its combination of narrative and performative qualities. A play is a story incarnated in real space and time by real people. It is a human-to-human interaction that can often communicate something transcendent. The actors tell the story by becoming the story. It is subject to all the vagaries and complexities of life. An actor might forget a part; the timing of curtains, lighting, scene changes could go awry. The story is told in the messiness of an imperfect world, and at its best the live performance of a theatrical piece can bring everyone involved in the play—audience, performers, and stage crew—to a transcendent moment. Such a moment might be reduplicated but can never be recaptured. It, like life itself, is ultimately transient. Every play contains the possibility that it might disintegrate because of external or internal forces. This quality is lacking in film. Even seeing a film of a live performance of a play is not the same as being at the live performance. The risks involved in a fallen world are part of the inherent quality of a live performance.

Max Harris explores the incarnational quality of theatre from a slightly different perspective in his work *Theatre and Incarnation*. Harris contrasts theatre with literature, not with film. For Harris, a script is not theatre but an opportunity for theatre. Theatre is primarily a "plastic art," with its context being primarily time and space, not concept. Theatre, like the incarnation, engages all the senses. While the exclusively plastic arts make use of space, and the narrative arts use time, theatre uses both simultaneously. This is exactly the Christian understanding of incarnation, the Word made flesh, God entering our temporal reality.[15]

Certain theological and cultural biases in today's world, however, are fighting against theatre from a Christian perspective. There is an inherent dualism in a good deal of Christian thought that can be traced back to the first-century use of Platonic philosophy to interpret Christianity. Plato believed that theatre became too sensual when it evolved from a poet reciting monologues into the acting out of the text. The fear of the sensual was only reinforced by Reformation thought, which privileged the Word read and proclaimed over all other expressions, such as the Word depicted in visual art or performed theatrically. This notion diminished the full understanding of incarnation and all but extinguished theatre in the Protestant churches.[16]

Harris, using the work of Peter Brook, pushes the incarnational aspects of theatre beyond the simple dualism of holy and secular to the idea of the "rough and holy" in theatre.[17] In his use of Brook's work, Harris insists that for something to be truly divine it must be honest in its portrayal of the reality of our world. He sees this reflected in the best medieval Christian drama because it depicts the pain and suffering of sin from which the crucifixion saves us. Ultimately the incarnation is the embodiment of the rough and the holy, the human and the divine.[18] Using this criterion, Harris critiques Christian playwrights such as T. S. Eliot and Christopher Fry who err on the side of ignoring the rough and focusing too much on the holy. Sanitizing theatre does not serve the religion of the incarnation well and disconnects art—and faith—from life in ways that God chose to avoid in the incarnation.[19]

When the actor playing Teddy was driving through the streets of Chicago, he was interacting with "Carl" and the relationship they had created from Ralph Conception's script as well as with our reaction as an audience in the backseat. All of us were interacting with life on Chicago's streets that night, but the actors had to expand or contract their dialogue to mesh with the traffic flow so that their dialogue fit where we were in the city at a given time. Although *Job Opportunity* was a unique performance, the demands placed on its actors were common: it was different in degree, and not kind, of spontaneity and attention to surroundings. Not unlike any live performance. Not unlike life.

Though all art to some degree reflects the existence of a Creator,[20] the live performance of a play communicates the incarnational quality of God and through this becomes a uniquely human art form. It is the incarnation of the narrative in flesh, space, and time that sets theatre apart. One could argue that sport—the drama of athletic competition—also has this quality. Yet sport lacks an intrinsic narrative to make it theatre's equal. A goal scored in the last minutes of a game has a meaning within the narrative of the game, especially if the goal breaks a tie and becomes the game-winning score. But extra narrative is added to make sport more dramatic, such as the story that the goalie giving up the game-winning score had never given up a goal in the last five minutes of a game, or he was playing against the team that had just traded him for his lack of ability to concentrate, and so on. It seems that the pregame show, the sideline commentator, the color commentator all serve to create these larger narrative contexts for our athletic events. A game-winning home run is placed within the larger story that the batter was 0 for 11 against that pitcher lifetime. The figure skater's fall is presented in the context of her recent broken ankle and her struggle to regain her previous form. The growth of sports talk radio, ESPN, and other sports networks all create drama around sport that becomes as important as sport itself. Still, one could watch a sporting event and not be aware of the multiple story lines intersecting in that event. However, one could not miss the narrative element of a play; it is essential to what makes a play a play.[21]

Witnessing the performance of *Job Opportunity* invited me to see the city in which it was performed differently. I began to see the streets filled not with anonymous people but with individuals with hopes, dreams, and stories. It reminded me that each one of these people is known and loved by God, is part of God's story of creation and invited into God's story of redemption. The conflict between Teddy and Carl raised issues of value conflict within my own life. Where do the values of family, friends, and money fall along the continuum of my priorities? Who or what is Lord of my life? Athanasius wrote that God became flesh that flesh might become God.[22] The incarnation becomes the hinge of our redemption (to borrow a phrase from Tertullian). So too, the incarnational quality of theatre allowed the story of Teddy and Carl to become flesh, that we might experience and transcend our humanity and gain a glimpse into the larger story of our life, our world, and our God.

Theatre as Corporate Enterprise: *Community*

Job Opportunity ended with the four actors taking a bow standing in the crossfire of the car's headlights. After the curbside curtain call, we were invited to get out of the car to stretch and converse with the actors. It was a feeling unlike many in my life. I had not uttered a word the entire time I was in the backseat, yet I had a sense of having communicated with both my fellow audience members and the cast. Through laughs and gasps, sideward glances and quizzical looks—but mostly through an immediate, shared common experience—I felt a bond with those who shared the backseat view of the play. It seemed only natural to strike up a conversation about the play, the reaction from people on the street, about our thoughts and feelings on the story and its characters.

This play was more than an experience we shared; it was an experience we created with one another. Like us, the actors were curious about our interpretations and thoughts, and they were particularly interested in checking their interpretations of our reactions. We as an audience had provided a new context for their interaction and in so doing had created a new play. Our presence and our responses, together with the haphazard occurrences on the street, had all contributed to an unrepeatable performance.

As pointed out earlier, *Job Opportunity* and its unique qualities only magnify what is true in general about theatre: the audience and the performers together form a community. There are those transcendent moments in theatre when the actor has so captured a character, or the ensemble has so incarnated the story, that the audience shares in something truly magical.[23] In these moments, the audience and the cast find a common center and draw together into a circle of trust and expectation, giving themselves over to the story and its possibilities. And the sense of this community is palpable.

Shared common experiences and the relationships they create are vitally important to the Christian understanding of what it means to be human. Orthodox theologian John Zizioulas has made a profound observation about the nature of reality, and in particular what it means to be a human being created in the image of God.[24] Zizioulas argues that nothing can live in isolation or autonomy. Beginning with the etymology of the term "person" and its use in the theatre to refer to the mask the individual wore as an actor, through its early philosophical interpretations, Zizioulas explores the term's meaning. He ultimately concludes that to be a person means being able to face another; to exist means to exist in relationship.[25]

Zizioulas's approach is both philosophical and theological. He begins by addressing stereotypes of Greek anthropological philosophy. He cites beliefs that ancient Greek philosophies are "impersonal" and fail to address the uniqueness of the individual. Zizioulas counters by noting how both Aristotle and Plato do in fact recognize the uniqueness of the individual. However, these Greek philosophical approaches promoted an understanding of the individual in relationship to the cosmos, which was being integrated into the universe. These Platonic and Aristotelian understandings of relationship even made God subject to this law: no person—including the Divine Persons—exists autonomously; rather, everyone exists in relation to or "in Dialogue with" creation.[26]

Zizioulas observes that one's integration into the cosmos was the key issue in Greek theatre, particularly the tragedies. In the tragedies the hero strove to resist and rebel against his fate, all the while learning that his fate could not be changed. His harmonious interrelationship with the universe, the gods, and himself was unavoidable. It is within this relationship that the person finds his or her unique identity.

Just as this understanding of relationship is conveyed by the Greek term *prosopon*, so also is it suggested by the Latin term *persona*. The Roman understanding of person as role is similar to that of the Greeks. *Persona* is not simply a role one plays; it is one's place in life that gives one his or her identity. And one's true identity exists in relationship with other people and the universe at large, not in isolation. One's personhood is not something one imposes on the world; it is an identity one inherits through relationship to the world. This concept of "person" underlies both the early doctrines of the personhood of Christ, fully human, fully divine, and the three persons of the Trinity.

Zizioulas makes a crucial claim for the Christian faith. He perpetuates the ancient Christian claim that the touchstone of the Christian faith is belief in the Triune God; the Christian understanding of the divinity of Christ derives from this central belief. This is a bedrock assertion for what it means to be human, for in this perspective something or someone can exist only in relationship with something else. God is not exempt from this requirement, yet God needs neither people nor creation to be God (let alone to exist), because God by God's triune nature is eternally in relationship. This relational quality both defines God and becomes the template for what it means to be made in the image of God.

Historically there have been two approaches to the concept of the Trinity. On the one hand, the concept of the immanent Trinity emphasizes how the three persons of the Trinity relate to one another.[27] On the other hand, the concept of the economic Trinity is concerned with the roles each person of the Trinity plays in God's saving relationship with humanity and, in fact, in relationship to all creation.[28] For years one of the distinguishing marks between the Eastern churches and the Western churches was the East's preference to speak of the economic Trinity and the West's preference to understand the Trinity in immanent terms. Even so, the Trinity was often at best a secondary theological category in Protestant and Catholic (Western) theology, lagging behind Christology in importance. Not until the mid-twentieth century, when Roman Catholic theologian Karl Rahner uttered his famous adage, "The immanent Trinity is the economic Trinity," was the Trinity revalued as a primary theological category. By this statement, Rahner meant that God relates to humans in the same way that God relates to Godself.[29] Rahner's insistence that the Trinity is the touchstone for Christian theology ushered in a renaissance of trinitarian thought that continues in the new millennium.[30]

The conclusions of much contemporary trinitarian theology illumine the unique divine quality of theatre versus other arts or even other performance arts. It takes an entire community working together at any one time to perform a live theatre piece. The actors and the stagehands, the director and the producer, the actors and the audience, all are necessary for a performance of a play. After all, if any one were absent, would there still be a play? A film or other piece of artwork is different because the audience has less interaction with the making of the art, less human contact with the performer, and hence a less truly human experience. Humans are created to live in community; theatre is an art form that naturally creates a community—an intimate and immediate community.

This realization invites the question of what is meant by "community," especially in the context of today's world. The dissolution of previous understandings of community has led to numerous books describing and bemoaning definitions of community, past and present. Authors such as Robert Bellah and Robert Putnam have described the deconstruction of community in which models of community with shared values and experiences, resulting in common goals and cooperation, are replaced by clusters of smaller, self-selected, often less formally organized groups.[31] Though we may agree with Harris that the audience in theatre is referred to in the singular because it functions as a unit,[32] we must acknowledge the diversity of responses within an audience. Still, even if in an ad hoc sense, the shared experience of a theatrical performance can and does create a community for many who have little other sense of community in their lives.

There have been recent attempts to play up this characteristic of relationship, especially between audience and performers. For example, the Broadway play *The 25th Annual Putnam County Spelling Bee* prescreens audience members as potential spelling bee participants within the play. Audience members sign up to become a crucial part of the play as they actually participate in a live spelling bee on stage. This game show-like quality, where one can go from being part of the audience one moment to central participant in the performance the next, is not the only way the interdependent and relational qualities of theatre are manifest. One does not need to be on stage to be a participant. One does not even need to attend a performance of improvisational theatre to interact with the actors.[33]

Peterson Elementary School on Chicago's far north side annually puts on a school musical. Each year a standard piece of musical theatre is performed by upward of two hundred students in a school where forty different languages and dialects are spoken. One year Peterson Elementary School performed *The Wizard of Oz*. Beyond the core cast of characters in the production, there were numerous choral numbers by large blocks of students playing munchkins, for example. There was an Indian Tin Man, a Korean Cowardly Lion, an Anglo Dorothy, and an African Toto, along with munchkins of every race and creed. Although most North Americans are intimately acquainted with this familiar tale, the parents and grandparents of many of these children were seeing this story for the very first time. Being in the audience with scores of people who, like Dorothy, find themselves far from home in a fascinating and frightening land, one begins to see this familiar play in a new way. For Peterson, these performances are the events that hold the neighborhood's community together in ways that academics and sports never could. The interdependence experienced in the live theatre performance establishes a bond that spills over into the way this diverse community sees itself as a single organic whole in which multiple stories blend into a context of empathic hearing. *The Wizard of Oz* gave this diverse community an opportunity to hear one another's stories through Baum's story of Dorothy. Seeing such ethnically diverse faces among the cast and hearing familiar lines spoken with a variety of accents allowed everyone to see this play for the first time all over again.

This experience cannot be explained by using the concept of incarnation alone. What is memorable about this production is the trinitarian dimension, not the incarnation dimension. To place the focus on the actors is to do a disservice to the whole, which is much larger than the sum of its parts. The process began with the way the school's students, teachers, and staff interacted with one another in creating this event into which the audience could enter. This secondarily led to the interaction of the performers and the entire supporting cast with the audience, creating a community of interpretation in the performance of this script. And finally, this resulted in the interaction of parents with the school staff and other parents in new and more personable ways.

Although not every play ends in a dialogue between artists and audience, as did *Job Opportunity*, indirect communication is always inherently a part of the art form. This relational quality embodies the essential human quality of community, which follows from our being created in the image of the Triune God. Like few other art forms, theatre underscores these very unique qualities of human life as it was intended by our Creator.

Theatre as Transformative Encounter: *Presence*

One of the qualities of live theatre is the thrill of being in the same room with the performers as they engage in their craft. When John Malkovich and Dustin Hoffman reprised Arthur Miller's classic *Death of a Salesman*, one of the draws of that run was the opportunity to see these two tremendously talented actors on stage, in the flesh, together. As noted earlier, one has a sense of immediacy being at such a performance that can never be replicated in a video recording of the same event.

This quality of intimacy was magnified in the play *Job Opportunity* because of the audience's close physical proximity to the actors. It is hard to imagine feeling more intimately connected to the characters in a play than I felt in this experience. We were close enough to smell the flavor of gum on Teddy's breath. Yet even in much larger venues, a good actor has the ability to create a sense of intimacy, a quality of presence that connects the audience to the performers and through them to the story they are enacting.

This raises the question of how one human person is present to another. How is it that we communicate to one another? What is it that allows us to express thoughts and feelings that are unique to us to another person in a way that is discernable and intelligible? When we hear the ubiquitous theme song from *Friends*, "I'll Be There for You," what do we understand by "being there"? How are we present to people in a way that communicates our care and concern?

Anyone who has tried to have a conversation with a teen playing a video game or instant messaging knows that they may be physically present with you but may not be present *to* you. The issue is one of attention. To what do we attend? How often do we focus our attention exclusively on one thing? In our culture of multitasking, we appear to be losing sight of the importance of "undivided attention," of how being single-minded in one's focus creates a sense of intimate presence with another. The category of presence ups the ante within the theological category of incarnation. When the Scriptures proclaim that Christ is the promised Immanuel, "God with us," the promise is not one of physical presence alone. It is a promise of God being present to us, not just present. God's presence is an immediate, personal presence. The issue of presence is the bridge between incarnation and sacramentality, or the theology of God's intimate presence to humanity.[34]

In the previous chapter we saw how theatre historians and theorists have identified the deep and intimate relationship between religion and theatre. The concepts of trance and possession—channeling transcendent spirits through the actor—are considered part of theatre's origins by many and as its very nature by some. These are themes of presence. The concept of God's presence to God's people runs deep in the Christian faith and at the same time has divided Christian communities. To understand the story of the concept of "presence" or "sacramentality" in the Christian faith—especially in its contemporary models—will help one understand both the history of the Christian church's relationship to theatre and the Christian understanding of presence as a way of interpreting theatre.

The Christian church has taken numerous approaches to understanding *how* God is present to humanity, particularly through the sacraments. Sacramental theology has often been characterized by defining how God is present in an object, such as bread, wine, oil, or water. In the past fifty years, however, there has been a shift from understanding presence as being within an object to focusing on presence in the sacramental action that a community performs. This approach to sacramentality assumes that God's presence is primarily "peopled," and that actions such as shared table fellowship in the Lord's Supper define the type of actions that manifest God's love between people.[35]

The question of how God is present to us returns us to our initial question of how people are present to one another. Augustine is the theologian who addressed this question most directly. He journeyed through many philosophies and religions before coming to rest in the truth of Christianity as the answer to his questions. Specifically, Augustine was strongly influenced by Manichean and Platonic dualism. This led him to believe that before the fall of humanity, humans were able to communicate directly—spirit to spirit, soul to soul—without the need for using their bodies.[36] With the infusion of sin into our creation, humanity could no longer communicate spiritually; it required the use of the physical world. Augustine was vexed by the question of how a person could share a unique experience that he or she had with another person in an intelligible way. His conclusion was that humans could communicate only through signs, words, and gestures. God could speak to us without signs, words, and gestures, but God chooses to communicate within the limits of our fallen humanity.[37]

For example, if I was thinking of an ice cream sundae made with soft-serve ice cream, smothered with hot fudge, and topped with whipped cream, nuts, and a cherry, most people could picture (maybe even taste!) what is simply an abstraction of a hot fudge sundae. I could also show you a sketch or photograph of such a hot fudge sundae and have similar results. In the end, the idea of a hot fudge sundae would be communicated to you through signs and words. Further, if I was physically present to you, I could use gestures as well, making my communication that much more intimate. You could hear the tone of my voice, see my facial expressions, and maybe even smell the aroma of hot fudge on my breath. This is simply the way humans communicate and therefore are present to one another. And this is what gives live theatre a sacramental quality, for the actors are present in an intimate way because of the immediate use of signs, words, and gestures offered with the intention of communicating to a particular group of people.

Unfortunately, the history of the theological category of sacramentality, like that of Christology and the Trinity, is the story of a move away from communication to realism and now back to communication. In understanding this theological trajectory, one can begin to see how theatre embodies the theological category of presence. The Platonic paradigm is used by the subapostolic church marked by the apologists.[38] A Platonic worldview invites one to see the world as a two-tiered universe. The real world of forms exists in the upper realms of heaven. "Real" is determined by the quality of permanence and changelessness. Over time, the physical world of matter changes, while the eternal forms remain static (or in stasis), and so the world of forms is understood to be spiritual, not physical. This notion led to the Christian embrace of an immutable God, one who does not change. The physical world is merely an image—an imperfect reflection—of the world of forms. Our spiritual side (our soul or psyche) can sense the spiritual reality or form reflected in the transient physical object. So a chair on earth is recognized as a chair because it reflects the eternal, perfect form of "chair" in heaven. Our eternal souls, having been residents in heaven before our birth, can recognize the earthly shadows of these heavenly forms. This devaluing of the physical and the sensual led Plato to demean theatre.

In the Platonic paradigm, everything on earth is simply a referent to what is truly real in heaven. Therefore, the "real presence" of anything depends on its ability to present an eternal reality in an earthly context. A sacrament, then, is different from an ordinary substance in that its eternal referent is divine. Whereas the earthly matter of bread may refer to the eternal form of bread in heaven, the consecrated bread of the Eucharist refers to the form of the eternal Christ, the Word made flesh. The result is the presence of God and its spiritual benefits. As Augustine preached, "These realities are called sacraments because in them one thing is seen while another is *grasped*. What is seen is a mere physical likeness; what is grasped bears spiritual fruit."[39] In fact, this Platonic dualism led early Christians to distance themselves from theatre, if not reject it outright, because it was too sensual or what we might now describe as too worldly. Still, presence was rooted in an understanding of something being communicated through signs, words, and gestures, a theme that would be lost over time.

This sacramental understanding of the power of these signs to communicate God's presence to God's people did not persist. For numerous reasons, the understanding of the presence of God in the Christian West became more literal, and "real" became analogous to "physical." This led to a crisis in the Reformation regarding whether one accepted God's sacramental presence as physical or spiritual, or whether one rejected the understanding of God's presence altogether. These interpretations of presence remain with us today, frequently dividing and subdividing Christ's church in the world, leaving the church to untie a proverbial Gordian knot.[40]

The resolution of this issue (at least theologically) came through a recovery of a more biblical understanding of presence in the mid-twentieth century by Roman Catholic theologians Karl Rahner and Edward Schillebeeckx, using a model of communication theory. Rahner's contribution to this paradigm was his concept of "real symbol" (at times referred to as "natural symbol" or "genuine symbol"), that is, those symbols that effectively communicate what they represent. Rahner follows in Thomas Aquinas's footsteps in understanding the human body as the symbol of the human soul, where the body is the expression or self-realization of the soul. The symbolic quality of the body to express the soul is limited and incomplete, but it is a natural relationship and corresponds to the soul. It is through the body that the soul is present in the world. Beginning with this paradigm, Rahner goes on to argue that all reality is in its nature symbolic, a process of self-expression through symbols that, though distinct from what they symbolize, have a natural affinity and correlation to the reality they communicate. Theology can be understood, Rahner would suggest, only as a system of symbols that point beyond themselves to God.[41] The relationship to theatre is self-evident: it is the actor's body that becomes the symbol of the character he or she plays.

To say that something was "reduced to symbol" is contrary to Rahner's thought. A symbol was the highest form of reality that something in the physical realm could achieve. This premise shaped all of Rahner's theology, particularly his Christology. Rahner argued that the primary symbol of God was Jesus Christ. However, God's gracious nature continues beyond the life, death, and resurrection of Christ in the body of Christ, the church. The sacraments function, therefore, as actions or events that are manifestations of the ever-given grace of God.[42] These were the key building blocks that Edward Schillebeeckx would use to develop his theology of transignification.

Schillebeeckx was convinced that Rahner and others were moving in the right direction in their interpretation of the sacraments. Yet Schillebeeckx was dissatisfied by the perpetuation of a dualism that separated the inner and the outer, body and soul, matter and spirit. His contribution known as the "Interpersonal-Encounter Model" is based on two premises. First, sacraments assume an "I-Thou" rather than an "I-It" relationship. A sacramental encounter is an encounter with a person, not an encounter with an object. Second, the action of God's grace accomplished in Christ continues in the church today. Sacraments are events that occur within a community and are done by the community.[43] Likewise, theatre establishes an I-Thou relationship within the cast and between the cast and the audience and hence can establish a community through the performance in ways that film and literature, for example, cannot.

Although Schillebeeckx's thought is rigorous and not uncomplicated, it is possible to boil it down to an analogy. If I were to give my wife flowers as a sign of appreciation and love for her, I have given her more than just flowers. I have given her an expression of my love and commitment to her and our marriage. The meaning and significance of the flowers have been transformed from signs of God's beauty and the wonders of nature to an expression of my love for, and my relationship with, my wife. The meaning of the flowers has changed, and they communicate more than just the presence of the flowers. They make my love present to my wife in the action of my giving them to her.[44] Sacramentality, then, the category of how God is present in the world, is seen as actions through which people are present to one another, embodying God's love. It is Schillebeeckx's recovery of both the symbolic and the relational/communal that makes the concept of sacramentality so appropriate to our discussion of theatre.

The discussion of sacraments in the past one hundred years creates a helpful backdrop for understanding the unique qualities of live theatre. As mentioned earlier, a dominant question in sacramental theology over the past centuries has been, how is God present in material objects? The category has been "present with" or "present in," not "present to." In much the same way, over the past one hundred years, film has become the lingua franca of drama, whether on the big or the small screen. In the past fifty years, many plays have been broadcast, either prerecorded or live, and often presented as if the broadcast version were the same thing as the live event. But just as sacramental theology has returned to a focus on the presence of Christ in the gathered community,[45] so too theatre has reasserted its uniqueness in the performative event. A person can be present to a film, but neither a film nor the people in the film can be present to the audience. Yet, in theatre the performers and the audience can be present to each other, interact with each other, and create a unique performance together.

The sense of presence in a live performance cannot be equaled in a recording of a performance. There is a power and immediacy possible in theatre that cannot be replicated in film. For example, Rodgers and Hammerstein's musical *The Sound of Music* had never been performed in a major theatre in Austria, in no small part because of the emotional proximity to the story. However, director Renaud Doucet brought the play to the Volksoper Theatre in Vienna in the spring of 2005. Doucet realized that many demons connected with Nazi control of Austria needed to be exorcised from the Austrian psyche. Rather than avoid the issue, Doucet addressed the matter head-on in a way that could be done only in live theatre. In the final scene when the von Trapp family performs in a competition in an Austrian theatre, Doucet used the entire Volksoper Theatre as the stage and placed actors in authentic Austrian Nazi uniforms in the aisle to give the audience a sense that they were the audience at the competition. The audience response was palpable as its members were confronted with a presence of their past. Some of the audience gasped as the Nazis streamed down the aisle, and still more rigorously applauded as the von Trapp family escaped their captors.

Doucet was able to elicit such a deep response because he knew the powerful presence that live theatre would engender. He specifically played on those signs, words, and gestures that would touch the audience in ways that anything less than a live performance would not. Film alone could not place Nazi soldiers within the comfort zone of an audience member and draw out such a response; this was achieved only by the actors playing the roles of the soldiers directing their attention (albeit through posture, expressions, gaze) with the audience.

The theological understanding of sacramentality gives us insight into why the *live* is superior to the *virtual* in communicating presence. It also has interesting parallels to the evolution of the Stanislavskian approach to acting. Konstantin Stanislavsky was a Russian actor and later acting teacher whose approach to character development revolutionized acting in the later nineteenth and early twentieth centuries. Stanislavsky's approach to acting involved creating multiple layers of a character by asking and answering questions about that character, and in this exploration establishing a depth and realism that would bring the character to life. The key to this technique was not actually becoming the character, or in some way merging one's life with the life of the character. Instead it was acting "as if," maintaining an objective distance from the character.[46] The students of Stanislavsky, known as "method actors," took this to another level. They maintained that you could not act out something you had not experienced, blurring the distinction between the actor's life and the "life" of the character. Just as in the history of the presence of God in worship, literalism and realism replaced symbolism and trans-significance. One need not become the character to play the character, any more than bread need become the flesh of Jesus of Nazareth for the intended presence to be communicated. And just as there has been a theological moderation in presence, so too there has been a moderation in acting.[47] As we will see in the next chapter, the sacramental quality of theatre is one of its most profound aspects, in both its past and its future.

Part of the power of *Job Opportunity* was the immediacy of the story created through the proximity to the actors. This play is one of the most memorable I have experienced. It was not the best-written play, nor was it the best-acted play. Yet the proximity to the actors and the stage being set literally in my neighborhood gave the story a level of reality that I had never before experienced in theatre. Although not every theatre experience is as intense as *Job Opportunity*, every play has a quality of human presence that is accessible in the live theatre performance. Every play utilizes the grace given us within the limits of our humanity to communicate in direct, profound, and intimate ways.

Theatre and Religion

There are many approaches to the relationship of religion and culture.[48] Without entering into the debate about Christianity and culture here, we would suggest that the most helpful model for understanding the relationship of Christianity and culture is in the work of Paul Tillich. Tillich saw an essential union between religion and culture. Part of Tillich's theological agenda was to create a synthesis of theology and culture, in particular a synthesis of theology and art. His desired synthesis was admittedly never realized. This, Tillich argues, is the result of sin. The existence of religion is, in fact, evidence of sin. Tillich writes, "Asked what the proof is for the fall of the world, I like to answer: religion itself, namely, a religious culture beside a secular culture, a temple beside a town hall, a Lord's Supper beside a daily supper, prayer beside work, meditation beside research, *caritas* beside *eros*."[49]

Tillich suggests that there are two essential modes of how the person (Tillich's term is "mind") interacts with his or her environment (Tillich's term, "reality"). This interaction between mind and reality (or person and environment) creates culture. In this interaction an individual can either grasp reality or shape it. Within either of these interactions, the human mind offers three types of reason: *autonomos, heteronomos,* and *theonomos.* Tillich describes this model:

> The words "autonomy," "heteronomy," and "theonomy" answer the question as to *where* the "nomos" or law of life is rooted in three different ways: Autonomy asserts that man as the bearer of universal reason is the source and measure of culture and religion—that he is his own law. Heteronomy asserts that man, being unable to act according to universal reason, must be subject to a law, strange and superior to him. Theonomy asserts that the superior law is, at the same time, the innermost law of man himself, rooted in the divine ground which is man's own ground: the law of life transcends man, although it is at the same time his own. Applying these concepts to the relation between religion and culture, we called an autonomous culture the attempt to create the forms of personal and social life without any reference to something ultimate and unconditional, following only the demands of theoretical and practical rationality. A heteronomous culture, on the other hand, subjects the forms and laws of thinking and acting to authoritative criteria of an ecclesiastical religion or a political quasi-religion, even at the price of destroying the structures of rationality. A theonomous culture expresses in its creation an ultimate concern and a transcending meaning not as something strange but as its own spiritual ground. "Religion is the substance of culture and culture the form of religion." This was the most precise statement of theonomy.[50]

The challenge, then, using Tillich's paradigm, is to understand the incarnational, even sacramental, presence of God in culture in a way that acknowledges the transcendence of God, while maintaining God's gracious condescension within culture. As residents in contemporary, postmodern culture, we have been duped into believing that we are autonomous and self-sufficient. The Christian response has often been "heteronomous Christian culture," which creates a parallel culture to the secular culture, while at the same time placing this Christian culture above all other cultures. Think of the rise of contemporary Christian music, with its Top Ten, its musical genres that ape contemporary genres, even a Christian "Grammy" award known as the Dove. At its worst this phenomenon leads to an autonomous destruction of religion and a heteronomous destruction of culture; as a result, humans, especially people of faith, have ontologically estranged themselves from culture and have distanced themselves from the source of their creativity and vitality. A heteronomous Christian culture ultimately points more to itself than to God.

Visualizing these three concepts in relation to one another might be a helpful way of summarizing them.

Where the law of life is found	How we live	How this shapes religion
Autonomy	Humans create their own norms, values, and laws, unrelated to the laws of the world around them.	Religion becomes an exercise in self-expression and is disconnected from the culture at large.
Heteronomy	Humans live in a world defined by laws completely external to themselves.	Religion becomes a system that expresses and/or creates an alternative world, separate from the interior world of the individual. Religion can become a counterculture.
Theonomy	Humans live in a world in which the laws of the universe are the same as the laws discovered within oneself.	Religion is congruent with the laws of the universe, creating a synergy of religion and culture.

Peter Berger in his seminal book *The Sacred Canopy* charts the development of Protestant Christian thought from Friedrich Schleiermacher to the mid-twentieth century.[51] Berger contends that the interior turn Schleiermacher made in defending Christianity against his "enlightened" colleagues, what Schleiermacher termed "the cultured despisers,"[52] ultimately led Protestant Christianity to abandon the three elements that are crucial to the existence of any religion: mystery, magic, and miracle. Schleiermacher's use of Enlightenment categories, including the diminishment of the miraculous and the supernatural, led to a Protestant interiority, what we would now call "spirituality," which increasingly took precedence over organized religion. Berger, writing in the early 1960s, argues that this trend has put the ministry of Protestant churches in jeopardy. In a secular, pluralistic world in which women and men see their relationship with God akin to the care and feeding of their own personal spirituality,[53] the need for any sort of mediation or accountability to a church becomes less important. Berger's work was written in a time when talk of marketing the church was both new and rare, well before the "seeker service" model established by Willow Creek Community Church. A half century ago Berger identified the beginnings of a trend that has led to a significant shift away from organized religion and a community of faith as a place for establishing one's own faith life.

The alternative is to understand God as primarily revealed in Scripture and ultimately in Jesus Christ, and secondarily revealed in parts of culture such as the arts. In particular, theatre as art stands in prophetic contrast to an individualistic, autonomous culture in which community and relationship are unimportant. This alternative vision is underscored in Tillich's theological critique.[54] Tillich asserts that God is the ground of meaning through which all cultures are founded. Issues of life and death, of love and hate, of charity and self-centeredness, define us and our relationship to the cosmos; these are universal issues of ultimate concern. Issues of ultimate concern are those concepts that point to God and indirectly reveal God. Tillich would insist that what makes art uniquely qualified as a vehicle for revelation is its symbolic nature. A symbol points beyond itself to God, while at the same time revealing that to which it refers. Using vocabulary introduced earlier in this chapter, we might say that symbols of ultimate concern are sacramental. And as we saw in the history of symbol and sacrament above, at its best, their use presupposes a community for interpretation.

For example, Shakespeare's *Hamlet* has been performed for centuries. And it will continue to be performed because it speaks to the universal questions of human existence. In that way it indirectly points to the answers to those questions, that is, the self-giving love of the living God. *Hamlet* complements, not competes with, the Christian message. In fact the symbolic nature of theatre itself, with its communal, interdependent nature, reflects the nature of the living God and God's triune nature.

Although art in general has the potential to reveal the nature of God, theatre has a unique opportunity to convey the reality of the Triune God. Humans are situated in an existential dilemma. They can imagine eternal life but cannot attain it. Our mortality is an anchor restraining us from attaining immortality.[55] This crisis and the anxiety it produces can be negotiated through art. At least art can provide opportunities for catharsis, such as Aristotle suggested.

Whenever issues of ultimate concern are raised, the possibility of faith exists. Tillich writes, "Faith is the state of being ultimately concerned."[56] This is not to equate faith with "the Christian Faith," but to suggest an openness to God, providing an opportunity for the Christian gospel to be introduced through the questions raised in art. Using Tillich's theonomous understanding of religion and culture, one can see how theatre conveys Christian themes by virtue of its performative nature, even beyond the religious quality of theatre's potential to communicate issues of ultimate concern.

A Graced Opportunity

Among the arts, theatre uniquely reflects the divine image in which humans are created. As with other live performance arts, the live quality of a play is subject to the limits of time and space. There is no editing to cover mistakes or provide a different angle. And unlike musical performances, in which a note sung or played a bit off can be electronically corrected before it is amplified to the audience, no such corrective exists for a missed line or cue. There is a quality in the craft of theatre—the performances, the writing, the direction, the staging—that pushes the boundaries of what is possible but ultimately still works within those limits. This incarnational quality is essential to a theatrical performance.

Though all art is intended for a community and can possibly even create a community, live performances engage the audience in dialogue and interaction. The dynamic of community created in live performance gives theatre its special appeal. After all, why spend the money to see *Hamlet* or *Cats* when you can rent the DVD much more economically? We do so because of the undeniable thrill of being in the moment when the play unfolds, knowing that as a part of the audience we are part of the performance. We are part of the community creating that unique theatrical moment. Theatre connects so deeply with our human nature because it speaks to the essence of who God created us to be, creatures in community, interdependent and integrated with one another.

What sets theatre apart from other dramatic or narrative arts is the concept of presence. It is the ability of the actors to attend simultaneously to the other performers, the story being enacted, and the audience that allows the play to come so close to one's inner self. Although this is possible in any play, it becomes most obvious when the play is performed by persons of no mean ability. For example, in one production of the play *The Value of Names*, Shelly Berman played an aging actor fingered in the McCarthy communist witch hunts in the 1950s. His character is confronted by his daughter, who wants to change her name so that she can make it into the business on her own, not because of her name. Yet at the same time, she admits being embarrassed by her father's bitterness over his being redlisted many years ago. In a monologue that closes the first scene, Berman delivered his lines to the actress playing his daughter with such passion and persuasion that even the actress was riveted by his words. But it was the way in which this skilled performer made eye contact with the audience during this monologue, and the way he paced his delivery, that so held the audience in his grasp. Without exception, each time the lights went up for the intermission, there was a breathless pause, betraying that everyone in the audience felt as if Berman had been speaking directly to him or her. As someone who had the opportunity to usher at this play many times, I saw Berman's ability to adjust his performance nightly to include feedback from the audience, which made this actor and this story intimately present to everyone in the room.

This quality of immediacy and presence—whether experienced from the backseat of an Oldsmobile or from the seat of a posh theatre—speaks of an incarnate God who is present to us, and allows us by God's grace to be present to one another. In a theatrical experience—even in the most faithless performance—the thumbprint of our Creator is evident.

live theatre
in a virtual world

Todd E. Johnson

Breakfast

I was looking forward to breakfast that morning. David McFadzean and I had been having conversations about team teaching a course at Fuller Seminary with the operative title "Drama and the Christian Faith." David is a television and movie producer and writer of some note who is also a committed churchman.[1] We had been discussing the place of narrative and ritual in the Christian journey and had been brainstorming ideas of how theatre, worship, and pastoral care are all narrative at their core. We had teased out points of convergence and divergence as we considered bringing theology and ministry students together with Christian theatre artists. These conversations had been pregnant with creative ideas for teaching. But this conversation was going to be different.

I had e-mailed David a draft copy of the previous chapter. I was curious to hear his feedback on my description of how live theatre was in some way reflective of God's nature and immanent presence to humanity. I wondered how he would react to the survey of theologies that I had argued are relevant to theatre. I wondered what he would think of current theologies that see God's presence as primarily "peopled" and especially regard the human component to Christian rituals as parallel to the theatrical experience. Though I was curious about David's feedback and insights, I thought this would be a sidebar conversation to the larger conversation involving our class, but this was not to be.

David was already seated when I arrived and began to talk before I had settled into my seat.

"Your chapter was fascinating. But it made me a bit concerned. You made such a good case for the divine quality of theatre that it left me saying 'Why bother going to church if you can experience the presence of the divine in theatre?' After all, theatre is usually more polished in both 'script' and 'performance' than church. In most cases, theatre is of better quality than worship."

I wasn't quite ready for this comment, so I tried to buy some time. "What did you think of the use of *Job Opportunity* as an example? Is it too eccentric?"

"No," David responded, "It was too good. It showed how creative use of theatre's greatest asset—the interaction between performer and audience—is a powerful tool in creating profound experiences. You see, the problem isn't that people come to theatre expecting something to happen; and they are disappointed when nothing happens. The problem is that people go to worship and expect nothing to happen—and what is worse is that usually nothing *does* happen. Why go to church when you can go to theatre? You have made a persuasive theological argument that theatre is a viable substitute for church."

I informed David that the chapter was the first part of a couplet of chapters and that many of the concerns he had in reading the first theological chapter would hopefully be answered in the second. Maybe the connection between the theology of sacraments and the theological nature of theatre was not persuasive or elicited an uncomfortable association for you. I hope this chapter, building on the previous chapter, resolves any unanswered questions.

To begin with, McFadzean's observation that people would settle for second best—for less than what is truly real, or in this case, truly divine—is one that echoes an ancient allegory with an interesting twist. In *The Republic*, Plato offers an illustration, an allegory, of how he understands the world. Plato describes the world through two types of people, those who are able to see the world as it is and those who are incapable of such direct contact with the real world.[2] Obviously these two groups have very different experiences of the world. The philosophers, who are able to address the verities of the cosmos directly, live, as it were, above ground in the light of day. Those who are incapable of experiencing the brilliance of such truth live in caves below ground. In the famous allegory of the cave, Plato describes how the philosophers interpret the world for those unable to experience it for themselves. They live with their backs to the mouth of the cave, the light of the world streaming in from behind them. Those who know, experience, and understand what is truly real present events of the world, casting them as shadows on the wall of the cave thanks to the sunlight behind them. This primitive projection of reality foreshadows movies and television and their projection of a virtual world. For example, we don't experience the events of the world; rather, we experience a distillation of these events processed for our easy consumption on the televised news. Our homes, wired as they are to the various electronic media of our day, have come to resemble Plato's view of the world. We may live in comfortable caves, but they are windows as much to the virtual world of the electronic age as to the real world outside the door.

The important distinction between our virtual world and Plato's allegory of the cave is that those who dwell in the cave don't know there is another world and believe that their experience is all there is. In today's world, however, we know that there is something more, but often we chose a prefabricated, virtual reality over actual reality. Increasingly, we prefer to interact with people through media rather than directly.

Put another way, two visions of the future were offered in the first half of the twentieth century. The first, and most famous, was George Orwell's vision of life under Big Brother in *1984*. This parallels Plato's vision, where those who know better control those who don't. Life in *1984* is one of oppression and control. The other vision is that of Aldous Huxley's *Brave New World*, where people are not so much controlled as anesthetized by entertainment, humored into a state of sedation and complicity. Although our fears have been dominated by the more familiar vision of Orwell, Huxley's prophecy, according to Neil Postman, is the one that has come to pass. Postman's study of contemporary society concludes that we are now held captive to our delights, choosing to be entertained in our caves rather than live in the real world.[3]

Substance, Sensation, and Spectacle

Postman's observation opens into the larger question of how live theatre functions in a world of spectacle and virtual reality. Here I find Postman's argument worthy of consideration. Postman, using Plato (along with Marshall McLuhan), argues that forms of communication determine the quality of a culture. This leads to his first conclusion: that in our post–printing press, post-telegraph era, we now see the world through the lens of our media.[4] The first great shift in media culture according to Postman was the printing press. The printing press radically changed our view of the world, expanding what was common knowledge about the size and diversity of our planet, its cultures, and its history. Protestant faith in particular was an early consequence of the printing press, as it became the religion of the printed book, giving people access to Scripture that was until then unthinkable.[5] The print media's growth advanced the orality of human culture. Now people could speak with great clarity and certainty about ideas that would have otherwise been unattainable. The printing press gave conversation both greater depth and breadth and offered deeper resources for people to critique what they had heard. It made information about the world—past and present—readily accessible, effectively shrinking the size of the world.

To summarize Postman's thesis: languages are our media, media are our metaphors, and metaphors create our culture. Postman maintains that cultures choose metaphors that most accurately reflect their understanding of truth, so as media changes, ideas of truth change with them.[6] For example, the metaphor of "book" dominated the worldview of literate peoples for centuries; now the world is dominated by a shift from print to "video" as the dominant world metaphor.[7] The intermediate step between the technology of the printing press and today's multimedia video culture, Postman asserts, was the telegraph. The telegraph (telegraphy) was the watershed in this change because it could communicate data over a great distance with what was at the time unimaginable speed. But what it communicated was brief and devoid of details and context. Telegraphy valued the immediacy of information over quality.[8] Radio, therefore, was merely a small step forward in terms of the effects of technology on culture.

The next major stage in the evolution of our culture, according to Postman, was the recording and transmission of images, more importantly in television than in motion pictures. The image functions differently than the word—either spoken or printed—in communication and culture. Postman argues that the shift to the image away from the word is a shift away from precision. Further, the televised image transfers the value of information into the value of entertainment to the point where our culture is based on entertainment more than information.[9] Postman maintains that the shift to a visual culture was a shift away from a rational culture to an emotive or affective culture. For example, in a television culture, advertisements no longer argue the worth of a product; instead, they create an aura of attractiveness.[10] Postman asserts that "advertisers no longer assumed rationality on the part of their potential customers. Advertising became one part depth psychology, one part aesthetic theory. Reason had to move itself to other arenas."[11] This observation is reiterated by Johannes Birringer, who concludes that television has become the paradigm for our present and future culture: a constant flow of information and entertainment that knows no geographic bounds and becomes increasingly self-referential. Television not only influences society but also defines it.[12]

Postman's interpretations about the role of technology in culture—creating metaphors that define our worldview—are as important to the realm of faith as they are to the world of live theatre. The culture established by telegraphy has effectively changed all our cultural expectations, religion and the arts notwithstanding.[13] For example, the technique used in producing a television show involves changing view every 3.5 seconds, never allowing the eye to rest. It is a medium that seeks to emotionally tantalize and titillate. Television by virtue of its impact on our culture has established entertainment—sensational and enticing entertainment—as the natural format to represent all experience.[14]

Technology does not simply contribute to culture but is a force in creating it. For example, the clock was invented by monks to allow them to keep a more regular schedule of daily prayer. A technology built by the church as a tool to make its life more regular in the end gained control and regulated both the church and society. Clocks have redefined time so profoundly that we can scarcely imagine a world without clocks and the schedules they produce.[15] Our North American culture is particularly susceptible to the influence of technology on society. Anglo North America was the first society to be established as a culture of print. From the arrival of the first European settlers in the New World, a technology of communication was at the core of their culture. Over time the type of communication technology has changed, but the assumption of such technology remains unchanged.

Like the assimilation of the technology of clocks in an earlier age, our communication media have created and defined our world.[16] And with the acceptance of technology as a centerpiece in our culture comes the assumption that technological progress is inevitable and inevitably good. This technological model of progress has initiated the trend of separating us from our traditions; where new is good, old is bad. This leads to a dismissal of the past, as in Henry Ford's "history is bunk" view of the world, and the uncritical acceptance of innovation as inherently good. These assumptions, which are so common in our day-to-day lives, were not, and are not, inevitable, but are the result of the choices we have made in our uncritical absorption of our technologies.

An invention as innocuous as a clock can create an entirely new set of values and expectations in a society, and given its religious roots, it had a cultural imprimatur. So too, the opportunity to broadcast the gospel by television seems to be a logical use of technology to accomplish the church's mission to proclaim the gospel. Yet truth does not look the same in the world of telegraphy, something the church has not taken into consideration. On television credulity has replaced reality as the basis for authority. Ministers have become personalities in the media sense of the word.[17] Thanks to television, religion has shifted from an encounter with the transcendent (what Postman terms "enchantment") to the personal (or entertainment). Television from its earliest years was seen as a medium for religious programming. However, "religious programming" did not mean that religion would be the content of television, but rather that television would be the format of our religion.[18] Religion, like all aspects of contemporary culture, has fallen under the spell of the entertainment culture. In a consumerist culture, religion is a commodity to be marketed, another lifestyle choice to promote.[19]

Postman repeats this observation when he describes the influence of technology on culture in general, for in the end, the history of technology and the scientific method have led to the victory of relativism. The earliest scientific paradigms were Newtonian, based on the belief that physical laws applied universally. But with the shift in science to Einstein's paradigm of relativity, our modernist culture followed suit, turning to what we now call postmodernity, in which "truth" becomes defined only by its context, not by its universality.[20]

Art, like religion, has had to adapt to this emerging culture. Live theatre has always employed some form of technology in its performance, be it as simple as the use of a stage for improved sight and hearing or as complex as the latest special effects and pyrotechnics for the finale of a Broadway spectacular. Yet technology, especially electronic presentational media, has the potential to dilute those unique human qualities described in the previous chapter. How does theatre exist as a live art medium when the surrounding culture is becoming increasingly drawn to the virtual and the sensational? After all, what happens to live theatre when people prefer to sit in their caves and watch electronic shadows and projections, especially when those projections are more vivid and engaging than the real thing?

The Super Bowl of Entertainment

Technology's effects on culture, in particular art and entertainment, have not been subtle. It has raised the bar from sensational to spectacular. Exhibit A in evidence of the dual effects of entertainment and technology on North American culture is the growth of the Super Bowl and its halftime shows. The first Super Bowl was played in January 1967. Though the game was not a sellout, it was broadcast by both NBC and CBS and became an immediate force in sports television. Today the Super Bowl is the single most-watched annual sporting event in the world.

Along with the growth of the game and its popularity has come the expansion of all the Super Bowl–related events and programming. None of these has grown as exponentially as the halftime show. The first Super Bowl halftime was a traditional football halftime, with the marching bands of the University of Arizona and the University of Michigan performing. Televised football games in the 1960s regularly showed the halftime show, which was usually twenty to thirty minutes long. For the first ten years of Super Bowls, marching bands accompanied by special guests were typical, while the halftime analysis of the game grew in prominence, taking away broadcast time from the halftime show itself. However, the tenth Super Bowl halftime show began a trend that would change the course of all subsequent Super Bowl halftime shows.

The Super Bowl X halftime featured the song-and-dance group Up with People, who staged a special show celebrating the United States bicentennial. The next year was a show produced by Disney titled "It's a Small World." Each year the halftime show became a larger production and stretched in length to beyond a half hour. Still the television audience for these performances was declining. To address this problem, the halftime show for Super Bowl XXVII became the first performance by a single performer: Michael Jackson. Jackson at that time was still one of the biggest names in entertainment, and his show involved a choir of 3,500 children along with elaborate staging, jumbotron projection, pyrotechnics, and a squad of Michael Jackson doubles. It was by any standard an extravaganza. From that point the halftime show has become a showcase for some of the biggest names in entertainment, including U2 and the Rolling Stones. The show is staged primarily for the television audience, and the hype surrounding the halftime show at times rivals that of the game itself. Today the halftime performers are not even paid, their profit is in the publicity they receive for performing at the now hour-long halftime show.

The growth of the Super Bowl over the past forty years, along with all the accompanying events such as its halftime show (not to mention the premiere of commercials during the Super Bowl), make it an entertainment event like few others. The halftime show especially chronicles the trajectory of our media culture driven by advertising, technology, and its goal of creating the spectacular: each year must outdo the previous year to attract more people. How does theatre, even presuming all its virtues, fit into a world driven by spectacle?

As easy as it would be to blame the growth of technology and our high-powered market economy for a culture focused on simulation and stimulation, the problem is not a new one. Aristotle in his *Poetics* describes the six elements of drama: plot, character, theme, dialogue, rhythm (or music), and spectacle. Of these six, spectacle is the least valued. Aristotle concedes that spectacle has an emotional appeal, but one that is less effective (and less poetic) than the other elements.[21] He goes on to chide those who rely on spectacle for diminishing the art form, suggesting that those who depend on this convention to accomplish what plot or dialogue could do create a sense of the "monstrous," not the "terrible" (or "awesome"), and demean their audience in the process.[22] Aristotle realized that human nature would be attracted to the sensational but in the end would not be sustained by it.

The same year the first Super Bowl was played, French filmmaker Guy Debord published his book *The Society of the Spectacle*.[23] In this seminal critique of the culture created by capitalism and its technologies of production and advertising, Debord defines the accumulation of spectacles, not possessions, as the goal of our consumer society. The accumulation of sensations, experiences, thrills, and pleasures is the endgame of capitalism. And from Debord's perspective, these spectacles are more than mere entertainment; they are social controls, masquerading as celebrations. Though drawing a similar conclusion as Postman about the pervasiveness of entertainment as a central value in our culture, Debord, unlike Postman, sees the future in more Orwellian terms. Debord writes in his opening chapter, "Separation is itself an integral part of the unity of this world, of a global social practice split into reality and image. The social practice confronted by an autonomous spectacle is at the same time the real totality which contains that spectacle. But the split within this totality mutilates it to the point that the spectacle seems to be its goal."[24] For Karl Marx, capitalism separates the worker from his or her product; for Debord, spectacle separates humanity from reality. Once again we find ourselves back in Plato's cave, entertained but ignorant—even ignorant of our own humanity.

Technology: It's the Reel Thing

We began this chapter with a discussion of the impact of technology on our contemporary culture and have explored the place of technology within the larger consideration of a culture of entertainment. The theme that has been constant throughout this exploration is the relationship between the virtual and the real. In light of our explorations of faith and theatre in the previous chapter, it would serve us well to consider the relationship of technology and faith, in particular, technology and worship. The Christian faith presupposes that God exists in a reality that is more real than our own temporal reality. Paul wrote that what we now understand as real will one day fade into a reality that is more real and more true.[25]

Technology has been a part of human existence as far back as we can trace human history. Technology, whether it is as simple as a lever or as complicated as a microprocessor, is the human use of an instrument or tool to accomplish a task better, faster, or easier. The Christian church has vacillated between a warm embrace of technology and a strong repulsion toward it. Sometimes the attitudes toward a given technology can shift over time or can vary among the Christian traditions at a given time. For example, many Christian churches would not think twice of showing videos in their worship space today, but those same communities seventy years ago might not have approved of a video recording or movie of any type anywhere, convinced that films in and of themselves were evil.[26]

Though technology has been a part of culture since before the inception of the Christian church, and though the church has always needed to respond to the technologies of a particular time and place, not until the Industrial Revolution in the West did the church confront technology as the dominant cultural force. There were many Christian responses to the Industrial Revolution and the "modernist" period that it initiated—Vatican I, evangelicalism, the Oxford and Cambridge Movements, and Christian socialism.[27] Sociologist Peter Berger has suggested that since the Industrial Revolution, technology has defined our culture as never before. Paul Tillich likewise observes that the mythology of technology in our world today might be akin to the story of the Tower of Babel, in that we believe that through human ingenuity and industry we are able to overcome our mortality and achieve divine heights. In fact, the Industrial Revolution's primary symbol was the machine—machines that produced goods, services, prosperity, leisure time, and an overall better quality of life. The machine had salvific overtones in this emerging culture, with its hopes of establishing a new earth and leading humanity to the promised land.[28]

Christian worship has always employed some forms of technology, whether in the architecture of the meeting space or written texts of Scriptures or prayers. But when confronted with technology that brings with it values that might be construed as counterproductive to the gospel, the church has paused to reflect. Allow us to illustrate this idea using amplification as an example. As the church grew in size, the need to communicate to larger groups became an issue. Numerous forms of amplification, most of them simple uses of acoustic properties, were developed. For example, a creative solution developed in the medieval church was the sound board, or a small "roof" placed above the pulpit, which prevented the preacher's voice from floating to the rafters of the vaulted ceiling and reflected it down and out toward the congregation. It seems an obvious next step with the invention of electronic amplification to use microphones and speakers. And in fact, most churches (even small churches that may not need it) have some form of electronic amplification in them. But what about amplifying sight? After all, if it is good to amplify sound, why not sight? Although some churches are reluctant to use video amplification of their worship services, others have rushed headlong into the use of video projection and broadcasting without critically reflecting on their use.

First, one must acknowledge that sight and sound are two different senses in our culture and that, as we have seen, we live in a predominantly visual culture. Further, it means something different to have your image projected than to have your voice amplified. Those who are regularly videocast are often people of some import: politicians, entertainers, athletes, and so on. By the use of videography, do we imply that our pastors and worship leaders have the same or similar cultural status—or that such status is a good thing? Further, sight is a more selective sense than hearing; we choose what to look at differently than the ways we choose what to hear. Using a camera in church limits what the viewer will see, defining the important people and events in worship.[29] Ironically, in the past fifty years there has been an emphasis on creating worship spaces where people's visual attention is drawn as much to the congregation as to the worship leaders, while the use of video projection frequently isolates individuals and most often individuals in leadership roles.[30]

The use of video has expanded beyond simply the amplification of sight within a worship space. It has, in some cases, replaced the presence of a live person. A growing number of churches broadcast part or all of their worship service to satellite locations. For example, North Coast Church in Vista, California, offers a "contemporary" worship service for baby boomers, which includes a block of praise and worship music followed by a sermon. Simultaneous to this service are "video venues," each of which has a different style of worship music—from traditional hymnody to alternative rock to country—performed by live musicians. All the music at these worship offerings ends simultaneously, followed by a live video feed from the main service to all the other services. At North Coast Church and the other churches that use video in similar ways, video does not supplement the live event (in this case preaching) but replaces it. In light of our theological analysis of theatre in the previous chapter, one must ask if something essential in the incarnational, communal, and sacramental quality of the ministry of worship is diminished if not lost in this practice.[31]

Stage Lights to Pyrotechnics: Live Theatre and Technical Ecstasy

How then do we evaluate theatre in light of this culture so clearly identified with the virtual and the sensational? Certainly any number of large theatrical productions could be accused of yielding to the temptation of utilizing the latest technologies and special effects with the goal of sensationalism. Yet we would suggest that the use of technology—even video technology—can underscore the human, not dilute or overwhelm it. For example, the Victory Theatre in Burbank, California, performed *The Elephant Man*. The play is based on the life of John Merrick, a man with tragically deformed features who goes from being a sideshow attraction to the toast of Victorian England's social elite. The challenge of staging this play is communicating Merrick's humanity without overlooking his deformities. When David Bowie famously played this role, he wore no special make-up to exhibit Merrick's physical malady but instead contorted his body to evoke his grotesque appearance. The Victory Theatre's production took a different approach. The actor playing the elephant man neither wore extensive makeup nor exaggerated Merrick's deformities through contortion. Instead the crew used translucent screens between the audience and the stage to project pictures of the historical figure, John Merrick, which reminded the audience of this person's condition without overwhelming the performance with overly realistic makeup. The use of video technology in this case enhanced the human quality of performance, creating both empathy for the Merrick character and a sense of the humanity behind the deformity. The technology contributed to the telling of the story without attracting attention to itself, in the same way an actor's performance is part of a larger whole more than it is a singular contribution. The technology creatively embodied the message of the play: to see what makes us truly human we must look both at and beneath the surface.

Still, the challenge of the future of theatre, with all its potential, in the current context of technological advances and a bias toward the sensational is a daunting one. As we have seen repeatedly, the effects of media on our society and its arts and culture have been profound. Electronic media can easily magnify and depersonalize life. Studies of the effects of mass media on ritual events have demonstrated that media frequently transforms such events "from a ritual to a spectacle."[32] Though this is obvious in the current trend in television and its plethora of "reality shows," it is by no means a new phenomenon. Early in the life of television, sociologists identified its ability to turn ordinary people and their lives into drama. Over time the rise of the reality show has only validated this observation made over a half century ago, which in television history is a long time.[33]

Television's impact on theatre in England, for example, went beyond the stimulating content with which it had to compete; it was a challenge because of the immediacy of the medium. In pretelevision England, touring troupes were able to take a first-rate production of a play across the country so that everyone was able to see the same high-quality performance. Television made this practice obsolete, since everyone could see the same performance on "opening night," as it were. The effects reached beyond the economic viability of touring theatre. The loss of theatre to television in England marked "a retreat from public consideration of what might seem to be public questions."[34] Those who work within theatre and look to the horizon ahead suggest that television culture's impact will push live theatre to the margins, diminishing its presence on the national and the regional levels. In response, theatre will become increasingly critical of society, increasingly multicultural, and create local "alternative-culture projects and community-based performance and media collaborations."[35] Such projections raise questions for our consideration: If theatre uniquely embodies central qualities of God and the life of faith, why is it losing out to other art forms? Was there ever a time when theatre actually embodied those theological qualities we have named in an explicitly Christian way? We now turn to an example offered as a response to the second query, with hopes it will provide clues to answer the first.

Corpus Christi: The Sacred Story

Technology, as we have seen, has changed both the larger culture in which we live and the culture of worship and theatre. Our expectations of what theatre is and can be have been shaped by a culture of sensation and personalization. These themes are a distinct move away from the theological themes of community and presence, which complement the incarnational aspects of theatre. The difference between theatre as a corporate enterprise and theatre as individual commodity is striking. This comparison is at the core of Sarah Beckwith's seminal study *Signifying God*.[36]

Beckwith's study is an analysis of the Corpus Christi plays in York, England, comparing their celebration in the fourteenth through sixteenth centuries to their reenactment in the past fifty years, both in York and in Toronto, Ontario. As we introduced them in chapter 1, these plays, also known as "mystery plays" or simply "mysteries," were a cycle of plays performed throughout the city retelling the history of God's saving acts, from creation and fall through redemption to final judgment. These plays seem to have had liturgical origins, as enactments of Scripture readings in the worship of the medieval church. These stories then were woven together as an entire story cycle. In York, for example, forty-eight individual plays comprised this cycle.

These plays were liturgy in the truest sense of the word. A liturgy (from the Greek *leitourgia*, meaning "work of/for the people") was a public act done for the good of the entire community. The Christian church chose this term to describe what Christians did when they worshiped God in Christ's name. For example, a person or a family would bring their offering to the church and leave it in an appropriate place before worship. Most of the offerings were food (i.e., olives, grapes, bread, wine, cheese, and so on), and not money as we think of offerings today. Some of these gifts would be set aside for the Lord's Supper in the worship that day; some of the food would be taken by the clergy as their rations for the week. This was their pay. The rest was distributed to the poor and needy. All of this was the *leitourgia* of the people: the support of the worship of the church, the support of the ministers and ministries of the church, and the support of reaching out to the world in Christ's name. The church's liturgy was incomplete without all three.[37]

In a similar fashion, each of the mystery plays in York was undertaken by a particular guild. These people would create a "pageant," or decorated cart, that would travel around the city from place to place staging this particular story. Each story was part of a procession arranged chronologically.[38] These plays were truly the work of and for the people, and though they included political and social elements, they were for the most part religious drama. And according to Beckwith's analysis, they were both tremendously popular and influential.

These plays were performed on or around the Feast of Corpus Christi. This feast has its origins in the thirteenth century and can be viewed as a direct result of the Berengarian controversy and the decision of the Synod of Rome that the presence of Christ in the bread and the cup was the physical body and blood of Jesus of Nazareth.[39] The result was a diminished practice of actually receiving the consecrated elements and an increased devotion to them, as they were seen as relics par excellence in the church.[40] The Feast of Corpus Christi is celebrated on the Thursday after Trinity Sunday, which is the Sunday after the Feast of the Ascension. Corpus Christi celebrates the presence of Christ in the "body" of the bread and the cup, even as the church has already celebrated the elevation of the body of Jesus into heaven at the ascension. The celebration of Corpus Christi took the form of a procession in which the people would parade through the streets of the city with the host in a vessel known as a monstrance. These processions evolved into the movable and multiple performances of these plays throughout the city on the days after the celebration of Corpus Christi.[41]

Beckwith's thesis follows the line charted in the previous chapter: there is a sacramental character to theatre. In the case of the mystery plays, the plays themselves were actually more sacramental than was the sacrament of the Lord's Supper as experienced in those days. Beckwith writes, "I understand the plays as sacramental theatre. How we present ourselves to each other (the classical domain of theatre) and how we are present to each other (the domain of sacrament) become, I argue, vital theological as well as theatrical resources in the York plays. In them theatre and sacrament become profound investigations of each other's opportunities and limits."[42] In an age of the church when the sacraments were distanced from the people, theatre became the vehicle of experiencing God's presence.

The mystery plays were the most popular events in York. Over 10 percent of the population was involved in staging the plays, and people from far and wide came to see them, along with the entire York community. Beyond theatre, they were the people's religion. This was possible because theatre and liturgy were, and still are, communal at their core. Both worship and theatre are acts of and judged by the community, and neither can be understood outside that community. Both worship and theatre are mutually reciprocal events, with what they offer and how they are received inseparable from what they are.[43]

Theatre, like corporate worship, does not communicate doctrine in a linear way. Religious theatre such as the Corpus Christi plays does not establish an analogue to orthodoxy or present doctrine in any systematic or even loosely structured way. Instead theatre creates a world of significance to be explored and inhabited.[44] In theatre, one person stands in for someone or something else. There is substitution and representation. In the Christian economy of salvation, Christ stands in for humanity; the priest and/or the host stand in for Christ, even as the community stands in for Christ. It is a matrix of corollary relationships.[45] And in worship, as in theatre, one understands the meanings of these relationships by participating in them.

The Corpus Christi plays in the medieval world presented the body of Christ as the paradigm of society and its values, in particular social cohesion and social identity. The Corpus Christi plays embodied this, reincarnating the life of Christ in the streets of the city. However, whereas access to the Eucharistic body of Christ was the sole proprietorship of the clergy, the Corpus Christi plays were the property of the people.[46] The celebrations of these plays made the story of God's salvation and the presence of God accessible to ordinary people in ways the church's worship did not. Placing the biblical narratives in the streets of the city implied a relationship between the here and now with the there and then, along with thread of divine presence stringing the two together, making the lives of the people part of the fabric of salvation history.

Beckwith's study makes a profound observation about both worship and theatre and their relationship to time: in both theatre and liturgy the dead come to life in the bodies of the living, in the enacting of a play or in the communion of the saints. Beckwith asserts, "If theatre, like resurrection, is the appearance of the dead in the bodies of the living, then its very liveness, our recovery from mortification, depends on the subtle linking of actor to actor, actor to audience, that sometimes happens in a theatre whose only existence is the present. It is from this spectral yet palpable bond that our mutual recognition and self-recognition take on life and meaning together."[47]

Beckwith argues that the mystery plays in York were sacramental in ways that their revival as spectacle never could be. In today's world these plays have become tourist attractions and fossils of a bygone era, but not an integrated part of the life of the people who view them. If one learns anything from the juxtaposition of theatre and sacrament, it is that neither is an object to be known or understood. Instead, theatre (like "sacramental" or presence-filled worship) is a process that demands our participation and our willingness to be known within the contexts of our unique lives. Quoting Stanley Cavell, Beckwith concludes, "Nothing can be present to us to which we are not present."[48] Reviving these plays in our contemporary culture failed to revive the meaning and experience they provided for the people of medieval York.

Beckwith has made a compelling case for the possibility of the incarnational, communal, and sacramental quality of theatre, as well as evidence for its having realized this potential. But is this a possibility today? How do plays staged before the invention of the printing press relate to our postmodern, post-Christian, wired world? Is it possible that these qualities will never be revived? This is the question to which we now turn.

Worship, Theatre, and Emerging Communities

Of all of the analogies between theatre and worship, the most famous was offered by the Danish pastor and philosopher Søren Kierkegaard. Kierkegaard addressed the issues facing his church in the early nineteenth century. He suggested that people came to worship expecting a performance put on by the clergy and church musicians for the congregation. This, he suggested, was a fallacious understanding. Instead, the clergy and other worship leaders were more like conductors of a symphony or choir—or director of a play—in which the congregation performed for the true audience, God.[49] It is important to note that Kierkegaard meant to imply not that God as audience is passive but rather that God is in fact very involved in the performance: audience and performers create a community, defining both relationships and meanings in the performance event. This understanding, offered in an age closer to our context than that of the mystery plays, offers a helpful guide for our application of Beckwith's analysis to theatre and worship today. How can and does theatre (or worship) communicate presence and create community?

The concept of *leitourgia* as a way of understanding worship is a good place to start. A truly liturgical understanding of worship is one not of elaborate ritual but of "full, conscious and active participation,"[50] an expectation that (as with Kierkegaard's belief) worship is done by all present, not merely observed by an audience. This reiterates a distinction made in the first chapter: theatre and worship are similar but not synonymous. Also mentioned in the previous chapter was the work of Shannon Craigo-Snell, who identifies performance as a process of becoming, one requiring practice. Others, such as Steven Guthrie, have applied this concept to the Christian life and particularly worship. Guthrie points to recent work in psychology, philosophy, and education that give evidence for strong connections between our physical existence and our rational thought. It can be summarized in these two rather pithy statements: 'We do not have bodies; we are bodies,' and 'we learn through our bodies.' The act of worship, then, is essential for learning our theology and rehearsing our faith.

This approach goes against the long-standing Christian bias toward separating the spiritual from the physical. Taking the incarnation seriously, however, requires us to see the spiritual and the physical as united; therefore, the physical act of worshiping affects us spiritually. As Paul noted, the offering of our bodies becomes the key to the transforming of our minds (Rom. 12:1–2). In worship we rehearse our faith, practice it, discipline it, and grow in it. Both the Hebrew word (*wayishtachu*) and the Greek word (*proskyneo*) translated into English as "worship" are literally physical actions of prostration and submission (e.g., bowing). Worship as described in the Bible is foremost a physical action and a participatory event—a performance of our faith.[51]

It is worth considering in more detail Craigo-Snell's work, for it illuminates the truths of theatre as they relate to faith and helps us understand Guthrie's conclusions. Craigo-Snell's work is a response to the thought of Nicholas Wolterstorff, in particular his metaphor of understanding revelation as moving from musical text to musical performance.[52] Wolterstorff begins with the assumption that God can speak and has spoken, particularly in the text of the Scriptures. The question, then, is how do we interpret God's speech? Wolterstorff uses the analogy of a musician reading a score and imagining its performance. The musician's imagination is influenced by communities of traditions, training, and theory, making the interpretation a result of a communal process. Wolterstorff establishes an interesting assertion from this process, that the text performed is the text created by the artist's imagination, not the musical score.[53] If we relate this analogy to Scripture, preaching becomes an art of interpretation bringing the text to realization but never becomes the "correct" realization, because it is always dependent on influences that lead one to interpret the text partially. In other words, no performance of a musical piece or a sermon text can ever exhaust its meaning.[54]

Craigo-Snell offers an alternative theatre analogy to Wolterstorff's musical analogue.[55] She suggests that theatre is a more apt paradigm for the Christian faith than music, as it is more directly a communal process. Craigo-Snell observes that the church, like theatre, is an interdependent community comprised of people with differing gifts, doing a variety of tasks with various degrees of commitment and involvement. In this model the person in the back pew, like the person working in the box office, is equally part of the community and its work, even if he or she is not as evident as those more directly identified as "performing" the community's main task. Furthermore, for both the church and the theatre, the text is the center of their reason for existing. Everything these communities perform is rooted in a text that has life only when enacted.[56]

The interpretation of this text in theatre is not done by a single person who sits at the nexus of several communities of interpretation as does Wolterstorff's musician, but by a community of people who work through the text over time through the process of rehearsing. Actors, directors, producers, set designers, and so on are all part of the process of interpretation. And this interpretation takes place in a specific place and time, contextualizing its interpretation. If the interpretation of the text fails to connect with the lives of the people outside the theatre, the theatre will soon shut its doors. And this is more like the church is—or should be—where each person performs a role in bringing the latent meaning in the text to life in ways relevant to the community at large.[57]

Using Guthrie's observation of Craigo-Snell's work, one does not move directly from text (whether real or imagined) to performance. There is a layer—a very thick layer—of rehearsal between text and performance. And as anyone who has been involved with theatre will testify, even after a theatrical production has moved from rehearsal to performance, the performance is constantly changing, evolving, and growing. In a very real way a theatrical production never completely moves out of the rehearsal phase. Likewise with the Christian church, worship is never a final performance but a rehearsal of our faith. Our life as disciples is an ongoing rehearsal of our faith, constantly reinterpreting the Scriptures in our lives as a part of the community of faith to which we belong. And in the process of our rehearsing our faith, whether in or out of worship, we are learning and growing in our faith. Placing the important layer of rehearsal between text and performance reminds us that it is in doing that we come to know, not in knowing that we come to do. The lesson one learns from theatre is that participation is vital to the full formation of our faith and its ongoing rehearsal of our life as disciples.

One could see the two latest trends in worship gatherings as embodying the ideal of "full, conscious, and active" participation through their rehearsal of the Christian narrative, making the individual integral to the act of worship by the community. The multisensory worship patterns generally categorized as "emerging worship" and the resurgence of home churches together exemplify a move to recover worship that is more corporate, more participatory, and enables a more immediate sense of presence to God and to one another.[58] Both of these movements provide an alternative to the traditional and megachurch offerings, in particular an alternative attractive to people under forty. There is also an open-ended quality to these worship styles, which value participation over polish, community over consumption.

The theatrical expressions of this same phenomenon are the smaller, local alternatives to large theatrical productions in black-box theatres around the United States in both major metropolitan areas and smaller cities and towns. One of the more interesting examples of this trend is the sporadic development of indigenous theatre, rooted in the story of a community and performed by members of the community. In marginalized communities, theatre has been used to provide a voice for people who are otherwise voiceless, to speak of their own lives with value, and to challenge those who seek to demean them. Theatre is being used in some communities as a means of preserving and telling the oral history of groups. Especially in African American and Latino communities in the United States, stories are gathered, collected into sequences, turned into dramatic texts, and then performed. Thus an oral history that might otherwise be lost in a culture of text and hypertext is preserved, passed on to the next generation of these communities. These stories are then given the chance to be interpreted and reinterpreted from generation to generation, as long as the dramas are performed. Further, it gives these communities a vehicle for communicating their stories, their values, and their challenges to those outside their communities.[59]

The use of drama in worship was, until recently, becoming more commonplace. These sketches, which can often be not only thought provoking but also profound, are very often simply an embodied sermon illustration. Often the opportunity to use theatre as a tool of the Holy Spirit to convict is lost.[60] This opportunity is not lost on other theatre groups, however. The Cornell Interactive Theatre Ensemble (CITE) is an extension of Cornell University's Office of Human Resources, which seeks to educate people about racism and sexism in the workplace. CITE members offer dramatic representations of workplace experiences and then facilitate conversation about them. These sketches and vignettes are intended to be both realistic and disconcerting, inviting participants in these workshops to reflect on their own lives, their own preferences and prejudices, their own sensitivities and insensitivities. CITE's artistic director, Martha Dewey, has degrees in both theatre and theology, which invites comparisons between Jesus's use of parables and CITE's use of theatre. One can only hope that Christian theatre—within or without the church—might follow suit.[61]

Our culture is far different from that of pre-Reformation Europe, and Christianity has a far different role in our world. To use Paul Tillich's categories from the preceding chapter, we do not live in the theonomous culture that gave rise to the mystery plays, but neither do we live in the autonomous culture that we often think we do. We live in a heteronomous culture that, as Dell deChant argues, is religious to its core. The faith of our cultural religion is not in a transcendent God but in an immanent market economy and the promises of success, fulfillment, and happiness.[62] These values are communicated efficiently and effectively through our virtual, multimedia world. Though we are in no way suggesting that we go back, we must not move forward uncritically. As Christians in particular, we must continue to value the human and the real over the electronic and the virtual. Live theatrical performances can become a prophetic statement about our headlong rush into "technopoly." Likewise, the qualities of live theatre can serve as benchmarks for the performances of Christian worship of all types, for Christian worship of any style or genre ought to embody qualities of incarnation, community, and presence.

Returning to Plato's Cave

Writing on a topic such as "live theatre in a virtual world," one can easily overgeneralize to the point of being misleading. I do not intend to persuade you that attending live theatre will make the artistic interpretation of life more valid or accurate than attending a movie or watching television will. Wonderful stories and tremendous performances can be found on the screen both large and small. However, there is a living, human quality in live theatre that television and movies can only imitate. When one watches a live performance, one is necessarily reminded of the transient, mortal, and finite qualities of our human existences, because one is in the presence of living human beings. This is something a recorded performance can at best approximate and at worst obfuscate. A recording of a performance can give the illusion of immortality, perfection, and exaggerated importance. Seeing live theatre can remind us as nothing else can of the role we play in life—and all life's limits.

The image of life as a stage, famously remembered in Shakespeare's *As You Like It* goes back at least as far as the first-century Roman philosopher Epictetus. This enduring image remains relevant because it underscores the unique, once-and-for-all quality of our lives by correspondence to the precious, unique quality of each theatrical performance. One could see this as reason for despair: our lot has been cast, our role has been chosen, and we play the part and then we are done, as we saw in the example of the *auto sacramentales*. On the other hand, one could see this as a great opportunity to play the role with enthusiasm and skill, to improvise and stretch the character, to push the cast to new levels. For Christians, this also extends to eschatological themes, that the performance of our lives anticipates what Jürgen Moltmann describes as the "final act," that is, the consummation of our time into the full realization of the reign of God. Our performance, whether as a secondary character or in a major role, contributes to the entire narrative trajectory of the movement of God's work in the cosmos.[63]

Our contemporary culture offers two basic entertainment options: to sit in our caves, watching the virtual world flash before our eyes, or to go out into the community and watch a performance as a community. The viewing of a film in the local Cineplex moves us out of the inner circle of our immediate family and friends and into the larger community, creating the opportunity for larger social interaction. Even more does the possibility of a live performance create the opportunity for us to catch but one small glimpse of the real light of day, and even more catch an image of a God who invites us into community with Godself and with one another in God's name, making God present to us and through us, all because of the choice to play the role of one of us to redeem us. When we attend live theatre, there is a possibility of redemption—a buying back of one's life. In a play I might see my life reflected on stage, respond to it as it enfolds, while the actors accept and integrate my response (and the responses of others) into the telling of their story. And this reminds us as Christians that we tell the Christian story by enacting the story in our own lives. This is the most important role any of us will ever play.

the christian at work

Being an Artist in the Theatre

Dale Savidge

Both theology and the art of the theatre are rooted in humanity. Christianity is not just a religion of dogma; it is a faith based on relationship. Likewise theatre is a relational art. "Christian" denotes a person who follows Christ; it isn't an adjective that describes things such as plays. What sets the Christian faith apart from other world religions is the belief in a deity who was incarnated as one of us, who lived in community among us, and who through redemption gave us a way to live in relationship with God and with one another. We turn now from abstract concepts of Christianity as a theological system, as a historical institution, and as a force in the creation of art works to its manifestation in people who call themselves Christians and artists.

How we as Christians live in our surrounding cultures overarches the relationship of how we perform theatre, experience theatre as audiences, and use theatre in our worship. How do we understand the relationship between our Christian faith and the art of theatre? Before delving into specific applications of theology to theatre, let's step back and briefly survey how we as Christians might thoughtfully interact with culture.

This book is one in the Engaging Culture series, which seeks "to help Christians respond with theological discernment to our contemporary culture." In chapter 2, Todd referred to Paul Tillich and his model for Christian interaction with culture. Similarly, Richard Niebuhr's classic *Christ and Culture* has been a guide for many Christians who have thoughtfully grappled with their interaction with the surrounding culture.[1] On one end, Niebuhr posits the "Christ against Culture" position, common among conservative Christians. It is based on the writings of Paul and John, especially the first Epistle of John, and pictures the culture, the world, as an antagonist to the spiritual walk and welfare of believers. Culture is the domain of Satan, the "Prince of the power of the air" (Eph. 2:2 NASB). John's admonition "Do not love the world or the things in the world" (1 John 2:15 NRSV) is taken to mean "separate from the world." The Amish and the Mennonites are examples of Christians who have taken this position to its logical and comprehensive conclusion; fundamentalist restrictions on social dancing, movies, and other "worldly" activities are selective manifestations of the same. J. Gresham Machen called this attitude the Christian attempt to destroy culture out of a recognition of the "profound evil of the world."[2]

On the other end of Niebuhr's spectrum is the "Christ of Culture" position. This accommodationist position, evidenced in modernist Protestant churches that pursue a social gospel, views culture not as a force to be feared but as an integral part of human experience capable of assisting the walk of the believer. The culture (especially Western culture, which has been shaped to a large extent by the influence of Christianity in history) is part of who we are, and therefore we turn toward it by choice and out of necessity. Practical manifestations of this view may be seen in the megachurches that seem to absorb each new cultural shift (or even fad) as quickly as possible in order to be relevant to their congregants. Machen called this Christianity "subordinated to culture."[3]

Two other positions that Niebuhr offered ("Christ above Culture," "Christ and Culture in Paradox") are alternatives between the two extremes. The fifth, "Christ the Transformer of Culture," has often been the choice by those interested in the arts. Here Niebuhr posits Christ as the Redeemer of culture as well as people. The world is cursed by the fall, and the redemptive plan of Christ is to redeem all creation. It is the mission of Christians not only to extend the gospel to people for their salvation but to carry the message of reconciliation to culture at large. It is easy to understand why this position is popular among Christians engaged in artistic, that is, culture-making, pursuits. Machen called this position "consecrating culture" and encouraged believers to cultivate the arts and sciences "with all the enthusiasm of the veriest humanist, but at the same time consecrate them to the service of our God."[4]

Some Christian traditions have embraced the "Christ the Transformer of Culture" position. Such traditions encourage cultural interaction because they value material life on earth now as evidence of the rule and reign of Christ the King. There is optimism inherent in such theology and a willingness and even eagerness to look for cultural indicators of spiritual progress. If God is at work in the culture, building the kingdom spiritually through the attention of God's people to their surroundings, then artists have a clear mandate to engage in culture-making activities. Many traditions view eternity for the believer as a perfect physical existence on the New Earth; this further validates attention to the material and cultural dimensions of this life.

A recent reading of Niebuhr's *Christ and Culture* is offered by Craig A. Carter.[5] If Niebuhr is optimistic about the role of Christians in the culture and the possibility of cultural (as well as personal) redemption, Carter calls believers to their roles as disciples of the suffering Christ and as missionaries to the culture that persecuted and crucified Jesus. Carter's Anabaptist perspective recaptures the important contributions of separatist communities (including Amish and monastic communities). R. A. Markus remarked of the ancient world: "Asceticism was coming to be the mark of authentic Christianity in a society in which to be Christian no longer needed to make any visible difference in a man's life."[6] In twenty-first-century Western nations, Christians can coexist quite comfortably with unbelievers. Believing artists are encouraged to ply their trades without being too overt about their faith. Perhaps an emphasis on discipleship and mission is necessary to recall for us how our Savior and namesake suffered at the hands of the prevailing culture. We view both God's grace in creation and the stain of sin on creation as the starting point for considering the place of arts in the practice of faith.

Later in this chapter, we address an underlying tension with which the creator and the consumer of theatre must deal. Jacques Maritain puts it succinctly: "It is difficult . . . for the Prudent Man and the Artist to understand one another."[7] Christian artists in particular live with the tension between morality and aesthetics—the sometimes contradictory demands of their conscience and religious traditions (or criteria set upon them by the keepers of Christian morality), on the one hand, and the freedom of imaginative expression demanded by theatre, on the other. As we suggest later, this tension is an inherent and healthy part of living the life of a believer artist. Also, the tension is inescapable for those who live now in anticipation of their ultimate redemption.

Having generalized about the role of the Christian in the culture from Protestant perspectives, we turn to the three arenas in which Christians interact with theatre. We will now look at Christians as participants in the creation of theatre. In chapter 5 we will switch our perspective and look at how audiences respond in both the theatre experience and in a worship setting.

Christian Artists in the Theatre

The remarks in this section apply to anyone engaged in the creation of theatre, but they have special application to those who practice theatre vocationally, that is, people who have given up earning their income by other, more predictable and reliable means. If you are one of these vocational theatre people, you may feel you are a minority in the Christian community. The life of a Christian artist, especially one who practices the art of the theatre, is not one to be entered into lightly. The road is narrow, and there may be few companions. There may be moral tensions and economic uncertainty: employed, unemployed, employed again (you hope). You experience the juxtaposition of intense ensemble relationships followed by periods of isolation. Theatre people follow the work; they may put down roots for the length of a show, a contract, and then they are transients again. In a way their lives resemble the life of the Lord during his tenure on this earth: "the Son of Man has nowhere to lay his head" (Matt. 8:20 par. Luke 9:58). Family life can be elusive, and actors are often seen as commodities to be exploited.

Even after all that, you pursue your dreams in the theatre because you realize it is a richly satisfying life for those who are called to it. You have the great privilege of incarnating stories that matter, of working in community and experiencing the presence of other human beings (and of God) in a way few other activities can provide. The theological categories we've been presenting—incarnation, community, and presence—aren't just concepts to you. They are principles for living, for your work, for your calling.

Theatre is a collaborative art. Even solo performers rely on the work of writers, directors, designers, producers, managers, publicists, and so on. Collaboration involves critique, and those who create any portion of a theatre event are subject to and are practitioners of critical feedback. The ethics of constructive criticism are the same for Christians and non-Christians. Patience, honesty, kindness, truthfulness, and many other virtues are equally important in the theatre and at church. Collaboration also means vulnerability, and that openness to our collaborators carries great benefits as well as the risk of pain.

Christians who are theatre artists face challenges and opportunities that are distinctive to their particular calling in the theatre: writer, actor, designer, and so on. The theatrical art is an amalgam of many arts, often including music and dance, and although theatre artists may be skilled in several of the composite art forms, they will typically have an area of specialty as well. The arts can be categorized as either *creative* or *interpretive* art forms. Generally speaking, artists involved in the creative arts work alone and communicate directly to their public (for example, painters and poets). Artists involved in the interpretive arts, typically the performing arts, base their work on something another artist has created (a piece of music or a play, for example), and they shade that original work by their interpretation of it in performance. A playwright may send a script directly to an anthology, to be read by individuals ("closet drama"), or to a theatre company, where it will be handled by interpretive artists: directors, actors, and designers. This section will investigate issues unique to the creators and the interpreters in the theatre, with special attention to those who engage in the *essential* art of the theatre: acting.

Consider yourself a part of two communities: theatre and church. Many challenges that face Christian theatre artists also confront Christians in general or artists in general. Everyone has to provide for his or her survival regardless of faith or vocation. The theatre is not necessarily a more difficult place to survive than the corporate world or the ministry of foreign missions, or any other calling. Jeannette Clift George, artistic director of the A.D. Players in Houston, Texas, is fond of reminding believer artists that they should pay attention to their growth as artists *and* as believers. To ignore either dimension of life is to risk drifting away from relationship with Christ or stagnation as an artist. Both the Christian life and the life of the artist presuppose growth and progress. There is no substitute for a community of other believers, a church family, for growth in the faith; we all, as artists, need to be in fellowship with other Christians, and not just other Christian artists. The body of Christ exists in the variety of its parts, even when those parts may introduce tension. Tension keeps the parts of the body together; it makes them flexible, taut, and strong. Tension isn't anxiety, unrest, or stress; financial uncertainty, constructive criticism, shortages of time and resources make you a better artist. The opposite of tension is flaccidity, malaise, stagnation. Art is created in adverse circumstances, under pressure, against the odds, and sometimes God uses people as the iron that sharpens you in your artistic pursuits. Artists are *passionate*, in the same sense in which Christ experienced *passion* (suffering). Jesus said this kind of life would characterize his followers.

Christian artists should also be accountable to other artists. We need the challenge of peer networking. We need to see good work done by other artists. We grow by investing time and money in theatre attendance, play reading, education, conferences, festivals, reviews, and articles about performances. Expand your network first to your local theatre scene, then regionally and nationally, and then to the theatre of other countries, cultures, and periods; your artistic imagination will be enriched and strengthened. Avoid working alone, in isolation, apart from other Christians and other artists.

You may notice in these remarks practical extensions of the theological underpinnings of theatre that we discussed in chapter 2. *Incarnation* in the theatre means grappling with the physical outworking of an essentially imaginative process. *Community* means interdependence on other people, both Christians and artists. *Presence* refers to the manner in which God is present to us and how we are present to each other through theatre. One reason that theatre is such an intense and rewarding experience is the quality of presence among the troupe or cast. Christian artists bring these concepts to bear in their lives as artists, and their lives as artists open them to understanding these concepts in unique ways. It is a challenge and an opportunity together—embrace it, explore it!

As Christians we should thoughtfully consider the content and subject matter we consume from the culture and that which we contribute to the culture. "Prepare your minds for action" (1 Pet. 1:13 NASB) means, among other things, making thoughtful choices about which plays to read as well as which plays to write, which theatre to see as well as which parts to audition for (see Phil. 4:8). Here are three guidelines for artists in this regard. They exist simultaneously and are not mutually exclusive. However, they will foreground themselves at different times according to the choices you face. Each principle can also be taken to an extreme position that distorts its true value.

First, consider what your particular discipline demands of you: what makes for good acting, what makes a good script, and so forth. A good artist knows and serves the art form. Writing a good play according to accepted standards of playwriting, acting a role with an understanding of what makes good acting, designing and directing with knowledge of the criteria for quality stagecraft are guidelines for choosing the content you will present. If a play is not a play, if it is a sermon in dialogue form, it hasn't measured up to the criteria by which drama is judged. When Bezaleel was commissioned to create works of art for the tabernacle, he was expected to honor the God of beauty by making every effort as an artist to meet the critical standards of his particular artistic discipline (see Exod. 28). So it is with the theatre artist who seeks to honor God with the offering of a play, a role, a production.

One dimension of producing a work of theatrical art is the entertainment value of the product. To amuse is to stop the thought processes; to entertain is to capture attention and through the conventions of the stage bring the audience to the threshold of another world for the duration of the production. A good play arouses, sustains, and satisfies the attention of an audience. Coleridge referred to a "willing suspension of disbelief," and if a production doesn't command that voluntary commitment of an audience, it has failed to meet a very important criterion for quality theatre. We won't list all the criteria for every theatrical discipline, but knowing these criteria and seeking feedback on your work from those who understand and can apply the criteria is part of reflecting the excellent character of God in your work.

An unhealthy extreme of serving the art is the "art for art's sake" attitude. Here the artist is released from any other considerations (moral, for example) and asked *only* to answer the criteria of the art. Christians, however, cannot sever their imaginative work from the presence of the Holy Spirit, the biblical revelation, the history of the faith, or the life of a Christian community. Honoring the art isn't the goal; honoring God in the art is.

Second, Christian artists should sense and respond to their own consciences, to the witness of the Spirit, to the voice of God. The witness of the Spirit is one manifestation of the grace of God that guides believers in their walk and in their choices. Seek for times of silence, and exercise patience in waiting for the voice of God in the choices you will face in the theatre. *Discernment* is a spiritual discipline to be sought and nurtured. Discernment is affected by maturity, and you will find that decisions on similar issues are resolved differently at different seasons of your life. The Scriptures are able to make you wise, not just to moral issues but to artistic ones as well.

Sometimes people believe they have heard God's voice telling them to do something creative. "God gave me this play" can be an expression of sincere intention, or it can be a mask for shoddy craftsmanship. God's leading is never apart from God's attributes of beauty and excellence. If God gives an artist a work to produce, God always expects the artist to use, attain, or hire the skills necessary to create the work with excellence—that is the way God created the world and that is the pattern God has set for us. It would be absurd for a musical composer to claim divine impetus for a piano sonata apart from training in musical composition and theory. Similarly, a writer must make the sacrifices necessary to learn the technique of playwriting and couple that with the leading of the Holy Spirit.

Third, Christian theatre artists bear a responsibility to their audiences. Theatre cannot exist without audiences, and we should respect our audiences. If your audience also represents your sponsor (a church congregation who pays for the production, a school community who provides the actors), you may be dealing with what Calvin Seerveld terms "encapsulated theatre." That is, the purposes for which you produce theatre are subsumed under the larger mission of the sponsoring organization, and your content choices are, to some extent, beholden to that overarching mission. The communities of which you are a part also influence your creative choices. It is not a sign of weakness or an artistic sellout to make content choices with the spiritual welfare of your family and friends in mind. Paul exhorted believers to "let all things be done for edification" (1 Cor. 14:26), and if a production choice (much like the choice of whether to eat meat offered to idols in the first-century church) would jeopardize the faith of someone who is depending on you for his or her spiritual health, you would do well to include that relationship in your decision-making process.

In a review of a Metropolitan Opera production of Arnold Schoenberg's *Moses und Aron*, Michael Linton touches on the challenge facing the artist attempting to write from a faith tradition: "Great religious art tends to be collaboration between an artist and the religious community of which he is a participating member. The faith community nurtures the artist through education, encouragement, commission, and performance; the artist in turn creates as an act of faith within that community. Certainly he creates as an individual (in the West at least), but as an individual who knows that his art grows out of a tradition and speaks back to that tradition."[8] Linton then notes that contemporary evangelical Protestants have "shown little interest in nurturing the serious artists within their folds." Artists react by "privatizing their religion" and taking their art to "extra-religious venues" because the tradition isn't interested in that dialogue.[9]

There is a danger in this third consideration. The audience can become a dictator, causing us to sell out for economic or spiritual reasons. Writers and actors who write and audition with an eye to the marketplace are smart; they will continue to find work. However, if the sole arbiter for decisions is the audience, whether expressed in ticket sales, popularity, or spiritual results, the artist risks selling out. You can arrive at the end of your career and, like the officer in the film *Babette's Feast*, lament that after winning all the battles, you've lost the war. Actors can sell themselves, even physically, to gain the favor of a director; directors can take projects that violate their conscience if the prospect of financial gain has a strong enough appeal; in so doing, they may lose their own souls (Matt. 16:26). Audience response then is a factor, but not the sole factor, in making Christ-honoring artistic choices.

From a general discussion of the Christian working in the theatre, we turn to two specific disciplines that contribute to the theatrical production. The first, playwriting, falls among the creative arts; the second, acting, is primarily interpretive. We take them in the order in which they typically occur: the creation of a play script forms the starting point for the work of the actor.

The Christian as Playwright

Capturing an action in language under the limitations of theatre (actors' interpretations, the vagaries of physical theatre, the fickleness of audiences) is challenge enough; add to that balancing the twin demands of art and faith, and the task of the Christian playwright is daunting. On the personal level of conscience and on the corporate level of community, writers balance diverse, often conflicting demands. Unlike actors and directors, writers tend to work outside organizational boundaries and so are not usually constrained by mission statements, personnel resources, or facility limitations. The downside of this position is that their plays may not find an audience, any audience, unless they admit production considerations into the imaginative process of writing. This means that they must also admit considerations of organizational missions, morality, and audiences without becoming bound by the same. It is a fine line, a tightrope that must be walked anew each time a play is begun. The line is there for any writer, but it is especially problematic for Christian playwrights.

Ideologues of any stripe often begin the creative process from their ideological starting point. This is not necessarily a bad thing; Bertolt Brecht proved how effective such writing could be, and Tony Kushner continues to produce works of dramatic power written from a distinctive ideological point of view. Christian writers are in fact liberated by their faith, because Christianity frees us to explore the world as God's handiwork and the place of God's continual presence. We don't ascribe pain and suffering to God, but even the pain in our lives is under God's sovereignty. God's presence makes sense of the pain, and it provides hope for redemption. That is a very liberating framework to work within.

Plays are created from one or more of the elements that constitute drama. Aristotle delineated these elements: plot, character, diction, theme, music, and spectacle. As we saw in the previous chapter, he placed them in a particular order based on their manifestation in the tragedies of his day. Since his time, writers have rearranged those elements to suit their purposes. Ideological playwrights often start with a theme, an idea. There are many fine plays in this tradition, and we would do well to understand how those writers (G. B. Shaw, for example) successfully married their worldviews to their plays. Because a Christian writer brings to the work the shared traditions of the scriptural record and the history of the church, we should examine how the ancient Greeks used irony in the telling of stories very familiar to their audiences.

Of the writing of books and of plays, there is seemingly no end. Why would anyone make the sacrifices necessary to add to that body of work? Playwrights need to ask themselves: "What hasn't been said that only I can say, or that I *must* say?" Only the deep desire to speak through the drama, and to say something that can only be said in a play, should motivate writers. Further, art and faith issue from an attitude of servanthood, which itself issues from a sense of calling. Consider your call to write plays as a gracious opportunity to serve both God and your audiences. It is worth the effort.

T. S. Eliot argued forcefully for writers to have a historic perspective on their creative endeavors in a 1919 essay titled "Tradition and the Individual Talent."[10] Even a cursory understanding of this essay raises significant challenges to the culture of contemporary Christian writers. Both the surrounding culture at large and the Christian subculture in particular militate against the time and effort required to acquire this background of artistic tradition. The pace of culture and of Christian ministry sadly does not permit artists/writers the leisure necessary to swim in the stream of dramatic tradition. In addition to the Christian tradition, you would do well to encounter the dramaturgical tradition, from the ancient Greeks to the twenty-first century, in your education as a writer. Plato demanded that art fulfill a utilitarian function, that it contribute to the education of citizens to be admitted into the perfect society. Aristotle upheld the value of art as a pleasure-giving activity, but he did not mean the shallow, physical pleasure that is in ready supply in contemporary Western culture. An evidence of this Aristotelian pleasure was the experience of "catharsis," or the purgation of emotion by a vicarious experience in the theatre. The debate on what Aristotle meant by that multifaceted word should be studied, grappled with, and embraced by Christian playwrights. Theatre may produce results: change in character, education, spiritual renewal, and so on. But writers should set out to write good plays and let the results follow on their own.[11]

Horace, writing in the first century BCE in his *Ars Poetica*, married the external criteria of Plato (drama must satisfy the demands of politics) with the internal criteria of Aristotle (drama is beholden only to its own generic demands) by declaring that the purpose of art is to teach (*educare*) and to please (*delectare*). This duality of purpose held sway throughout the Renaissance under the prescriptive rubrics of the neoclassicists. It became, like Plato's dogma, an external set of rules applicable to the imaginative work of writers. The Romanticists, led by Victor Hugo, returned to internal criteria by way of the cult of genius, the elevation of the writer's imagination to a position of sovereignty. This culminated in the nineteenth-century aesthetes (Oscar Wilde in the theatre), who proclaimed that they would produce "art for art's sake" without attention to any external referents.

Christian playwrights don't write in a vacuum, apart from their faith, their audiences, and dramatic tradition. These considerations are buried deep inside writers and are reflected in their plays without conscious servitude to them. It is said that we become what we eat; it may take a long time, but eventually our bodies will surely reflect our diets. In the same way the ingesting of these streams of tradition doesn't bring about automatic results.

Just feed on them and let them work themselves into you, and your writing will be better for the effort.

The development of a distinctly Christian aesthetic, or theory of art, has been the pursuit of numerous artists and aestheticians. Playwright and theologian Dorothy Sayers (b. 1893 in England) wrote, among other works, the Lord Peter Wimsey mysteries and a twelve-part cycle of plays, *The Man Born to Be King*, which was broadcast on the BBC. Sayers also wrote nonfiction, and in 1941 she published *The Mind of the Maker*, in which she tried "to demonstrate that the statements made in the Creeds about the Mind of the Divine Maker represent, so far as [she was] able to check them by [her] experience, true statements about the mind of the human maker."[12] She notes that when the writer of Genesis records that man was created in the image of God, to that point the single attribute of the Deity recorded in the Bible was that of a Creator. "The characteristic common to God and man is apparently that: the desire and the ability to make things."[13] From this initial assumption, Sayers proceeds to apply the doctrine of the Trinity to the creative process. Her thesis is an expansion on the concluding speech in one of her plays, *The Zeal of Thy House*:

> For every work of creation is threefold, an earthly trinity to match the heavenly.
>
> First, there is the Creative Idea, passionless, timeless, beholding the whole work complete at once, the end in the beginning: and this is the image of the Father.
>
> Second, there is the Creative Energy begotten of that idea, working in time from the beginning to the end, with sweat and passion, being incarnate in the bonds of matter: and this is the image of the Word.
>
> Third, there is the Creative Power, the meaning of the work and its response in the lively soul: and this is the image of the indwelling Spirit.
>
> And these three are one, each equally in itself the whole work, whereof none can exist without other: and this is the image of the Trinity.[14]

Sayers believes that the Idea (parallel to God the Father, who exists only as a spirit) cannot be known apart from the Energy (parallel to the Son, incarnate in human flesh): "The Energy . . . is something distinct from the Idea itself, though it is the only thing that can make the Idea known to itself or to others and yet is . . . essentially identical with the Idea—'consubstantial with the Father.'"[15] The Power (parallel to the Holy Spirit) is the means "by which the [Energy] is communicated to other readers and which produces a corresponding response in them."[16] Sayers observes that in both trinitarian doctrine and trinitarian aesthetics, the three are distinct but inseparable—in short, a mystery.

Playwrights will begin to recognize in Sayers's essay how tightly woven their calling and craft is to the very essence of the Creator and to their own, sometimes mysterious, creative impulses. Some may find their work an offering of worship. Like much Christian doctrine, the application of the Trinity to creativity is not restricting but liberating. Francis Hodge hints at this in *Play Directing: Analysis, Communication and Style* when he remarks on the writer's "dream-flight, his improvisation,"[17] which takes shape on a stage in the embodiment of an ensemble of actors and as received by a live audience. There is a distinctly Christian dimension to this process, involving spiritual (imaginative) creation being incarnated in order to create a communal experience.

The twentieth century presents playwrights with a bewildering smorgasbord of dramaturgical choices, from the extreme form of realism that recreates life on stage (naturalism) to the many departures from realism that recur in various guises by breaking the appearance of reality in some way. We embrace the physical and the transcendent, seeing in both realms evidence of God's grace and presence. In the incarnation Jesus continued to be God even as he humbled himself and took on the form of a servant. His coming to earth reminds us that God created the material world (including people) and that the image of God remains intact in creation (including people), even in the fallen state of our world. Jesus sent the Spirit upon his return to heaven to favor us with the presence of God in this world, a reminder that Christians coexist in spiritual and material realms simultaneously. Our plays should reflect that coexistence.

The two overarching dramatic structures that subsume the various styles available to the writer are the *climactic* and the *episodic*. Theatre, television, and film are dominated by narrative, climactic drama. But consider also the rich tradition of literature in our Christian tradition, from the epics of the Old Testament, to the parables of the New Testament, to the episodic drama of the medieval period; you will discover a wedding of content and style/structure that could point you in some fruitful directions. Some work in more episodic dramatic structures is being done by writers seeking a voice in the mainstream theatre; much more should be attempted. Again, we can't just look at what is being done now; we have to look backward to the traditions.

The model of epic theatre suggests changes in the structure of plays as well as the integration of music and the juxtaposing of comedic and serious elements. It also points the way to a theatre with intellectual tendencies, a welcome antidote to the rampant sentimentalism that regularly floods the Christian subculture. At the height of the religious drama revival in England, when the plays of T. S. Eliot and Christopher Fry were being staged in the West End of London, the president of the Religious Drama Society of Great Britain, E. Martin Browne, surveyed the landscape of plays written by Christians and proclaimed: "The vast majority of religious drama is sentimental mush, abominably presented."[18] Melodrama is pervasive in our culture, and sometimes it may be the appropriate genre for a play, but we also need epic, comic, and tragic plays to fully express the breadth of perspective Christianity affords. One reason some people don't take Christianity seriously as a way to view the world is that we have limited and dumbed down the creative expressions of our faith to reach a large segment (and a low common denominator) of audiences.

In addition to steeping themselves in theatrical and historical traditions, playwrights should also understand and explore the implications of theology for their work. This goes deeper than inserting references to Christianity, setting the play in a church, or basing the play on the Bible, all of which can be appropriate things to do. Allow the theological categories that resonate in the theatre to germinate in your imagination, and they will work themselves into the deep structures of your plays. Francis Schaeffer has suggested that the arts must capture both the minor theme of Scripture (the fallenness of creation) and the major theme of Scripture (the redemptive work of Christ). Plays that are not anthropologically correct, that present humans as better than they are by nature, that fail to convey the reality of a fallen universe, do not serve the purposes of the kingdom of God. On the other hand, plays that present a world devoid of the potential for redemption, either in the plot, characters, or language; that present a universe outside the control of the sovereign God; or that are not informed by the incarnate Christ are equally off balance.

Consider also the manner in which God has revealed truth to us. We turn to the Bible as God's revelation. Theologians call this *specific* revelation. In the Scriptures God speaks with clarity to us, and we hear the truth of God: "Whoever believes in the Son has eternal life; whoever disobeys the Son will not see life, but must endure God's wrath" (John 3:36 NRSV). God has also chosen to communicate with us through nature, culture, and our consciences. Theologians call this *general* revelation. This is revelation through picture, experience, metaphor, and image. Consider the implications of this less specific and more artistic means of revelation. Some Christian audiences fail to see the truth of God being revealed in a general way in those plays that are not explicitly "Christian." I'm not sure whether Shakespeare was a Christian, and I wouldn't call his *Taming of the Shrew* a Christian drama. But the interplay between Petruchio and Kate, the balance of movement of these two headstrong characters to a place of mutual submission and respect, mirrors the teaching of Scripture in Ephesians 5. Examples from Shakespeare could be multiplied.

In chapter 1, we considered evidence of drama in the stories of the Bible, which may have been acted out in Hebrew worship. There is a very clear parallel to this type of drama in writing plays today for worship or church audiences. But we also noted evidence of theatre in the ministry of the prophets, and there are fewer examples of this type of drama in the contemporary church. In fact, writers who are given a calling to prophetic theatre may not write drama for the church; their work may speak from the margins to the church, as did the work of their Old Testament predecessors. Consider also the Lord's use of parables, to which he resorted only after his very clear teachings (in the Sermon on the Mount, for example) were consistently ignored or rejected. He turned to parables to enflesh the truth. His disciples sometimes had to ask for interpretations. The parables were intended to subvert the expectations that the people had of the Messiah and the reign of God on earth. So too, the church today needs writers who will use the example of general revelation, prophetic ministry, and parabolic structure to bring the unexpected news of God's holiness and judgment to the contemporary church and society. The church has its share of "priests" creating drama that reinforces and celebrates the belief systems of their congregations; we need priests, and we also need theatrical prophets.

Many people rush into playwriting with a mission: to illustrate/communicate/preach the message of Christianity through the potent medium of drama. An example of this in the church is the short play (sketch) format. The conscious effort to dramatize theology results in sermons-in-dialogue that are further weakened by the constraints of a short playing time. A ten-minute play can succeed, and a didactic play can succeed (again, witness Brecht), but a short message-play written by someone with little understanding of or training in dramaturgy will often fail as drama and as message. People who want to communicate on a piano dedicate themselves to learning how to play the instrument; so too writers should dedicate themselves to learning how to play the instrument of drama before performing in public.

"The term *thesis* will be applied to any intention extrinsic to the work itself, when the thought inspired by such an intention does not act upon the work by means of the artistic habit moved instrumentally, but puts itself in juxtaposition to the habit so as itself to act directly upon the work."[19] Jacques Maritain goes on to call this kind of influence "alien" to the creation of a work of art, for it short-circuits spontaneity and evidences a kind of calculation aiming for an end foreign to the work itself. Of course, any play can have, and most plays do have, a thesis, because plays issue from the intellect of the playwright. The question is whether the writer has sufficient grasp of dramaturgical technique and a confidence in his or her imaginative powers to allow the work to flow spontaneously from the imagination without superimposing a thesis on it. Maritain views the builders of cathedrals as exemplars: "They had the Faith, and as they were, so did they work. Their achievement revealed God's truth, but without *doing it on purpose*, and because it was not done on purpose."[20]

Again, Dorothy Sayers is instructive. In 1955 she published an article in *World Theater* called "Playwrights Are Not Evangelists."[21] In it she argues forcefully for writers to keep their eyes on their craft, not on a "spiritual box office." We should care about the spiritual results of our writing, but we need to do so only after first giving attention to writing a good play.

A strong position on the quality of what Christians write is not ivory-tower elitism, nor does it discount the sincere attempts by God's children to do the work of the kingdom through drama. The Holy Spirit can and does use a variety of tools, some of which confound human wisdom. We celebrate that work; at the same time we encourage you to consider the importance of learning the craft of playwriting and the lessons of theology as a way to honor God, who embodies excellence and beauty. Dependence on the power of God does not excuse us from seeking training and experience. Christians depend on God for the *results* that issue from their work. They make every effort, with the opportunities God gives them, to become the best artists they can—all the while giving God the glory for whatever is accomplished.

Many Christian playwrights embody their faith in the theatre through plays of first-rate quality. The Fall/Winter 2004 issue of *Christianity and Theatre* contains essays and excerpts by several of these dramatists.[22] It gives evidence that a body of work is being produced by Christians in the theatre who seek to integrate their faith with their dedication to drama. These authors meet regularly, at conferences, symposia, and productions of their plays, to further explore how to become better writers and better at grappling with the surrounding culture through their writing. Is the work difficult? Yes. Is it being done? Yes.

The Christian as Actor

In our description of theatre history, we mentioned how theorists often distill theatre to its essential components: an actor performing for an audience. Acting is the primary art of the theatre; all other arts may be dispensed with, but if there is no actor there is no theatre. Acting is also more than speaking or storytelling. It is imitation, taking on a character with the resources of imagination, voice, and body, in a way that is different or elevated from everyday discourse. Acting is fun, and many people engage in it for the pleasure of being in front of an audience and eliciting a response; acting is also hard work, and those who pursue it as their calling enter into a lifelong process of developing their resources for the challenges of the stage. You know good acting when the hard work fades into the background and you experience a performer truly enjoying the performance. An actor's hard work will make her or his craft seem effortless.

I'm often asked about challenges Christians face in the acting profession: the interviewer assumes they will be related to morals. I don't downplay those challenges, but if you are not an actor, you need to understand first how difficult it is to make a living as one. The economic pressures can be intense; they can also impact moral choices. In America, repertory companies are almost nonexistent, so actors are contractors jumping from job to job. Students with aspirations to the stage are encouraged to get graduate degrees, so that they can fall back on teaching for health and retirement benefits (the early twenty-first-century economic climate has made these all but essential). Actors Equity, the union of professional actors, and the Actor's Fund try to address these concerns, but a very low percentage (roughly 10 to 20 percent) of union actors are actually acting for pay at any given time. A small percentage of athletes can expect to play sports professionally, and a similarly small percentage of thespians can expect to be paid for their acting.

Some Christians working in the theatre express their situation as "between a rock and a hard place": misunderstood by their peers in the theatre because they've embraced Christianity and misunderstood by their community of faith because they work in the theatre. It is rarely that simple or that severe, and at the risk of sounding unsympathetic (which we are not), we suggest that such a martyr complex is neither healthy nor productive. Christian actors have learned to be nonconfrontational with their faith, and the Christian church as a whole no longer views the profession of acting as tantamount to moral failure. Even conservative churches and colleges now offer drama ministries and courses/majors in theatre. In point of fact, the Christian actor now enters the workforce with some distinct advantages: faith in Christ, which can provide peace and joy in any circumstances; the support of Christian brothers and sisters through church and parachurch communities; God's Word for inspiration and guidance; and the indwelling presence of the Holy Spirit.

Murray Watts notes that Christian actors can choose to ignore the implications of their faith on their work, "in any other sense than being a good professional." Others may obsess with the relationship and "agonize over the moral implications of their work." He challenges the actor to remember that "Christ dwells within him at all times, and this profound knowledge of inner sanctity, given by the grace of God, must surely bring the choices facing every actor into sharp focus. The Christian regards his body as 'the temple of the Holy Spirit.' What are the artistic implications of such an astonishing belief?"[23] Watts makes an important point: Christian actors can approach their calling and craft confident of their position in Christ. This is true of every Christian, regardless of vocation, but it has direct application for actors, who use their bodies and imaginations as the instruments of their work.

Acting is the essential art of the theatre, so the history and theology of the theatre should be brought into the consciousness of the actor. Actors are part of a community, an ensemble, which is usually reconstituted for each production (unless they are members of a repertory company). Knowing the value and obligation of being in a community will inform the actor's process. Acting relates to incarnation; actors give flesh to the imaginative creation of a playwright and/or to their own imaginative processes.[24] It is in the fleshing-out of a character within a community of other artists that theatre happens.

Actors should explore a theology of the body, and this begins by disavowing themselves of the notion that Paul the apostle was referring only to the body with the word "flesh" (Greek: *sarx*). In Paul's writings the flesh may be the body, but it is also much more. Since we are both spiritual and corporeal creatures, there is a systemic link between body and spirit: the things actors do with their bodies or allow to be done to their bodies are not just "as the character"; these choices have an effect on their spiritual welfare.

In *Good Taste, Bad Taste, and Christian Taste*, Frank Burch Brown writes, "We belong with and to our bodies. We recognize, for example, that what happens to our bodies happens in some way to ourselves."[25] Actors may view their bodies as disconnected from their spiritual life; such a view is founded on a false dichotomy between spirit and body.

Christians must reclaim an essential biblical truth: we do not have bodies; rather, we are bodies.[26] A persistent antimaterialism in Christianity handed down from the ancient gnostics, perpetuated by the Puritans, and still in evidence in some quarters of the church, fosters the notion that the body is itself evil. "There is no physical or fleshly pleasure without some spiritual harm," Meister Eckhart wrote.[27] In the culture at large, there is a general revulsion to nature (including the body) in its organic, decaying condition. The cult of celebrity and beauty fixes an ideal physical state at an age shortly after pubescence, in a particular body type and photographed under carefully prepared conditions. Charles Davis writes, "The rejection of matter, in particular of the living matter of the body, is characteristic of our culture today. . . . We can say that people in general have no feel or appreciation for the texture of material things." He advocates an "asceticism of achieved spontaneity" to reconnect physical sensitivity to spiritual pursuits.[28] Praying with the body ("enacted prayer" in Jeff Barker's words)[29] is one application. Learning the techniques of an art to "the saturation level" allows the artist to "respond connaturally and spontaneously in his art, in a manner analogous to our everyday responses, but on a different level. He achieves an artless art."[30]

A trained actor will detect echoes of Stanislavsky's theory of psycho-physical actions in these comments. Stanislavsky recognized a connection between emotions and physical action. Changes in the emotional state result in physical changes; actors get at the emotional state of a character by physically performing those actions that in real life evidence the particular emotion being sought. Actors who accept in full their spiritual and physical existence and understand, through theology, the connectedness of spirit and body can explore in depth that connection as they incarnate characters in plays.

> I find then a law, that evil is present with me, the one who wills to do good. For I delight in the law of God according to the inward man. But I see another law in my members, warring against the law of my mind, and bringing me into captivity to the law of sin which is in my members. O wretched man that I am! Who will deliver me from this body of death? I thank God—through Jesus Christ our Lord! (Rom. 7:21–25)

Paul is clearly locating at least some of the impetus for his sinful nature in his "members," his body; Charles Davis can only conclude, "Paul . . . has the human condition wrong."[31] No, Paul has it correct, and while Christian actors must recover a theology of the body that accepts its unity with their spirit, they must also recognize their fallenness, especially as people whose instrument is their body. "Because we are embodied souls, and spirited bodies, the physical senses can themselves be spiritual senses, when rightly used and enjoyed."[32]

People drawn to the profession of acting tend to be sensitive, sometimes insecure, and often vulnerable. Those attributes, channeled into creative work, are invaluable. Those very same attributes expose the actor-artist to the potential for physical, spiritual, and emotional harm. Unfortunately, in our fallen world, there are all too many individuals ready to take advantage of the very traits that make for a naturally gifted actor. What will see an actor through the challenges of this profession, economic and moral, is a sense of *calling*. A calling from God to a particular work is a deep sense in the mind and in the heart that you are doing the only thing you can do and that you will continue to do it no matter how hard it gets. This sense of calling is confirmed by Scripture and by the witness of those closest to you. When all three indicators agree—your conscience, your understanding of Scripture, and your closest advisors—you can be sure of your calling and have faith that God will be faithful to you while you are in it. Faith is not a feeling; it is holding on to someone: the faithful God. Faith has an object, and believer-actors absolutely must come to a position whereby they recognize their calling and daily hold on to their God in the face of success (which is sometimes hard to live with), failure, or rejection.

The apostles admonished believers to think energetically and critically (1 Pet. 5:8), to be vigilant against the enemies of their souls—the world, the flesh, and the devil (1 John 2:16)—and to use discernment in every choice they make (Phil. 1:10). Actors, given the prospect of a job on stage, sometimes forget these admonitions, especially when the choice involves an "on the spot" decision (as these choices often do). We encourage you to be strong in your spirit and full of discernment *before* you are tested. These character traits are not learned once only. Pursue them continually; what is necessary for one stage of life is not enough for the next. The challenges of the Christian walk are not static and predictable; they increase in number and severity as we mature: that is the privilege God gives to those who follow Christ as his disciples.

The actor who is in Christ is a child of God, under God's wings, and looked after by the one who sees the fall of a single sparrow. In Exodus 28 the artist Bezaleel is called to contribute to the construction of the temple through the exercise of his artistry. He is called to do this "by name," and his name means "in the shadow of the Almighty." The believer called to pursue the art and vocation of acting will do so in God's shadow and with immediate access to God through prayer. No challenge or choice will ever be entered into alone. "Whatever removes an obstacle removes a source of strength; whatever removes a difficulty removes a glory."[33]

"The work of art always ends by betraying, with infallible cunning, the vices of the workman."[34] G. K. Chesterton once remarked, "Art, like morality, consists of drawing the line somewhere."[35] We all draw lines every day in the choices we make. Every actor has his or her limits, be it certain words, certain physical actions, characters, places, collaborators. Don't be ashamed of or shrink away from drawing lines based on your understanding of Scripture, the counsel of other believers, and your conscience. Words have power, actions matter, and choices add up to a way of life. The challenge to Christian actors is to know, in advance and through thoughtful consideration, where the lines will be drawn before a question arises. As you mature and as your circle of influence changes, those lines may change, and that is also a function of growing in grace; you may find more or less liberty down the road. Adding children to a family makes for different decisions. Taking a leadership role in a church makes for different decisions. Moving from academic to professional theatre makes for different decisions. Such changes are a part of living; enjoy them and be ready for them.

the christian
at play

Being an Audience in the Theatre

Dale Savidge

All theatre artists are also audience members—or at least they should be. Attendance at plays is a necessary component of training and ongoing growth in the discipline. However, many more Christians attend the theatre than work in the theatre. Going to live theatre is not the same as going to a film or watching television. What does our theological reflection on theatre suggest about attending theatre? And, in turn, how can going to the theatre inform our understanding of theology?

Theatre is an experience that, at its best, ennobles the spirit and challenges the intellect. As Neil Postman reminds us, much popular culture is like eating cotton candy: it may taste good at the time, but it doesn't last long or provide any nourishment. There is nothing wrong with the lighter fare, but seeking out unfamiliar, classic, or difficult art of any type can nourish our spirits.

Don't take this analogy too far: going to the theatre is not like eating your vegetables! To those who take the time to understand how theatre works, and who make the effort to attend enough to develop a taste for it, theatre is anything but brussel sprouts. Experiencing the creative energies of a performing arts group and contributing to the performance by your presence in a live audience can be both invigorating and rewarding. When you take a Christian perspective into the theatre and make an effort to reflect on the performance, no matter how much it may challenge your worldview, you are certain to grow as a person and as a Christian. The theatre has traditionally been a forum for exploring ultimate concerns, especially those touching on interpersonal relationships. It is also a place for Christians to experience some of the greatest imaginations in human history and in the history of Christianity. If you have never experienced the genius and insight of Shakespeare, stop reading right now and go buy a ticket to a live presentation of a Shakespearean drama; very likely one is playing in a theatre near you. You will be glad that you did.

Recreation is an important but often neglected part of being a human and being a Christian.[1] While giving credence to the serious potential of theatre as a communicator of valuable cultural ideas, we recommend live theatre as a diversion from the work of everyday life. "No man can live without pleasure. Therefore a man deprived of the pleasures of the spirit goes over to the pleasures of the flesh."[2] This was written by Thomas Aquinas, not by a network television executive. The theatre provides such spiritual pleasures. "The power to laugh, to cease work, and frolic in forgetfulness of all the conflict, to make merry, is a divine bestowment upon man, and its absence in any case is as sure a mark of the blighting effects of sin, as is the frothy life of the devotee of miscalled pleasure who never contributes anything to the work of his generation."[3]

Audiences at a live theatre event possess the ability to influence the performance, something missing from the experience of television or movies. The theatrical event is reciprocal; the communication flows from actors to audience and back again, in a cycle of reciprocity. Audience response definitely impacts performers, and performances change from night to night depending on the audience response. Individuals in an audience collectively form an entity that also influences their individual responses. This is especially true at a performance of a comedy. Where and when the audience laughs is partially dependent on the collective response of those watching. When theatre is at its best, when it works as more than entertainment and gives the patrons an "aesthetic experience," you will feel part of a community, however temporary; it is a powerful and rewarding experience.

The Christian at the Theatre

We encourage you to be an audience in the theatre regularly and to take your seat as an active participant. Passively or uncritically receiving anything is hazardous to your spiritual health, so enter ready to engage, react, and reflect on what you experience. The experience of theatre, with its incarnational nature, the sense of community among both audience and actors, and the presence that happens in the shared space and time is a powerful and necessary antidote to the virtual world of the twenty-first century. Here are some examples of the kinds of plays that, while not overtly religious, are worthy of your consideration.

David Rambo's *God's Man in Texas* tackles tough questions, including questions of faith. It deals with the transfer of power from one pastor to another, and although it does not shrink from the dark side of ecclesial politics, it offers a balanced and fair depiction of Christians. It is a contemporary play that features a person praying without a trace of sarcasm or cynicism. Tracy Lett's *Man from Nebraska*, which was featured in the September 2004 issue of *American Theatre*, is a crisis-of-faith drama that ends, quite surprisingly to readers conditioned to expect such a crisis to end in disaster, with the reconciliation of husband and wife. Ken, the husband, returns to his wife, and the play ends with his line: "I choose you. Choose me."

Other examples: the *New York Times* review of August Wilson's last play *Gem of the Ocean* (which played on Broadway in 2005) called it "grandly evangelical." The influential avant-garde director Robert Wilson combines African American gospel songs with the literature of Gustave Flaubert in *The Temptation of Saint Anthony*. That play echoes T. S. Eliot's *Murder in the Cathedral* (1935), a successful mainstream drama of an earlier generation. The Magis Theatre Company mounted a successful off-Broadway adaptation of C. S. Lewis's *The Great Divorce* in the winter of 2007, and in June of that year the innovative theatre artist Rinde Eckert performed *Horizon* at the New York Theatre Workshop. In *Horizon* Eckert pays homage to the theology of Reinhold Niebuhr in a multidisciplinary performance piece that places the "man of God in a sort of spiritual laboratory."[4] In May 2007 the *New York Times* carried this article:

PERFORMANCE SPACE 122, the East Village center known for telling heart-on-its-sleeve theater to take a hike, is undergoing a religious conversion of sorts, with two new shows on Christian themes. "Church," written and directed by Young Jean Lee, is being performed until next Saturday. It's an unorthodox contemporary worship service, complete with sermon, praise dancing and a gospel choir. The playwright and director Lear DeBessonet upends Brecht's "St. Joan of the Stockyards" in a revival that begins June 15, transplanting the dark Joan of Arc story to 1920s Chicago, with bluegrass music by the singer Kelley McRae and handouts of warm bread. Young Jean Lee . . . and Lear DeBessonet are both directing plays that address religious themes at Performance Space 122. Ms. Lee, 32, and Ms. DeBessonet, 26, sat with Erik Piepenburg to discuss how Christian fundamentalism influenced their plays; what it means to lose, gain and question faith; and how downtown theater mistreats the evangelical mind.[5]

Dramatizations of the Bible also frequently appear in the theatre: in the fall of 2004 Val Kilmer took the stage in Los Angeles in the pop opera *The Ten Commandments*. (In spite of a $10–15 million capitalization, the musical opened to lackluster reviews and closed for revisions a month later.) Other well-funded theatre with Christian/biblical content is being planned for New York City, and biblical epics continue to play in outdoor drama venues as well as in state-of-the-art facilities such as Sight and Sound Theatres (Lancaster, Pennsylvania, and Branson, Missouri) and the Holy Land Experience in Florida. Recently, fund-raising began for a major new musical on the life of John Newton, *Amazing Grace: The True Story*.[6] Professional theatres with a Christian worldview operate in several cities across the United States and Canada, producing full seasons of quality theatre. These include the A.D. Players in Houston, the Lamb's Players in San Diego, Taproot Theatre in Seattle, Pacific Theatre in Vancouver, and Saltworks Theatre near Pittsburgh, among others. Not every play staged by these companies is based on the Bible, but their season choices derive from their Christian perspective and taken as a whole reflect a commitment to biblical themes or at least themes of ultimate concern.

The Epistle of James is emphatic: "Every good and every perfect gift is from above and comes down from the Father of lights" (1:17). There is much beauty and truth to be found in the artistic offerings of nonbelievers because all good gifts issue from God. Any theatre piece with integrity that truthfully presents itself to us can open a door for theological reflection. The contemporary issues that theatre engages touch us as Christians and our neighbors.

Jack O'Brien, artistic director of San Diego's Old Globe Theatre, looked to the future of the theatre in the November 29, 2004, issue of *Time*: "It seems that hot, young playwrights and directors are attacking stereotypes and breaking new ground—and not only in New York . . . [in] forward-thinking, cutting-edge, often controversial plays."[7] O'Brien credits a 1993 Broadway production with leading the charge: Tony Kushner's *Angels in America*. "Thanks to *Angels*, provocative issues will hit stages across America. Kushner inspired us to lead with our chins, and not shy away from controversial themes. It was a wakeup call for artists in theatres large and small that the times are ripe to examine socially challenging material and concerns and get them quickly on stage."[8] The contemporary theatre, aside from tourist musicals on Broadway and on tour, is a place for vigorous, often heated, exploration of real life issues—with issues of sexuality at the fore.

Angels in America drew a firestorm of controversy after its appearance in New York in 1993. Subsequent productions in regional theatres and now on college campuses continue to be lightning rods for criticism from Christian organizations. The 2004 HBO film brought the work to an even larger audience. The two parts (*Part One: Millennium Approaches* and *Part Two: Perestroika*) take six hours to view. *Angels* won the Pulitzer Prize, a Tony award, the Drama Desk award for Best Play, and was named one of the ten best plays of the twentieth century by the Royal National Theatre of Great Britain.

The controversy attending this play is an unsurprising result of the subject matter. It is an epic melding personal and political, individual and corporate themes in a work whose subtitle is *A Gay Fantasia on National Themes*. Every play has a point of view, a worldview within which action unfolds and by which the choices of the characters are filtered. Kushner's is unapologetically the worldview of a homosexual male; in fact, except for the minor role of a doctor who attends Roy Cohn's AIDS-induced decline, there isn't a straight male in either play. The central character, Prior Walter, is a homosexual dying of AIDS and given to hallucinations brought on by the medications he takes in his battle to slow the disease. He is visited by an angel and later ushered into "heaven" on a flaming ladder. Heaven turns out to be San Francisco (after an earthquake), where Prior declares his independence from "God" since "God" has abandoned creation.

Prior's partner, Louis Ironson, deserts him in his battle at the same time a Mormon lawyer, Joseph Pitt, deserts his Valium-addicted wife, Harper, because he realizes he is a homosexual who has been forced to suppress his identity by his Mormon upbringing. The two dysfunctional relationships mirror a common human tendency: to take the easy way out and escape a relationship when things aren't going well. Soon the lives of these four are intertwined (Joe becomes Louis's lover) and interdependent.

There is enough objectionable content in this play to arouse calls for censorship and boycotts from some Christian communities wherever it plays. A militant ideology permeates the plays, summarized by Prior in the closing lines of part 2:

> We are not going away—the world only spins forward. We will be citizens, the time has come. The great work begins.

That this work has received such wide critical and popular acclaim is attributable to the excellence of its dramaturgy and breadth of vision, as well as Kushner's unambiguous political and social agenda. The tone of the play champions the cause of gays, in particular as an oppressed if not neglected segment of society.

In *Angels* the homosexual male is a victim, personally and corporately, and AIDS, or the failure to focus enough resources on the treatment of AIDS, is the physical manifestation of the hatred of a religiously motivated, Republican-dominated society.

A transcendent presence is evident in this play: after all, angels appear and are seen by Prior and later by Hannah Pitt (Joe's observant Mormon mother). But the message of the angel is to empower Prior's homosexuality and ordain him a prophet to the world, a prophet who will carry the homosexual agenda summed up in those final lines (just as the angel Moroni appeared to Joseph Smith and sent him on his way with the message of Mormonism).

So what is the response of a Christian to such a seminal work of theatre, one that confronts the Christian community with one of the most divisive issues in contemporary church and society? Christians have both rejected and accepted this play in the same way churches have rejected or embraced homosexuality. Certainly Christians have every right to make their voices heard in their communities. The prophets of the Bible did not shrink from speaking out, and a play like *Angels* invites and provokes public responses. We should also consider this play and others with its subject as representative of a culture that has raised questions of sexuality above nearly any other concern in life. Christians need to address this mistaken emphasis and offer a more balanced perspective on our humanity.

But another, more personal response is called for. *Angels* is not just a political soapbox; it is a poignant story of people trapped in dysfunctional relationships, fighting a debilitating and painful disease, searching for personal peace. If you read/view past the ideology to the characters in the world of the play, you will not just see and hear the pain of the characters; you will feel it in a profound and powerful way. Such an experience should move Christians to action, not just sympathy but active love for our neighbors who are represented by the characters in *Angels in America*.

Christian playwrights do not have an exclusive hold on truth, nor are plays written by non-Christian writers devoid of portions of God's truth. The theatre as an art form is open to spiritual truth and to content that hints at a spiritual world. In 1991 several theatre artists discussed the relationship of theatre to spirituality. John Guare (author of *Six Degrees of Separation*) recognized the fear of audiences that art might undermine their morals (something it is admittedly able to do); he wondered why they "do not see the opposite viewpoint just as clearly. If art has such power, it can also renew life. But today we don't know what to do with art. . . . Why do people see the power of art to destroy and not its power to heal?"[9] Director Andre Serban says, "Theatre must look for spiritual truth—but now formulas of sociology are offered up as panaceas. Today's theatre is trapped in a sewer. Characters sit around in the muck without looking up. Art must inspire faith. But in our time, trying to provide spiritual weapons is difficult. Audiences resist."[10] According to Peter Sellars, "Theatre is a Nautilus machine for the soul," and Richard Foreman remarks: "The art that interests me most in the 20th century . . . is a form of spirituality."[11] The theme of spirituality in theatre was addressed directly in a more recent issue of *American Theatre* (November 2000). Celia Wren attended the summer networking conference of Christians in Theatre Arts (CITA) in North Carolina, where over six hundred participants gathered. She summarized the various issues Christians face in creating and experiencing theatre. Other articles in the issue focus on faith-based theatre from non-Christian religions.

The evangelical subculture has offered believers a steady diet of sentimental entertainment, in painting, literature, television, film, and music. Live theatre can provide, after this "orgy of sentimentalism," a "rude contact with reality."[12] Because it often stands outside the stream of popular entertainment, which must for economic reasons appeal to a low common denominator, theatre can speak like a prophet; its voice is often strident, sharp, and painful. It is in Victor Turner's phrase in the realm of "antistructural life" in that it is not part of everyday (i.e., work and family) life but is weighted with significance.[13]

The question of attending the theatre involves both *what* to see and *how* to see. Christians are called to exercise thoughtful caution ("keep your heart with all diligence" Prov. 4:23) and that includes being selective consumers of all culture. Philippians 4 bears consideration, especially the admonition to think on truth rather than error. The presence of objectionable content (language, violence, sexuality) may be the deciding factor in whether experiencing a play is a healthy choice; but the presence of philosophical error is far more insidious and harder to detect and will be far more harmful to the spirit of a person. We need to develop critical sensibilities as audience members, and part of this process is making good aesthetic choices.

From the theatre of ancient Greece until the 1800s, dramatic literature generally fell into two dominant genres: comedy and tragedy. The expected response to the first was laughter and to the latter silence. It was not until the advent of melodrama in the nineteenth century that audiences were moved to tears through various sentimental devices (e.g., a fiddle in the wings). It has become a staple of much drama, filmed and live, to manipulate the emotions through the use of continuous musical accompaniment: melodrama. This lowest of dramatic genres is also characterized by a black-and-white portrayal of good and evil and a penchant for spectacle. Certainly the Bible differentiates between good and evil, but in human nature the two are comingled, and truthful portrayals of dramatic characters must acknowledge the fallenness of even heroes. Further, good and evil are sometimes viewed as equal forces locked in combat, à la *Star Wars*. Such a portrayal is not biblical; it is a theological heresy that posits good and evil as two sides of a single force. A part of making good choices is distinguishing among the genres we regularly encounter.

Exercising taste in our theatrical choices involves three steps: first perceiving the work, then enjoying the work, and finally judging the work.[14] Too often audiences permit the work to so engross them emotionally that they fail to understand it. It is also possible to become so critical that the necessary enjoyment of the work never happens. More often than not, however, audiences fail to take the final step and think critically about the work. Great theatre always challenges us to take that final step. David Hume distinguished between merely liking a work and thinking critically about it. "All sentiment is right . . . because no sentiment represents what is really in the object."[15] Hume suggests *judgment* as a necessary next step.

Christians often add to their response to drama a spiritual sentimentality. Not only do we like what moves us emotionally; we blur the distinction between aesthetics and edification. Certainly God can use even the rocks to build the kingdom and work in the hearts of people, and it is through human weakness that God's strength is revealed. But beauty and excellence are also divine attributes, and art that aspires to beauty and excellence honors God; in the words of Dorothy Sayers, "Before everything let us not forget that to do good it is necessary first to do well."[16] Audiences, like artists, need to develop the sensibilities that can discern the divine attributes of beauty and excellence in the theatre and support those works, whether by Christians or not, that aspire to them.

Although it is true that almost any piece of theatre can be taken as a positive experience, one that strengthens a believer's walk, it is not true that all Christians should attend every play available to them. We should consciously control the things we experience, and this is particularly true of the powerful medium of drama. Mature Christians understand themselves and listen to those who know them well. They voluntarily deny themselves in areas that would hinder their growth and damage their relationship with Christ.

For example, Edward Albee's powerful drama *Who's Afraid of Virginia Woolf?* is a searing indictment of failed marriages and dysfunctional relationships. The play is filled with violence and profanity, to the point that the audience is beaten down with the utter hopelessness of the two couples. But at the end George offers a prayer, a Latin requiem, and the dark night of the play issues in the rising of the sun. In performance this is a power-fully redemptive and hope-filled moment, but it has come at the end of two hours of depravity. Does the play tell the truth about fallen humanity? Yes. Is the experience appropriate for everyone? No. Another example is Samuel Beckett's *Waiting for Godot*, a masterpiece of absurdist drama. Again, this is a play that takes its gloves off in its treatment of fallen humanity, and it presents a worldview absent a deity. It masterfully brings us face-to-face with our spiritual condition apart from God—without any hint of sentimentality. These plays, and many others like them, are the works of brilliant writers, and when produced well they are powerful dramatic experiences—but they can also be sources of despair and pessimism.

I attend theatre in my local community (Greenville, South Carolina) with some regularity. I do this because I love theatre and I believe purchas-ing tickets helps encourage and sustain the artists and organizations that produce it here. Still, I'm selective about what I spend money to see; my choices are made based on the content of the piece as well as the quality of the production. I think purchasing wisely helps encourage arts presenters to make quality choices in their seasons and, also important, protects my meager budget!

In the 2004–5 season, one of our local theatres presented work by Thorn-ton Wilder (*Our Town*), Arthur Miller (*Death of a Salesman*), Shakespeare (*Midsummer Night's Dream*), Harold Pinter (*Betrayal*), and Suzan Lori-Parks (*Top Dog, Under Dog*). I went to the Wilder, Miller, Pinter, and Lori-Parks shows (I've seen *Midsummer* many times at the community level). Pinter and Lori-Parks were hard choices because I knew their plays would contain a lot of difficult content. I chose to see Pinter because his work is consistently recognized as masterful, and the Lori-Parks play won the Pulitzer Prize for Drama in 2002. Both plays deal with the underside of human nature, and neither shrinks from presenting the presence and consequences of the de-pravity of humans (though neither used the word "sin"). I stayed throughout the entirety of *Betrayal*, even though I found the play difficult. Pinter uses sparse language and action to take us back in time through the progression of an extramarital affair and in so doing lays bare the downward spiral of broken relationships. I found it affirmed what Francis Schaeffer has called the "minor theme" of Scripture: humans are fallen and tend toward destruc-tive behavior. The play understates, suggests, and subtly calls up a specific incidence of this destructive behavior, unfaithfulness, in short, betrayal.

Top Dog, Under Dog was a more difficult experience. The play takes us into the urban ghetto, a world of despair where card tricks on the street are the primary means of survival. It is an unsparing presentation. Profanity assaults us, first in the rap-music environment and then as the two characters move violently through the first half of the play. That was the only part I saw. When pornography and masturbation entered the scene, I checked out. I know these are part of the fallen world, but I didn't feel comfortable staying. You may think I copped out, and perhaps you wouldn't have left, but the decision was mine to make and I made the one that was right for me at that time. It isn't often that I can't find a reason to stay through the second half of a play, but in this case I couldn't. The last time I remember leaving a play at intermission was at a London performance of Chekhov's *Cherry Orchard*. In that case it was the quality of the production, not content, that sent me home. These were entirely personal decisions, and my point is not that you make *my* decisions but that you make conscious decisions *for yourself*, and that you consider how they will affect you and those around you.

There are no hard and fast rules for how you, as a Christian in an audience, should choose what to see, what not to see, what to sit through, and when to exit. What we experience in the theatre affects us emotionally, intellectually, and spiritually. The important thing is to *choose* and not just naively assume you can be part of any experience without being affected by it. You can't.

In October 2007 I spent two hours with two hundred strangers in the small rural town of Rosebud, Alberta (Canada), at a performance of the musical *Tent Meeting*.[17] There are occasions when an investment of time bears dividends far beyond the amount invested. Theatre is for me very often such an experience. Here we were among the hills and livestock of western Canada, reliving a Depression-era story of gospel music and tent-meeting evangelism. I only knew a few people in the theatre; I was in a foreign country and at a distant time with a story that I had very little experience with—and I felt right at home. Theatre has a way of making communities of people, and when the story is about our faith, about people who share our faith, and the experience is shared with many people who resonate with the story, the experience can be profound. Both theatre and Christianity invite us into community.

Living in community means I should temper my criticism with an awareness of the mutual obligations of membership. I live and work in the theatre community in my hometown, so my response to the work done by other members reflects the respect I have for them. I don't always need even to express my opinion. My pastor defines humility as "having a low opinion of my opinion." Christians are experts at criticism. I've heard people criticize a play because it didn't give the whole picture; usually that means the play didn't offer a redemptive moment at the end. It is incumbent on us to weigh not only the individual work under consideration but also the oeuvre, or total body of work, produced by the artists. If a given work seems not to represent the total scope of Christian revelation, that is because no one work can adequately convey all of God's truth. Artistic productions are limited by the constraints of their medium. If you think a play is too overtly Christian, this may be due to the producing organization and its mission, to the particular event for which the play was written, or because the artists were in need of giving direct expression of their faith at the time of the creation. The obverse is also true; plays that seem not to be Christian enough in their content may be reflecting external and internal considerations weighing on the artists and of which you can have no direct knowledge. Consider everything that the company or artist is doing, and be charitable.

No true artist shrinks from intelligent, constructive, and vigorous critique of her or his work. Unfortunately, it is more often the case with Christian critics that spiritual and moral criteria are intermingled with aesthetic criteria, resulting in comments that are given undue weight by their spiritual overtones. Being "swift to hear, slow to anger" means suspending judgment until you are sure you understand the context in which the art was produced. If a Christian actor uses a word on stage, and you are offended by that word usage, then try to hear *from the actor*, not from any other source, the reason that choice was made. Realize that you may still not agree with the choice the actor made, and that's okay. There is a place for exhortation and rebuke, and the New Testament spells out the proper role of these and the proper method of using them. We've tried to encourage Christian artists to live in a faith community wherever they work. In so doing they can be vulnerable to the sharpening influence of other Christians, especially of those who do not work in the theatre. Unfortunately, many artists (who are often sensitive by nature anyway) shrink away from church because they've been wounded by thoughtless and even venomous criticism. Community is a two-way street that requires respect and charity in order to avoid head-on collisions.

The Christian church has an opportunity to encourage artists, just as it should encourage Christians in any vocation to which God has called them. To ignore, or worse to exclude, any member of the body from the support of the community is unconscionable. We plead for leaders of churches and those who are members of the body to understand and support those who are called to make their living in the theatre. Encouragement and correction, edification and exhortation go together in this reciprocal relationship to which Christ has called all of us as disciples.

Because theatre is a local phenomenon, as opposed to the unbounded availability of television and film drama, an element of community is involved in the support of theatre companies and their productions. Part of "loving your neighbor" means engaging and experiencing your neighbor's cultural efforts. Christian love is evidenced by participation in and dialogue with artists in one's local community. In Greenville, South Carolina, the Caleb Group encourages Christians to attend local theatre companies by sponsoring talk-back sessions after select performances.[18] In this way the theatres are supported, and we have an opportunity to live out our faith in our community. In other cities faith-based theatre companies rely on Christian participation to maintain economic viability so that they can continue to offer quality theatre with a biblical worldview to their communities.

We return now to the tension introduced earlier in this chapter: the tension between morality and art. In an essay titled "Art and Morality," Jacques Maritain grappled with this tension:

> The artistic habit is concerned only with the work to be done. It certainly makes allowance for the objective conditions (practical use, object intended, etc.) which the work must fulfill—a statue made to be prayed before is a different thing from a garden statue. . . . The sole end of art is the work itself and its beauty. But for the man working, the work to be done of itself comes into the line of morality, and so is merely a means. If the artist were to take for the final end of his activity, that is to say for beatitude, the end of his art or the beauty of his work, he would be, purely and simply, an idolater. It is therefore absolutely necessary for the artist, *qua* man, to work for something other than his work, something better beloved. God is infinitely more lovable than Art.[19]

Artists and audiences, as Christians, recognize the independent demands of the art and the artistic process concurrently with the demands of morality on the life of the artist as a person. The problem lies in the too-common conclusion that morality is based in the law or in a set of constrictions imposed on the Christian. Maritain assumes, rightly, that the fulfillment of the law in Jesus Christ means that all morality is now motivated by love, and not by slavish obedience with the hope of satisfying the demands of a just God. Paraphrasing Augustine, he writes, "If only you love, you may do as you please, you will never offend love."[20] It sounds very simple and even simplistic: the mark of a Christian is love, and the Christian artist who creates out of that love will create only work reflective of that love: love for God and love for our neighbor. Art and morality may pull in opposite directions, but they are bound inextricably together by love, and through their tension living works of art may be created.

The theatre arts are rooted in our humanity. Both actors and audiences must be present in their bodies and spirits for theatre to happen. What passes between them (the text of a play, a characterization, etc.) is on both ends, the senders and the receptors, a product of their humanity. A relationship is established, however fleetingly, and like all relationships for a Christian, this one is governed by the greatest commandment: to love. Such an ideal is not achievable without the empowering presence of the Spirit of God, and only in submission to God will the Christian artist and audience satisfy God's demands.

> Realize that you are summoned to a task far beyond your strength. Get to know yourself so well that you cannot contemplate yourself without flinching. Then there will be room for hope. In the sure knowledge that you are "obliged to do the impossible" and that you can do the impossible in Him who strengthens you, then you are ready for a task which can be performed only through the Cross.[21]

The Christian at Church: Being a Worshiper

The role of theatre in the context of church services is part of a larger discussion among Christians on the very nature of worship, approaches to corporate worship, and the relationship of churches to the surrounding culture. Sometimes lost in this discussion (or debate) is the reality that worship is not confined to a church service, and for the Christian artist the very act of creating theatre can be an act of devotion to and worship of the Lord. Frank Burch Brown offers ways in which art can be worship:

> We can dedicate art to God, address art to God, consecrate it, receive it on God's behalf, invite God to share the enjoyment, and look at it as something from God. But finally, and most mysteriously, we need to say that a work of art can be loved in God when it has become, itself, a medium whereby God *becomes present* to us. The artwork or artistic medium is then transformed into something by which the transcendence of God is celebrated or genuinely mediated, not simply reported or honored. Then it is as though God adopted the medium as God's own.[22]

Consider that every church service, whether historically liturgical or not, has a structure to it and is, *generically*, dramatic. The service itself has a rising action, a moment of climactic action, and a period of falling action or denouement. The drama of Christian worship is evident in its narrative origins. Christian worship was first celebrated on Sunday, the Lord's Day, which commemorated the day of Christ's resurrection. Soon the church commemorated the anniversaries of the deaths of believers, in particular martyrs, as a way of telling their story of faith within the larger story of God's faithfulness. Over time the church set one day aside for the commemoration of Christ's death and resurrection, distinct from the weekly celebration of Sunday. This, of course, was Easter. Once the date of Easter was fixed, other events in the life of Christ were commemorated (nativity, baptism, transfiguration, etc.). The Christ cycle, from Advent to Ascension, is essentially one half of the church year. The second half, from Pentecost to Christ the King, is the story we now live, the story of God's people living between the first and the second coming (the "advents") of Christ. For churches who maintain this ancient practice of telling the story of God's salvation history throughout the course of the year, the dramatic quality of each worship service is obvious; each liturgy is one episode in the story of God's redemption of creation.[23]

The dramatic quality of worship is nowhere more obvious than in the Easter Vigil, the service that begins on the evening of Holy Saturday (the day before Easter) and often lasts until midnight or later. This ritual begins in darkness, only to have the dark pierced by a bonfire and the passing of light from candle to candle within the congregation. This serves as the prelude to the telling of the story of the church year; beginning with creation, through the covenants with Noah, Moses, David, and finally Christ, the story of God's redemption is told. At the climax of this service, new believers (who have been preparing for this occasion for months) are baptized into the Christian faith, and then they receive the Lord's Supper for the first time, received at the table of fellowship by both Christ and Christ's body, the church. Anyone who has ever witnessed the Easter Vigil knows the raw dramatic power of this ritual. Much of its power comes from the way the story of an individual life is grafted into the story of God's salvation history, a story that will be repeated each and every Sunday and holiday through the drama of the church year.[24]

The description of these traditional worship practices may be completely new to you. This is but one indicator of the varieties of worship that can be found among Christian churches today. In his helpful essay on categorizing worship, Lester Ruth has suggested that it might be more helpful to avoid terms such as "traditional" and "contemporary." As alternatives, Ruth suggests different questions to ask, for example, whose story is told primarily, the individual's story of faith (common in a great deal of evangelical worship) or the cosmic story of salvation history (as seen in the description of the church year above)? Ruth also asks where the primary focus of worship is found. For some it is in the music, for others in the sermon, for still others in the Lord's Supper. Each of these foci determines a different way of organizing the worship service. Using these categories, we can see that both the story being told and how the story is told affect the drama of worship in a community.[25]

The recognition of a dramatic structure in worship services urges us to bring aesthetic concerns to bear on our worship. Directing ourselves to God and to God's attributes means considering God's attribute of beauty. Theatre artists can bring to their worshiping congregations a sensitivity, either innate or learned, to the dramatic rhythms of life, of story, and of ritual. Human history begins in the garden of Eden, a place of balance. That balance is upset by the fall, and subsequent millennia of conflict and crises evidence the disequilibrium that characterizes the human condition. The incarnation interjected a moment of crisis that led to the climax of the resurrection, when death was defeated in history and as an enemy of God's people. If worship leaders will consider the structure of the service in light of dramaturgical structure, the experience will not only be more effective but it will also connect to the humanity of the congregants in a powerful way.

Beyond the application of theatre to the structure of the service, there are numerous applications of theatre as interpolations in worship settings. The insertion of a dramatic element into a service has become a popular element of much contemporary worship. The sacraments/ordinances of the Lord's Supper and baptism are two scripturally prescribed interpolations with obvious dramatic qualities. Both involve participation, role-playing, symbolism, and reenactment of historic events. Aside from their theological significance, they can be seen as theatrical experiences. They are not performances because the congregation is asked to participate. Since the 1970s churches have added other dramatic interpolations to the worship setting: dances to Christian music, sketches that raise an issue the sermon will deal with, and more recently short films. These tend to be performances because no audience involvement is expected. Even so, community is created in the rehearsals, and the sharing of stories familiar to the congregation can deepen the sense of corporate worship.

Theatre in worship settings must serve the broader purposes of the church. When any art is asked to meet the external demands of another endeavor, tension is sure to develop. Jacques Maritain speaks of the autonomy of the artist, who must remain free of political, moral, or religious encumbrances; artists bring a political, moral, and/or religious *person* to their work, but they do not admit the demands of politics, morals, or religion to the artistic process. When art is at the service of a religious organization, however, a degree of submission is called for, and the artist may be expected to sacrifice some artistic autonomy in order to serve the ends of the organization. In the theatre, this tends to result in more discursive and less ambiguous (more priestly and less prophetic, more Pauline proposition and less parabolic, more sermon and less story) theatre.

A lot of time is wasted, artists are discouraged, and churches are not served by the hasty integration of drama into worship settings—hasty in that the right questions about theology and the local congregation are not considered in a rush to be relevant, contemporary, and cutting edge. We hope now to slow the process, prompt some reflection, and challenge you to begin by examining principles regarding the relationship of theatre and worship. Doing so may lead to relevant, contemporary, and cutting-edge applications—or it may not—but wherever you land, we hope it will be on solid theological ground.

Theatre in Worship: Community

A major misconception about theatre in church is that the product—that is, the performance, the content to be presented—is the sole or the primary point of the ministry. No one would deny that the message of a script, acted out rather than narrated or preached, has ministry potential. You may be reading this book because you've experienced the power of the dramatic medium in church or theatre. But it is also in the process of preparing the product, in the collaborative effort of actors, directors, designers, and others, that the intersection of theatre and community is found.

The behind-the-scenes work of theatre, that part of the discipline not visible to the audience, is more time-consuming and less glamorous than the performances. The work of mounting a piece of theatre can be tedious and filled with tension. It is also less predictable. Although directors/producers may exercise careful control in the choice of content, plan for a particular audience response in the staging and design, and even manipulate the response to the performance through marketing, they have less predicable control over the process of interacting with actors and designers. Certainly directors plan their rehearsals, but part of their job is to remain flexible and respond to the creative input of their collaborators; it is in these relationships that ministry may flourish, nurturing the body of Christ.

If Christianity is a relational religion, and theatre is a relational art, there is no better place for relationships to take root and grow than in the rehearsal process. Actors are at their most vulnerable in the studio, as they stretch their resources to fit the role and experiment with ways to play the characters. As directors we should be sensitive to the pressure actors work under and take opportunities to encourage their work artistically and spiritually. It is through the rehearsal process, which cannot be planned in minute detail, that grace is so often evidenced. When believer-artists are truly filled with God's Spirit, so that even their spontaneous responses under tremendous pressure are gracious, kind, and loving (evidence of the Spirit's fruit), God is most glorified; only supernatural power can explain human beings treating one another with virtue through this process.

Theatre directors in church or other Christian organizations recognize the value of the product, but they also cherish the ministry that happens among their community of artists. Many churches sponsor artist gatherings, where Bible study, prayer, and encouragement are directed to the distinctive needs of the theatre artist. Outside church networking organizations, such as CITA,[26] function to facilitate gatherings of artists to encourage and equip them to minister in both religious and mainstream theatre situations.

Theatre in Worship: Presence

A popular application of mime in contemporary churches is "human video"; a contemporary Christian song is played while a dancer, or dancers, mimes the action of the song. The movement of the dancer mimics the lyrics, so the content of the song is reinforced (often to the point of redundancy) by the mime. It is a kind of sign language for hearing people, and it illustrates the penchant in much contemporary Christianity to be direct and unambiguous with the message of the Bible. Mystery, uncertainty, and doubt are pejoratives in some Christian circles.

Revelation is God's communication, or unveiling, of Godself to humanity. Theatre is a medium of communication, revelation, an unveiling. Just as God is revealed in "specific revelation" (the person of Christ and the Bible), so too theatre sometimes communicates in a specific and direct manner. Most plays used in worship settings or in the context of the ministry of a local church are overtly Christian in the sense that their subject matter and objective are concerned with the message of Christianity. But God also uses "general revelation," through nature and the conscience of humankind. Theatre people should not be afraid to bring less-specific, less-overt drama into the context of the church. Jesus certainly was not unambiguous in his parables. There is a proper role for theatre to communicate mystery, the ineffable—to hint at the spiritual forces that are very real but not easily grasped by our literal, linguistic forms of communication. Because theatre is an art form that relies on music and dance in addition to language, it has the power to bring spiritual forces and celestial worlds to us through its manifold conventions.

Bernard Beckerman differentiates between *iconic action* and *dialectic action*.[27] Iconic action celebrates the audience's values. In the Old Testament the priests affirmed the values of the Israelites in the temple worship, which in itself had a dramatic structure. Theatre has a place in worship that reminds the congregation of its shared history and that connects our human stories with God's story. Dialectic action challenges the audience's values; the Old Testament prophets used theatre as one way of communicating God's displeasure with the Israelites. This is far less common but equally important to the health of a worshiping congregation.

Churches have largely tended toward concrete and literal, easily assimilated communication because many contemporary churches are now geared to reach unchurched people, and it is thought that being culturally relevant and direct is the means to accomplish this goal. The gauge for cultural relevancy is popular culture: television, movies, advertising, and popular music. There is a certain logic in these choices. Survey any group of Americans in any area of the country and ask them to identify either the characters in *Seinfeld* or the plot of Andrew Lloyd Webber's *Evita*, and their cultural biases become clear. Ask any congregation about their television habits, and you can understand why pastors draw on pop culture via electronic media. This practice doesn't always serve the end of worship, however.

Biblical scholar Bruce Chilton, in his study of the practice of organizing worship in yearly patterns, argues that one of the key building blocks to worship is mimesis, or the ritual representation of another event. To truly engage in mimesis, Chilton contends, remembrance must take place in community, and to be fully human one must have mimetic experiences. He concludes, "Only the plural of the species can be human, because a person in isolation—robbed of mimetic possibilities—is not a person."[28] When Christians gather to offer their sacrifice of thanks and praise to God, they do more than remember the past acts of God's interventions in human history; they rehearse and encounter the events as present realities. Mimesis becomes one of the keys to sacramentality or presence in worship, a truth we saw in Beckwith's description of the sacramentality of the mystery plays.

Churches often embrace a diversity of styles in music, and the theatre itself is a flexible communicative medium. Realism continues to dominate the theatrical landscape, but the theatre can make use of symbolism, conventions, and flights of fancy that transport the audience in time and space. Congregants may seem to have little imaginative capacity, conditioned by the literalness of televised drama and materialistic culture in general, but perhaps the church is the place where the ability to imagine can and should be recaptured. Francis Schaeffer writes: "The Christian is the one whose imagination should soar beyond the stars."[29] Theatre is one medium that can encourage such soaring.

More questions present themselves: Is the communication from those leading the worship directed toward God, or is it directed toward the congregation, or both? Can an actor become so wrapped up in the offering of a performance to God in worship that he is not aware of communicating to the audience? If so, has he ceased to be an actor, a *hupokrite*? If the actors in worship theatre are concentrating, as good actors, on their communication within the ensemble and toward the audience, can they also be offering worship to God? If the audience is focused on the performance by virtue of the entertainment quality of the ensemble, can it also be in an attitude of worship? Answers to these questions will vary in each church; therefore, the questions are worth asking and discussing in your own congregation. Asking them is a way of engaging in community. Better yet, engage your group in theatrical experiments and explore how, through theatre, both actors and congregants may be led into the presence of God.

This section on the Christian at worship would not be complete without a reference to the quality of theatre offered in the context of the local church. Theatre in church, like theatre in any other amateur/avocational setting, doesn't always rise to the level of theatre in organizations who hire trained, experienced artists. When churches reach the size that allows them to hire professional artists, the quality generally rises. Are there theological causes for the dissipation of the arts in general, and theatre in particular, in our churches? Paul Claudel identified one root cause in a letter he wrote in 1919: "[It] may be summed up in one: the divorce unhappily consummated last century between the propositions of the Faith and the powers of imagination and sensibility which are pre-eminently the privilege of the artist."[30]

The imagination is a frightening thing; Jeremiah attests to its tendency toward wickedness in humankind (3:17; 7:24; 9:14; 11:8; 13:10; 16:12; 18:12; 23:17), and his testimony is evidence of the power of the imagination. That power can also be used for good, and when the church is able to entrust its message to its artists (artists must first earn that trust), the worship of Christians and the proclamation of the gospel will be made more effective. Theatre artists can bring their intuitions and talents to the church, not just in staging sketches and pageants, but in understanding and maximizing the inherent theatricality of the life of the church—its worship, services, programs, and seasons. One goal of this book is to encourage clergy and theatre artists to build the mutual trust that will permit such collaboration for the good of the kingdom of God.

Those of us who integrate theatre in worship settings should acknowledge that sincerity is no substitute for accountability to the standards of the art and ultimately to the excellence epitomized in God, the Creator. Any artistic attempt by fallen people is imperfect, so we shouldn't shrink from offering our imperfect work to God. But we should cultivate dissatisfaction with even our best efforts and make it our constant desire to offer to God a better artistic sacrifice.

Artists need to be able to measure their progress. We do this by interacting with the best work being done in our field, both in religious contexts and in mainstream cultural institutions. Learn the criteria for excellence in theatre. Have a system for evaluating your work in the church. Invite theatre artists to see and comment on your work—even if they're not Christians. Be humble enough to accept criticism and be motivated enough to constantly seek out more training and experience. God will accept the best that you can do at each stage of your life, and God will honor your desire to constantly do better for the kingdom and God's glory.

conclusion

Dale and Todd Return to the Theatre

In the introduction we invited you into a conversation between theology and theatre. It is a conversation that has been ongoing for a few years between the two of us. It has taken us to a few plays, to a few classrooms and conferences, and to more than a few delightful meals. And this is the way it ought to be: theatrical conversations, in which we share ideas, ask questions, and allow ourselves to be surprised by what we find. At the conclusion of the process of creating this book (but far from the end of our conversation), we again shared a meal in yet another hospitable albeit bohemian café, anticipating our attending another play together. The one we had chosen was a new production of Martin Crimp's *Attempts on Her Life*, the Los Angeles debut of what has been called his "masterpiece of avant-garde theatre."

This particular production celebrated the tenth anniversary of the play's debut at London's Royal Court Theatre, where Crimp's plays are regularly performed. It was coproduced by the Evidence Room Theatre and the Unknown Theatre in Los Angeles. The play itself is a cluster of seventeen scenes with no common character, but all concerning a common character—or so it would seem. Each scene introduces a perspective on Anne, who is also called Anya, Annie, Anny, and Anissa. In each scene a different side of Anne is offered: is she a victim, a perpetrator, a suicide casualty, or a success? Each of the scenes is an attempt on Anne's life and an attempt to understand who this person is.

The play was creatively mounted on a sparse stage overcast with furniture and props suspended from the rigging. As each scene began, the staging for that scene descended ex machina from above, only to return and be replaced by other items for the next scene. The performances, like the scenes themselves, were uneven. At times there was riveting acting; at other times the actors seemed as confused as the audience. But the performance was not the end in and of itself. The performance—and the reason for the existence of these two theatre companies—was intended to create a community of dialogue, to be an oasis of personal relationships in an impersonal, urban world.[1] To accomplish this, the Unknown Theatre offers after every performance a "Fifth Wall," an opportunity to interact with cast members and audience members alike to discuss the play, to discuss theatre or art, or simply to meet like-minded people. The evening we were there, a performance by a live band and a dance followed the play. Even the collaboration of the two theatre companies was emblematic of the search for a sanctuary in a frenetic world: the Evidence Room Theatre was a company without a space and had been taken in by the Unknown Theatre for this performance. This was art offered to make an impersonal world more humane to anyone who wished to come.

This is but one example of the many manifestations of theatre in our rapidly changing world. Needless to say, this experience gave the two of us even more to talk about. Why don't you pull up a chair around the table and join us in what was our final conversation in this project.

Theatre and Theology in Dialogue

Dale: As a theologian, what have you learned about theology from your experience and study of theatre?

Todd: The distinction between theatre and drama, where drama is the narrative or text and theatre is the performance of the text, is a helpful way of looking at theology because theology has often been about texts; but now in the last forty or fifty years there has been a move to consider the importance of action as a theological text. Truly Christian theology has to be embodied belief; you just can't believe something and not have it impact your behavior. And that necessarily invites us to consider how we can enact, embody, and perform those things we believe. So in some ways it has reinforced a current theme in practical theology, where you just can't stay with theory; you have to put it into practice. Just as theatre does not exist outside of practice, I suggest that Christian theology does not exist outside of practice.

Dale: We take for granted in theatre that the goal of a playwright is to get the text onstage, to see it performed; that the drama or the text is in a sense incomplete until actors bring it to life on a stage. What I see about theatre by looking at your three theological categories—incarnation, community, and presence—is that theatre is much more than just actors putting words on a stage; it's about the relationships it creates. It's about their relationship with the audience; they are entering into a community, and they're entering into a dialogue with people not only on stage but in the audience. I think theology helps us understand that in a more profound way.

Todd: If we take seriously the theological assertion that God became flesh in Jesus of Nazareth, that means we have to take our humanity seriously—not just some of it but all of it. And you can't deal with ideas in isolation and be a fully human person because ideas have to be translated into body experiences: you have to live them; you have to do them. It's not enough for me to say that I love my wife; I have to embody that love, and I have to communicate that love to her. And theatre reminds us that there is an art to communication, that not all communication is effective. There are some people who are gifted to tell stories by performing them. And that, in terms of evangelism, becomes a benchmark of how well we tell our story of Jesus Christ, the most important story in the world. Do we tell it with all the rehearsal, all the expertise, all the investment of capital, human and other-wise, that we do to tell the story of *Wicked* or *The Producers*, and all those other productions that have so much energy and money spent on them? How seriously do Christians take telling the story of the gospel?

Dale: From the perspective of theatre, you are right; actors, set designers, writers, directors spend their whole lives trying to tell their stories. This is especially true for actors; the essential art of the theatre is the art of the actor. You can have theatre without a script, theatre without a designer, theatre without directors, stages, auditoriums, but you can't have theatre without actors or without audience members. Among the arts, the theatre has more often than not been the most uneasy fit within the church, with the pos-sible exception of dance. Working on this book as a theatre person, I came to see in a new way that theatre is very closely allied with theology because of the incarnation, because of community, and because of the potential of God's presence. The theatre is the art in which those theological categories can best be experienced together as a narrative art form.

Todd: Looking back through church history, one can find an interesting example of how theatre became a very concrete theological reality for Chris-tians. When the medieval church and its worship had transformed into a sort of clerical spectacle, and the people had been relegated to the role of passive observer, they were distanced from the sacrament of the Lord's Supper, which was to be the point of contact between God and God's people. Yet, the Holy Spirit did an end run by connecting people to God's presence through theatre in the performance of the mystery plays. It is fascinating to observe how important theatre was—not just to a little bit of the life of medieval Christians, but to their entire life—the entire community came alive in the Corpus Christi performances. Theatre defined communities, and the people understood fully the stories they participated in through theatre, in ways they could not understand through the worship of the church. As Sarah Beckwith points out, theatre was more sacramental than the Lord's Supper ever could have been because people were able to perform their faith. This is in fact the ideal that Christians maintain for worship: "Full, conscious and active participation."[2]

Dale: The play we saw last night is an interesting example; the content of the play didn't strike us as much as did the ensemble's commitment. One of the two troupes in the show had worked together for twelve years. They didn't have a performing space, so they went in with another group of actors in order to put this piece of theatre on. It reminded me of how many theatre people do theatre not because they can make money—they're doing it in spite of the fact they won't make any money—but they're passionate about telling stories on stage through the medium of theatre. We were part of an audience of about sixty people, and yet there they were, ten or fifteen people on stage telling us stories through the theatre because they had to do it—they just have to do it; it's a consuming passion for them.

Todd: It is interesting that their raison d'être really comes from their desire to start a conversation. It is in the purpose statement that they want to have a place where all of the Los Angeles community can come and be respected for who they are and enter into conversation about the topic of the play, so they have a party after the performance every night, and the actors and actresses were hanging around and you could talk with them and it was very much, "Let's be a community, even if it's an ad hoc community, for a short time."

Dale: The attempt to create a community began as soon as we walked into the auditorium; when we walked through the curtains to find our seats the cast was already on stage engaged in conversations. We found out later that this had something to do with the content of the play. But before we knew that, what we saw were people talking to one another on stage: the conversation began before the play began and obviously was going to carry on after the play. For twelve years, these people have been having conversations about things that are important to them and inviting audiences to join them.

Todd: Last night's play was provocative and out of the box, but it's not a play that is going to be done twenty years from now, let alone a hundred years from now. But at the same time, it had relevant themes and it created a community; it created a space. I can imagine people wanting to come back to have that experience again, and I can only think of Christians who look at something like that and say, "You know, church should be like that." That concerns me because the text they were operating from, the center of their theatrical performance last night, is so different from the gospel because their performance was about there being no truth. I am not necessarily suggesting that there is one way of interpreting Scripture; certainly there have been multiple interpretations of the Scriptures over the centuries and across denominations, but there is a limited range to the dialogue the gospel creates. Christian faith invites you to come and be transformed into the posture of the cross. We can learn from theatre, but it is important to note where theatre stops and the Christian faith begins; theatre doesn't replace the church.

Dale: When I go to church, I often think about worship in dramatic terms. I think about the structure of the service, I think about the conversations that happen before and after, and I begin to think about how church parallels theatre, and I have to catch myself and remember that church isn't theatre nor is theatre church. We can't let one substitute for the other. And it is interesting that you and I chose to go see things—*Hillbilly Antigone* in Chicago, the piece we saw last night in Los Angeles—that were not mainstream Broadway musicals, spectacles, entertainment-oriented pieces. We chose to see things that were experimental, fringe, that were communicating on a smaller scale maybe with a small ensemble, with significant things to say. One thing I would like to advocate in this book is that we not think of theatre as only the large, flashy road tours out there; also in our local communities artists are putting on plays that are worthy of our attendance, our dialogue, and our attention. In the same way, all Christian churches aren't polished megachurches, but they are important communities of faith.

Todd: The series of books in which this volume appears, Engaging Culture, begins with the assumption that there are people outside the Christian faith who are using art to raise questions about the world we live in, its values, its meanings, and so on. If art becomes decorum, if it fails to move us and be provocative or evocative, in particular if the theatre ceases to be a place of public conversation, something essential has been lost. I really want to applaud what the theatre production that we saw last night was trying to do because there really are few forums where you can meet face-to-face with people in your community. People are meeting all the time on the Internet, but you never see these people; you do not know these people; you don't live with these people. Here is the chance for face-to-face interaction with people.

Dale: This is a way to show that you love your neighbor. To love your neighbor the way Jesus describes it requires immediacy. To really love your neighbors, you need to make contact with them directly, not just post a blog, or send a text message or an e-mail to people. You need to be in the same room with them. In all our communities there are artists doing theatre. I think if Christians spent more time in the theatre than they do watching film and television, we could have a greater impact on the culture and, what's more important, on our neighbors. If we want to engage the culture, we Christians need to have our perspective, our worldview, and our voices in the conversation. We have to be creating our own theatre, and we have to be in the room with people who are creating theatre, so that after the play is done we can talk about it with them or carry on a conversation about hopes, fears, and values. We also make a difference by being there. You spend ten, fifteen, twenty dollars to get in the door. You support what they're doing. You're saying what they're doing has value. I think that is a way to show that you love your neighbor. It also brings your faith out into the public in ways that it isn't when you go to a movie or stay home and watch television or cruise the Internet.

Todd: It is interesting that many of the most insightful voices about the world today come from outside the Christian faith. If we disconnect ourselves from listening and speaking to those voices, then we disconnect ourselves from important conversations going on in our world right now. And that is not to say that we swallow what we believe for the sake of tolerance, or political correctness, or however we want to define it, but simply to say that the Christian faith has to be in conversation with these very sensitive women and men, these gifted artists who are in our case writing and performing very important pieces of art speaking about our world today.

Dale: This leads to another thing that I hope our book has done: make our readers better listeners in the theatre. We can go to the theatre and listen as we see the current and eternal human questions played out on stage. So we listen to what they are saying, and we can learn from it. I learn things every time I go to the theatre, and it informs me about my faith. I read my Bible for an understanding of my faith, I go to my church, I hear sermons, and I study the Bible in a small group study. There are lots of ways that I nurture my relationship with Christ; but I find that every time I go to the theatre, I take things away from it that deepen my understanding of who God is, often without that being an intentional choice of the group putting on the play. For example, I just finished directing Arthur Miller's *All My Sons* at the university where I teach, and I found myself encountering so many important truths about sin, responsibility, guilt, and considering the consequences of choices—really big issues for life and for the Christian life in particular. All of this through a play that was not written as a statement of Christian truth, but it is truthful and it resonates with so many important truths—and if I had not been involved with the community that produced it, I would have missed such a valuable experience.

Todd: It is an old Christian adage that says, "We need to pray with the Bible in one hand and the newspaper in the other." In some ways we need to pray with the Bible in one hand and all the sections of the newspaper, not just the first section . . .

Dale: Even the Arts section?

Todd: The Arts, Sports, Fashion—all of them are relevant for Christian conversation. If we fail to engage these conversations, we fail to engage a large part of the world, and we lose the opportunity to bring the gospel into dialogue with these corners of the world.

Dale: I would like to change the direction of our conversation and discuss what we learn from staging a play. In a sense, every performance is a rehearsal. It doesn't matter if you have a limited run or an open-ended run; every performance is a unique experience of the play. The audience changes, you get different reactions, your ensemble grows, and the chemistry deepens, so every performance is in a sense an exploration of the play. That's why one of the things that is really disappointing about an end of a run is that you are done exploring the text. Chekhov is a playwright who to my way of thinking doesn't work all that well on the page when you read him, but when you put him in the mouths of actors and begin to explore his work on stage—physically explore it—it is completely different. The relationships, the eye contact, the gestures, the movement, the blocking choices (which are of course limitless), all create the possibility for something far greater than reading the script. You can't ever get to the bottom of Chekhov; his work is too deep, too rich. Shakespeare is the same way. When you end the run of a Shakespeare play, you feel as if you've just begun to understand something of that play, and you are ready to start from the beginning again. The great texts are that way. In some profound ways theatre is a metaphor for discipleship: you're never done.

Todd: As a Christian, you're always in process, you're always becoming; the work of the Holy Spirit in gifting us and encouraging us to grow is an ongoing process. It's not either you have it or you don't; instead you are always on the journey. The first name for the Christian community according to Acts was "The Way," and in Luke's Gospel, Jesus teaches what it means to be a disciple on the way from the mount of transfiguration to Jerusalem. Not insignificantly, it is on the journey that he teaches what it means to be a disciple, for life as a disciple is a journey.

Dale: That's why the live quality of theatre is so crucial. You can't go back; its ephemeral nature mandates how you will experience it. You will never get to experience that rehearsal again; you will never be able to experience that performance again. Even if you go back to a performance the next night, it is a different performance. And so you lose a little bit of it, and yet at the same time you retain it. It's a part of you. The plays we have seen together—*Hillbilly Antigone*, *Symmetry*, *Attempts on Her Life*, and *Taming of the Shrew* at the Los Angeles Shakespeare Festival—they're gone. It's impossible to reexperience them. Even if we were to record a performance with a video camera, it would not be the experience that we had in the theatre with those people.

Todd: But how different it is to be a member of an audience at a play like *Attempts on Her Life* last night and the community we created, rather than being a part of the cast and crew and being part of that community, and the rehearsals and the laughs and the tears, and the frustrations. Those memories burn deep in your heart, more so than even the most profound performance you could watch, because when you commit to something as part of a community, you work and literally share blood, sweat, and tears together. The story you tell in your performances is the product of everyone's interpretation of the story working in concert. Again this becomes an interesting paradigm for inviting people into the performance of the faith, from outside to inside. But people who read our book who have never had the privilege of being on stage may never fully understand this. It is an experience like no other; in some ways it is being part of a team more intensely than being on an athletic team. You are connected on so many emotional levels; it is such a

144 ———— conclusion

vulnerable experience, yet empowering. I think that in some ways people turn to theatre as religion because they cannot find a community like that outside the theatre. Theatre becomes a support system and a threshold to transcendent experiences that the church should be providing, but people aren't finding them there.

Dale: When an actor steps into the shoes of a character, he or she experiences a certain amount of vulnerability, first to do that in rehearsal and then to put that in front of an audience; you really expose yourself. There is a real risk involved—a real risk and a real pleasure—the thrill of transcending your own existence. One of the significant challenges to this very human, person-to-person experience we call theatre is the explosion of virtual media in our culture. We can't escape the fact that our culture has become more and more virtual—electronic media, instant messaging, and all the things that we have mentioned previously in this book. This raises the question, is theatre an art that pushes back against the intrusion of the virtual media in our culture, and is that a good thing?

Todd: My daughter and I were looking at colleges this past fall, and while walking across campus at a prominent East Coast school, we saw a young woman talking on her cell phone. As she was talking and walking along, she saw the person to whom she was talking and literally passed within two feet of her, and the two of them never stopped talking on the phone. They waved to briefly acknowledge each other, but although they were literally face-to-face, this was never face-to-face communication. It seems that we are becoming more and more comfortable with less and less direct human interaction. And as believers in a religion that insists that God became flesh, which is, to quote one of the early church fathers, "the hinge of our salvation," we cannot lose the value of our humanity, because God did not redeem us virtually. This is in no way to diminish the joy and convenience that electronic media provide us. But the conveniences that they afford can diminish the human qualities that are so unique. I gave you an illustration yesterday of how a father who lives in another country may speak to his children by e-mail, by phone, and the like. But that is not the same as being there to tuck them in at night, to be present with them. And if we become a culture in which we are disconnected from bodily interaction and literally have platonic relationships, where our bodies don't interact and don't touch, then we have lost something of the image of God that is in us. I think we as Christians cannot uncritically embrace the technological advances available to us, especially in our ministries of worship, because the media we use have symbolic meaning beyond just being tools. They symbolize values.

Dale: You and I have much in common: our common faith, our common love of theatre, and the friendship we have developed through our work on this book over the past few years. The work on this book has been an interesting exercise in that we have done a good bit of our work virtually, exchanging documents by e-mail, having discussions on the phone, e-mailing suggestions for each other's chapters, but the real progress on this book has always been made when we have met face-to-face. Each time we have made significant progress on the book, it has been when we have been able to be in the same room with each other to discuss it, to share meals together, to attend plays together, to discuss our families, to share our lives with each other. Theatre can deal with profound questions of our humanity in ways that film and television cannot because it puts people together in the same room and creates a space for direct interaction. It simply feels like life. And it is a more powerful and more frightening medium.

Todd: My fear is that you and I have children who are part of a generation of human beings who are more comfortable with less interaction than we are. I think it feels better, that it feels more comfortable, to be in a room together. We use e-mail and the phone because it is so efficient. But I am apprehensive that we have created a generation of people who don't see the distinction between the virtual and the real, and that frightens me. So promoting theatre as a Christian promotes our humanity, promotes the image of God in our humanity, and promotes community.

Dale: Which, after all, is good for theatre and good for Christians . . .

Final Curtain: Last Thoughts on Theology and Theatre

And we hope this has been as good for you as it has for us and that you have entered into this conversation and will spread it in your local church and your local theatre. Both are communities in the making and are similar in some very startling ways. Though theatre is not the cure for everything that is wrong in the world or in the church, the way theatre reflects the nature of God, through incarnation, community, and presence, is a salve for the soul. And so we embrace theatre, experience and create it, and make it a part of the conversations we have about how best to worship God.

As we concluded our work on this book in the summer of 2008, a North Hollywood theatre produced an original play called *Stories from the Bible*. The ensemble of actors chose a series of Bible stories to perform, and then they used the words of the NIV Bible verbatim as their script, divided the words among nine actors playing multiple roles, and presented a forty-five-minute performance at Zombie Joe's Underground Theatre. That's right, a company called Zombie Joe's Underground Theatre became transformed by the power of God's Word, and in all sincerity—and with a great deal of professionalism—put the Bible on stage for paying audiences in North Hollywood, California. Their performance of the Scriptures read so commonly in churches became an uncommon experience of grace for audiences of all types of Christians and people of every imaginable faith—even people of no faith. It's remarkable where God is found in our world, even in the world of theatre.

notes

Introduction: Todd and Dale Go to the Theatre

1. Chris Jones, the *Chicago Tribune* reviewer, panned the play, calling it "Sophomoric, not Sopho-clean," and objected to its "rural stereotype" (tempo, p. 3), June 7, 2008.

2. Some performance art forms such as dance may be theatrical but are not included in our study. We examine primarily theatre, which is narrative at its core, and exclude other forms of performance art.

3. Ben Brantley, "As a Nun Stands Firm, the Ground Shifts Below," *New York Times*, April 1, 2005, online edition, http://query.nytimes.com/gst/fullpage.html?res=9801E4D8123CF932A35757C0A963 9C8B63&scp=4&sq=as%20a20nun20&st=cse.

4. See Ronald Grimes, *Beginnings in Ritual Studies* (Lanham, MD: University Press of America, 1982).

5. Recent Broadway successes based on popular music groups (*Movin' Out, Mama Mia*, and *Jersey Boys* to name a few) are the exception. They derive from their pop-culture sources a penchant for rapid delivery, short scenes, and high-decibel orchestrations. Dale knows one Drama Desk voter who takes earplugs to these musical-tribute shows.

6. Thornton Wilder, *Our Town*, in *Three Plays* (New York: Bantam, 1958), 62.

Chapter 1 A Survey of Christianity and Theatre in History

1. Pedro Calderón de la Barca, *The Great Theater of the World*, in *Masterpieces of the Spanish Golden Age*, trans. Mack Hendricks (Singleton, NY: Holt Rinehart and Winston), 369.

2. Ibid., 374.

3. Ibid., 377.

4. Ibid., 395.

5. See, for example, Arthur T. Buch, *The Bible on Broadway* (Hamden, CT: Archon, 1968); Kay M. Baxter, *Contemporary Theatre and the Christian Faith* (New York: Abingdon, 1964).

6. See Thomas Postlewait, "Criteria for Periodization in Theatre History," *Theatre Journal* 40, no. 3 (October 1988): 299; see also Bruce McConachie, *Interpreting the Theatrical Past* (Iowa City: University of Iowa Press, 1989).

7. Richard Southern, *The Seven Ages of the Theatre* (New York: Hill and Wang, 1961).

8. In the Fall 2003 issue of the *Journal of Religion and Theatre*, Eli Rozik describes the theory articulated in three major steps: the Cambridge School of Anthropology ritual theory (see the works of Jane Harrison, Gilbert Murray, and Francis McDonald); E. T. Kirby's shamanist theory (see his *Ur-Drama: The Origins*

of Theatre [New York: New York University Press, 1975]); and Richard Schechner's performance theory, which he developed in collaboration with the anthropologist Victor Turner (see Schechner, *Performance Theory* [New York: Routledge, 1988]; Schechner, *Between Theater and Anthropology* [Philadelphia: University of Pennsylvania Press, 1985]; Turner, *From Ritual to Theatre* [New York: PAJ, 1982]; and Turner, *The Anthropology of Performance* [New York: PAJ, 1987]). Eli Rozik, "The Ritual Origin of Theatre—A Scientific Theory or Theatrical Ideology?" *Journal of Religion and Theatre* 2, no. 1, http://www.rtjournal .org/vol_2/no_1/rozik.html; see also his *Roots of Theatre* (Iowa City: University of Iowa Press, 2002).

9. A. W. Pickard-Cambridge, *Dithyramb, Tragedy and Comedy* (Oxford: Clarendon, 1927).

10. Cited in Kirby, *Ur-Drama*, xii.

11. Margot Berthold, *World Theater* (New York: Frederick Unger, n.d.), 5.

12. Rozik, *Roots of Theatre*, 139.

13. "Unlike the Egyptians and the Greeks and some early Eastern civilizations, the Hebrews made little use of drama. Indeed, they dabbled very little in art since they were forbidden by Exod. 20:4 to make 'any likeness of any thing that is in heaven above, or that is in the earth beneath, or that is in the water under the earth' (KJV). There were dramatic elements in their religious observances . . . the Hebrews came close to some genuine theatre with the acts of the prophets, and with the dramatic literature of the Book of Job." Gordon C. Bennett, *Acting Out Faith* (St. Louis: CBP, 1986), 15. In reality, religious theatre goes back further than the Greeks and the Romans. There is evidence that religious ritual was central to the lives and activities of the earliest cultures. Early tribes of hunters used drama, often in the form of dance, to ask the gods for help with the coming hunt and to thank the gods for success on their return. See David W. Eggebrecht, *Spirit in Drama* (St. Louis: Concordia, 2004), 8.

14. Harold Ehrensperger, *Religious Drama: Ends and Means* (New York: Abingdon, 1962), 77.

15. See, for example, Paul M. Miller and Dan Dunlop, *Create a Drama Ministry* (Kansas City, MO: Lillenas, 1984); Steve Pederson, *Developing a Drama Ministry* (Grand Rapids: Zondervan, 1999); Lawrence Waddy, *The Bible as Drama* (New York: Paulist Press, 1975); Fiona Bond, *The Arts in Your Church: A Practical Guide* (Carlisle, England: Piquant, 2001).

16. Brian G. Magorrian, "For What It's Worth: Theatre and the Church," *Quodlibet Journal* 3, no. 2 (Spring 2001), http://www.quodlibet.net/magorrian-theater.shtml.

17. Robert E. Webber, "A Brief History of Drama in Worship," in *The Complete Library of Christian Worship*, ed. Robert E. Webber, vol. 4, bk. 2 (Nashville: Star Song, 1994), 657–59.

18. Because of the transformative potential inherent in role-playing, especially among people with psychological disorders, psychodrama should be used only by qualified and trained counselors.

19. For an interesting analysis of Old Testament texts as essentially dramas, see Thomas Boogaart, "Drama and the Sacred: Recovering the Dramatic Tradition in Scripture and Worship," in *Touching the Altar: The Old Testament for Christian Worship*, ed. Carol Bechtel (Grand Rapids: Eerdmans, 2008), 35–62. In this essay Boogaart argues that a proper interpretation of the texts of the Hebrew Scriptures requires acknowledgment of their explicit dramatic structure.

20. *The Dramatized Bible* (n.p.: Jubilate Group, 1989).

21. Michael Perry, ed., *The Dramatized Bible*, vol. 2 (Grand Rapids: Baker, 1994), 9.

22. Jonas Barish, *The Antitheatrical Prejudice* (Berkeley: University of California Press, 1981), 1.

23. Cited in Bernard F. Dukore, *Dramatic Theory and Criticism* (New York: Holt Rinehart and Winston, 1974), 92.

24. Cited in Barish, *Antitheatrical Prejudice*, 54.

25. Cited in ibid., 281.

26. *The Soliloquies of Saint Augustine,* cited in Barish, *Antitheatrical Prejudice*, 54–57.

27. Cited in Barish, *Antitheatrical Prejudice*, 265.

28. Ibid., 82.

29. J. M. Buckley, *Christians and the Theater* (New York: Nelson and Phillips, 1876), 118.

30. "There was no formal theatre in the middle ages; theatre had to begin all over again. . . . It is often argued that the roots of theatre lie in religious rituals, and this seems to be substantiated by the Greek theatre's initial connection to rites honoring the god Dionysus, the Roman theatre's relation to the festival of Jupiter (Zeus), and the medieval theatre's close tie with the Roman Catholic church."

Edwin Wilson and Alvin Goldfarb, *Living Theatre: A History*, 4th ed. (Boston: McGraw Hill, 2004). "The Middle Ages, then, were an extended period in which a new order came into being—and a new theatre. . . . It is impossible to say what the origin or origins of early mediaeval drama and theatre were. A combination of causes, or different causes in different places, would be the somewhat waffling solution to the dilemma." Patti P. Gillespie and Kenneth M. Cameron, *Western Theatre: Revolution and Revival* (New York: Macmillan, 1984), 155 and 165. "The displacement in Europe of a bewildering variety of gods and goddesses—Greek, Roman, Celtic, Norse, and Teutonic—in favor of an undivided Trinity of God the Father, Son, and Holy Ghost, which had become an accepted political fact of life by the tenth century AD, not only determined the development of the theatre during the next five centuries, but has contributed significantly (if decreasingly) to it ever since." Glynne Wickham, *A History of the Theatre* (Cambridge: Cambridge University Press, 1985), 68. "Dramatic tendencies of Christian worship declared themselves at an early period. At least from the fourth century, the central and most solemn rite of worship was the Mass, an essentially dramatic commemoration of one of the most critical moments in the life of the founder." E. K. Chambers, *The Medieval Stage*, 2 vols. (New York: Oxford University Press, 1933), 2:3. "After a four-hundred-year absence from Western culture, the theatre experienced revival in the tenth century AD, and this rebirth took place in the church." Robert Smyth, ed., *Lamb's Players Present: Developing a Drama Group* (Minneapolis: World Wide, 1989), 13.

31. Oscar Brockett, *History of the Theatre*, 9th ed. (Boston: Allyn and Bacon, 2003), 74.

32. Ibid., 75–76.

33. Karl Young, *The Drama of the Medieval Church*, 2 vols. (Oxford: Clarendon, 1933), collects numerous examples of these tropes.

34. Cited in A. M. Nagler, *Sourcebook in Theatrical History* (New York: Dover, 1952), 39.

35. http://www.unc.edu/depts/outdoor/dir/religious.html. At the time of this writing there were nine religious plays included in the institute directory.

36. See George Kernodle, *From Art to Theatre: Form and Convention in the Renaissance* (Chicago: University of Chicago Press, 1944), 16–17.

37. Charles Davidson, *Studies in the English Mystery Plays* (New York: Haskell House, 1965), 6.

38. Benjamin Hunningher, *The Origin of the Theater* (New York: Hill and Wang, 1955), 4.

39. Ibid., 7.

40. Ibid., 8–9.

41. Ibid., 61.

42. Corpus Christi was a very popular feast that reinforced the "magical" aspects of the Mass. The first evidence of a Corpus Christi play was in 1324; the form was most fully developed in the baroque period, when the entire liturgy assumed many theatrical elements.

43. Glynne Wickham, *The Medieval Theatre*, 3rd ed. (Cambridge: Cambridge University Press, 1974), 63.

44. See Peter Senkbeil, "Faith in Theatre" (PhD diss., Northwestern University, 1995).

45. "Today, as we enter the twenty-first century, much of the church is once again embracing the value of drama. In fact, one can argue that a true renaissance of this art form in the church is taking place." Pederson, *Developing a Drama Ministry*, 14. "Today, the church is experiencing a surge of activity in the dramatic arts. Christians are now producing theatre both within the church walls and outside them." Smyth, *Lamb's Players Present*, 15. "Today many congregations use drama as the medieval priests did, performing brief plays to enhance or exemplify the scriptural message or story." Eggebrecht, *Spirit in Drama*, 11. "It is safe to say that nowhere and at no time since the Middle Ages has more Christian theatre been produced than in America today, in Protestant and Catholic parishes, by professional touring groups, and in church-related and independent Christian colleges." Bennet, *Acting Out Faith*, 66.

46. Christopher Fry, "How Lost, How Amazed, How Miraculous We Are," *Theatre Arts* 36 (August 1952): 27.

47. In 1950 Christopher Fry made the cover of *Time* magazine for having four plays, either original works or translations, playing on the commercial New York stage simultaneously. Fry has also composed music for theatre, most notably Peter Brook's production of *The Winter's Tale*, and he wrote the screenplay for the movie *Ben Hur*.

48. Robert Steele, "Looking Over in Anger," *Motive*, issue titled "Religious Drama 1958," April 1958.

49. Carl S. McClain, *Morals and the Movies* (Kansas City, MO: Beacon Hill, 1970), 25.

50. See Angela Latham-Jones, "The Anti-theatrical Prejudice and the Church of the Nazarene: A Late Twentieth-Century Perspective" (paper presented at the Association for Theatre in Higher Education National Conference, August 7, 1991, Seattle).

51. David Cole, *The Theatrical Event* (Middletown, CT: Wesleyan University Press, 1977), 8.

52. Ibid., 10.

53. Ibid., 14.

54. Ibid., 15.

55. Jacques Derrida, "The Theater of Cruelty and the Closure of Representation," *Theatre*, Summer 1978, 15.

56. "Andre Serban on Artaud: An Interview," *Theatre* (Summer 1978): 2.

57. Antonin Artaud, *The Theatre and Its Double* (New York: Grove, 1958), 53.

58. Christopher Innes, *Holy Theatre* (London: Cambridge University Press, 1981), 14.

59. Ibid., 16.

60. Eugenio Barba and Nicola Savarese, *Beyond the Floating Islands* (New York: PAJ, 1986), 45.

61. Jerzy Grotowski, *Towards a Poor Theatre* (New York: Simon and Schuster, 1968), 33.

62. Ibid., 37.

63. Ibid., 41. Joseph Chaiken, the founder of the Open Theatre movement, openly acknowledges his debt to Grotowski in his book *The Presence of the Actor*. Chaiken also considers the actor as a mediator between our world and other "zones of being." He is rather more conventional than Artaud and sees a distinction between theatre and life, though "they are absolutely joined." Like his predecessors, Chaiken is unable to give satisfactory discursive explanations for the actor's art. "The actor is able to approach in himself a cosmic dread as large as his life. He is able to go from this dread to a joy so sweet that it is without limit." Later, in discussing the concept of "stage presence," he calls this quality a "deep libidinal surrender" and an offering of the voice and body in performance. Chaiken finds that an actor has access to "additional energy, like an electric field." This is another way of describing the dangerous power of which Andre Serban spoke. Joseph Chaikin, *The Presence of the Actor* (New York: Atheneum, 1972), 6–9.

64. Victor Turner, *From Ritual to Theatre* (New York: PAJ, 1982), 79.

65. Ibid., 14.

66. Ibid., 79.

67. Ibid., 121.

68. Ibid., 25.

69. Ibid., 11.

Chapter 2 The Theology of the Theatrical Process

1. I later learned that the police had actually pulled Teddy and Carl and their audience over during one performance for looking suspicious. Teddy and Carl remained in character the entire time and used it as part of their dialogue in that performance. Suffice it to say that this play had very porous boundaries to the stage.

2. Karl Barth, *Church Dogmatics* 3/3, as quoted in Max Harris, *Theatre and Incarnation* (Grand Rapids: Eerdmans, 2005), 6–7.

3. Ibid., 7.

4. Hans Urs von Balthasar, *Theo-Drama: Theological Dramatic Theory*, vols. 1–5 (San Francisco: Ignatius, 1988–98). Balthasar and Barth were frequent conversation partners, and their theological works, though very different, have interesting points of contact, such as this common use of theatre as analogy. Balthasar develops it much further, needless to say.

5. For a helpful introduction to *Theo-Drama*, see Ben Quash, "Real Enactment: The Role of Drama in the Theology of Hans Urs von Balthasar," in *Faithful Performances: Enacting Christian Tradition*, ed. Trevor

Hart and Steven Guthrie (Burlington, VT: Ashgate, 2007), 13–32; and Ivan Patricio Khovacs, "A Cautionary Note on the Use of Theatre for Theology," in Hart and Guthrie, *Faithful Performances*, 33–50.

6. Kevin Vanhoozer, *The Drama of Doctrine: A Canonical-Linguistic Approach To Christian Theology* (Louisville: Westminster/John Knox, 2005); Shannon Craigo-Snell, "Command Performance: Rethinking Performance Interpretation in the Context of *Divine Discourse*," *Modern Theology* 16, no. 4 (2000): 475–94.

7. Noticeably absent in Vanhoozer's theological paradigm is the audience. Is the audience God the Playwright, or those outside the theatre company? For further critique, see Joshua Edelman, "Can an Act Be True?" in Hart and Guthrie, *Faithful Performances*, 51–75, quote from pp. 54–55.

8. Khovacs, "A Cautionary Note," 47.

9. See David Davies, *Art as Performance* (Malden, MA: Blackwell, 2004).

10. The place of personified Wisdom is found throughout wisdom literature, both in the Hebrew Scriptures and the apocryphal Wisdom books. One could note, for example, that Wisdom is presented as a proclaimer, a street preacher, in the book of Proverbs (see Prov. 1:22–33 and again 8:1–36). Wisdom is crucial for the vitality of faith in God, for "whoever finds me [i.e., Wisdom] finds life and obtains favor from the LORD" (Prov. 8:35 NRSV). For a survey of Wisdom as it relates to incarnation, see Elizabeth Johnson, *She Who Is* (New York: Crossroad, 1994), 86–100.

11. The requirements of the law, in terms of ethical living and holiness, were an expectation because the one, true, holy God dwelled among the people of God. See, e.g., Deut. 23:14.

12. The creeds of the first few Christian centuries (Apostles' Creed, Nicene Creed, Athanasian Creed, etc.) have at their core the purpose of clarifying the relationship between the human and divine natures in Jesus Christ. See Jean Laporte and Finian Taylor, "Genesis of the Creed: God and Christ," in *Understanding Our Biblical and Early Christian Tradition* (Lewiston, NY: Edwin Mellon, 1991), 191–211.

13. There are many surveys of the history of the christological controversy. Some of the more accessible are Alister McGrath, *Christian Theology: An Introduction*, 3rd ed. (Malden, MA: Blackwell, 2001), 345–405; Robert Krieg, "Who Do You Say That I Am? Christology: What It Is and Why It Matters," *Commonweal* 129, no. 6 (March 22, 2002): 12–17. Also noteworthy is an essay by Roger Haight, who has been the subject of a good deal of controversy himself, "The Future of Christology," in *Christology: Memory, Inquiry, Practice*, ed. Anne M. Clifford and Anthony J. Godzieba (Maryknoll, NY: Orbis, 2003), 47–61.

14. To see this painting, go to http://www.artofmonet.com.

15. Harris, *Theatre and Incarnation*, 19. Harris notes an interesting contrast between theatre and incarnation. In the incarnation, God unmasked Godself, reversing the theatrical model. God is no longer figuratively represented but actually present; see p. 10.

16. Ibid., 69.

17. Peter Brook, *The Empty Space* (New York: Avon/Discus, 1968).

18. Harris, *Theatre and Incarnation*, 99.

19. Ibid., 109–10. Having said all of this, Harris asserts that theatre can never fully imitate life but instead approximates life through general terms or universal concepts. Using Aristotle, he notes that art has an imitative function. Therefore, the dramatic arts "imitate" (mimesis) history, audience, and universal truth. See p. 41.

20. For an extremely cogent argument to this affect, see George Steiner, *Real Presences* (Chicago: University of Chicago Press, 1989).

21. Although some performance arts that are not inherently narrative (such as dance or mime) might nonetheless be placed under the umbrella of "theatre," for the sake of this work we will assume that theatre in the main includes narrative.

22. Athanasius, *On the Incarnation of the Word (De Incarnatione Verb Dei)* 54:3.

23. As Evelyn Underhill observes, the term "magic" has its reference "in the science of those Magi" whose quest led them to the truth of the incarnate God. Those "magical" moments in a performance are those when we touch simultaneously what is truly human and truly divine. See Evelyn Underhill, "A Defence of Magic," in *Evelyn Underhill: Modern Guide to the Ancient Quest for the Holy*, ed. Dana Greene (Albany: State University of New York Press, 1988), 31–46.

24. John Zizioulas, *Being as Communion* (Crestwood, NY: St. Vladimir's Seminary Press, 1997).

25. Zizioulas evaluates the changing meanings of the term "person" in its early Greco-Roman context, and particularly its theatrical references. He begins by identifying the origins of the term "person" as an anatomical term describing "the part of the head that is 'below the cranium'" (ibid., 31). It came to mean "mask" in theatrical terms because of the understanding of the temporary union of the soul with the body in human beings; that is, our bodies—our soul's masks—are our person in this world. It became the means of our interacting with others and with all creation. Much later "person" was seen as equivalent to the individual's essence or nature. Zizioulas concludes that "person" finds its most complete expression in the triune nature of God. See 27–37, esp. 37.

26. Ibid., 27–29.

27. The classic treatment of the immanent Trinity is Augustine's *De Trinitate*. Augustine, *The Trinity*, trans. Edmund Hill (Brooklyn, NY: New City, 1991).

28. The Cappadocian fathers all addressed the issue of the economy of God's trinitarian nature in response to the threat of the teaching of Bishop Eunomius, who maintained that the Son was unlike the Father. One of the most accessible works by the Cappadocians is Basil the Great, *On the Holy Spirit*, trans. David Anderson (Crestwood, NY: St. Vladimir's Seminary Press, 1997).

29. Although God is the same God in God's relationship to self and to other, there has been a corrective offered by Piet Schoonenberg and Yves Congar, who seek to maintain a distinction between God as we can know God economically and God as God knows Godself immanently. In other words, no matter how fully God has revealed Godself to us, God is never as completely revealed to humanity—nor understood by humanity—as God is to Godself. See Catherine LaCugna, *God for Us* (San Francisco: HarperSanFrancisco, 1991), 209–21.

30. Many works on the Trinity in the last fifty years have in some way responded to Rahner, for example, the writings of Catherine LaCugna, Jürgen Moltmann, Miraslov Volf, Robert Jensen, and Terrence Torrence. Of all those who have begun building on Rahner's work, possibly the most notable is Catherine LaCugna, who uses Zizioulas's understanding of personhood and the Trinity to further develop the relationship between the economic and the immanent Trinity. LaCugna concludes that what we learn from the Trinity is that godly relationships are egalitarian, interdependent relationships. Human interactions that best embody the dialogical nature of human relationships (and best manifest the divine image in which we are created) are relationships in which all parties are equal, regardless of their role. LaCugna's great work in this area is *God for Us*, though her thought is distilled nicely into her short essay "God in Communion with Us," in *Freeing Theology*, ed. Catherine LaCugna (San Francisco: HarperSanFrancisco, 1993), 83–114.

31. Robert Bellah et al., *Habits of the Heart: Individualism and Commitment in American Life* (Berkeley: University of California Press, 1985); Robert Putnam, *Bowling Alone: The Collapse and Revival of American Community* (New York: Simon and Schuster, 2000).

32. Harris, *Theatre and Incarnation*, 68.

33. In *The 25th Annual Putnam County Spelling Bee*, another effect of this porous barrier between audience and performer is that the audience feels more a part of the ensemble because people from its world now inhabit the world of the actors, creating a unique and fascinating dynamic.

34. Sacramentality is the category of which sacraments are a subcategory. Sacraments are those actions within the Christian tradition in which God's saving presence is said to be encountered by the community of people celebrating them. For a helpful introduction to this theological concept, see Bernard Cooke, *Sacraments and Sacramentality*, rev. ed. (Mystic, CT: Twenty-third Publications, 1994).

35. This is exactly Cooke's thesis in *Sacraments and Sacramentality*. It is also Zizioulas's thesis, in which the divine nature of human relationship is incarnated in the sacred actions of the sacraments.

36. The common phrase "platonic relationship" actually refers to Plato's aspiration that the highest human relationships would be those where the souls touch but the bodies do not.

37. Augustine addressed questions of language, communication, and signs throughout his writings, but his most concentrated treatment is found in *De Magistro*. For an exposition of Augustine's philosophy and theology of communication, see Peter King, "Augustine on the Impossibility of Teaching,"

Metaphilosophy 29 (1988): 179–95; see also Michael Cameron, "Sign," in *Augustine through the Ages: An Encyclopedia*, ed. Allan Fitzgerald (Grand Rapids: Eerdmans, 1999), 793–98.

38. Bernard Cooke argues that the introduction of Platonic thought into Christianity was an inappropriate intrusion of a philosophical distance between an immanent God and God's selfgivenness to people in what Cooke calls the "abba" experience. See Cooke, *The Distancing of God* (Minneapolis: Augsburg/Fortress, 1990). Andrew Louth offers a contrasting opinion suggesting that Judaism was thoroughly Hellenized before Christianity; see his *Origins of the Christian Mystical Tradition* (New York: Oxford University Press, 1981).

39. Augustine, "Sermon 272," in *Patrologiae cursus completus: Series latina*, ed. J.-P. Migne (Paris: Migne, 1844–64), 38:1246–48.

40. For a more detailed description of the history of sacramental theology, see Todd E. Johnson, "Recent American Protestant Sacramental Theology: Two Decades On," in *In Spirit and Truth*, ed. Philip Anderson and Michelle Clifton Soderstrom (Chicago: Covenant, 2006), 121–43.

41. Rahner's theology of symbol is found in his "Theology of the Symbol," in *Theological Investigations* (Baltimore: Helicon, 1966), 4:221–52. For a helpful exegesis of his thought, see Michael Skelly, *The Liturgy of the World: Karl Rahner's Theology of Worship* (Collegeville, MN: Liturgical Press, 1991), 36–42.

42. For Rahner's full argument connecting symbol, Christology, ecclesiology, and sacraments, see Karl Rahner, *The Church and the Sacraments* (New York: Herder and Herder: 1963); see also Skelly, *Liturgy of the World*, 133–58.

43. The most accessible presentations of Schillebeeckx's theology are his "Transubstantiation, Transfinalization, Transignification," in *Living Bread, Saving Cup*, ed. Kevin Seasoltz (Collegeville, MN: Liturgical Press, 1982) , 175–89; *The Eucharist* (London: Sheed and Ward, 1968); and *Christ, the Sacrament of the Encounter with God* (New York: Sheed and Ward, 1963).

44. This illustration is similar to one that Schillebeeckx offers in "Transubstantiation, Transfinalization, Transignification," 188–89.

45. For example, when Paul speaks of "discerning the body" in the context of a Eucharistic meal in Corinth (1 Cor. 11:29 NRSV), it is a reference to the local church as the body of Christ (1 Cor. 12:27), not the presence of Christ in the Eucharistic elements. This Pauline understanding of presence has driven much of contemporary sacramental theology.

46. See Konstantin Stanislavsky, *An Actor Prepares*, trans. Elizabeth Reynolds Hapgood (London: Geoffrey Bles, 1936).

47. For a helpful survey of acting methods since Stanislavsky, see Joshua Edelman, "'Can an Act Be True?' The Possibilities of the Dramatic Metaphor for Theology within a Post-Stanislavskian Theatre," in Hart and Guthrie, *Faithful Performances*, 51–74.

48. This relationship may be most famously encapsulated in the models offered by H. Richard Niebuhr in *Christ and Culture* (New York: Harper and Row, 1951). This is explored in greater detail in chap. 4.

49. Paul Tillich, "Religion and Secular Culture," in *Main Works*, vol. 2, ed. Michael Palmer (New York: De Gruyter, 1990), 201.

50. Ibid., 199.

51. Peter Berger, *The Sacred Canopy: Elements of a Sociological Theory of Religion* (New York: Doubleday, 1967).

52. The reference is to Schleiermacher's seminal work defending Christianity against the attacks of Enlightenment thought. His argument was that the proof of the truth of religion is a feeling (German: *gefühl*) of being utterly dependent on God. See Friedrich Schleiermacher, *On Religion: Speeches to Its Cultured Despisers* (New York: Harper and Row, 1968).

53. Robert Bellah gives the example of a Shelia Larson, who mixes and matches to create her own religion she calls "Shelia-ism." See Bellah et al., *Habits of the Heart*. The shift from corporate religious identity to private spiritual identity is chronicled by sociologist Meredith McGuire in her essay "Mapping Contemporary American Spirituality: A Sociological Perspective," *Christian Spirituality Bulletin* 5 (1997): 1–8.

54. For an introductory survey on Tillich's approach to a theology of culture, see Michael Palmer, "Paul Tillich's Theology of Culture," in *Main Works*, 2:1–32.

55. For the classic articulation of this issue, see Ernst Becker, *The Denial of Death* (New York: Free Press, 1973).

56. Paul Tillich, "Dynamics of Faith," in *Main Works*, vol. 5, ed. Robert P. Scharlemann (New York: De Gruyter, 1988), 201.

Chapter 3 Live Theatre in a Virtual World

1. David McFadzean was a professor at Judson College in Elgin, Illinois, and head of the theatre department there. Since then he has written and produced for both television and film. He has contributed to *Roseanne*, *Home Improvement*, and *What Women Want*, among other productions. McFadzean is a cofounder of Wind Dancer Films.

2. The Platonic concept of reality is not without complications, and it will not be addressed here. Instead, we simply suggest that Plato understood that some—not all—people are able to grasp what is truly real directly. Others, out of necessity, must experience reality indirectly.

3. Neil Postman, *Amusing Ourselves to Death: Public Discourse in the Age of Show Business* (New York: Penguin, 1985). Postman offers many contrasts between Huxley and Orwell. One of the most poignant is, "What Orwell feared were those who would ban books. What Huxley feared was there would be no reason to ban a book, for there would be no one who wanted to read one" (vii).

4. Ibid., 9–10.

5. Ibid., 41.

6. Ibid., 23–24.

7. Ibid., 28.

8. Ibid., 65, 70.

9. Ibid., 80. Here Postman defines his thesis, "that television's way of knowing is uncompromisingly hostile to typography's way of knowing, that television's conversations promote incoherence and triviality, that the phrase 'serious television' is a contradiction in terms, and that television speaks only in one persistent voice—the voice of entertainment."

10. Ibid., 61.

11. Ibid., 60.

12. Johannes Birringer, *Media and Performance: Along the Border* (Baltimore: Johns Hopkins University Press, 1998), 5.

13. Postman extends his study of the culture of technology in his book *Technopoly: The Surrender of Culture to Technology* (New York: Alfred A. Knopf, 1992). The observation that no technology is value-less but is always value-laden is as helpful as it is startling, for Postman demonstrates how we have embraced technologies and their inherent values uncritically. For example, he describes how computers not only transmit and transfer information; they contextualize and define information. Our use-*cum*-dependence on computers is not without its effect on our culture and our presuppositions of what is real (107–8).

14. Postman, *Amusing Ourselves to Death*, 86–87.

15. Postman, *Technopoly*, 27.

16. Ibid., 66.

17. Postman, *Amusing Ourselves to Death*, 123.

18. Ibid., 125.

19. Evidence for Postman's assertions here are not hard to find. Two obvious examples of the accommodation of religion to a consumerist, entertainment-oriented culture are George Barna's *Marketing the Church* (Colorado Springs: NavPress, 1988); and Walther Kallestad, *Entertainment Evangelism: Taking the Church Public* (Nashville: Abingdon, 1996).

20. Postman, *Technopoly*, 54–55. A similar conclusion was reached by sociologist Peter Berger, from a different starting point, in his study of the effects of the Enlightenment on religion in his work *The Sacred Canopy: Elements of a Sociological Theory of Religion* (New York: Anchor Doubleday, 1967). Berger concludes that in a context where the individual is the primary locus of authority, religious ministry is reduced to sales.

21. See Aristotle, *Poetics*, VI.

22. Aristotle, *Poetics*, XIV.

23. Guy Debord, *The Society of the Spectacle*, trans. Ken Knabb (Oakland: AK Press, 2006).

24. Ibid., 8.

25. For example, "For to me, living is Christ and dying is gain" (Phil. 1:21 NRSV), as well as "For now we see in a mirror, dimly, but then we will see face to face. Now I know only in part; then I will know fully, even as I have been fully known" (1 Cor. 13:12). Paul implies not that the world we live in is not real but instead that this world is less complete and less valued than the eternal reality that is God.

26. For a survey of the church's response to film, see Robert K. Johnston, *Reel Spirituality: Theology and Film in Dialogue*, 2nd ed. (Grand Rapids: Baker Academic, 2006), especially chap. 2.

27. Susan J. White, *Christian Worship and Technological Change* (Nashville: Abingdon, 1994), 18.

28. For a survey of Christian responses to technology after the rise of industrialism, see White, *Christian Worship*, chap. 1. For an insightful description of the cultural consequences of the Industrial Revolution in the rise of a culture whose primary religious paradigm is consumerism, see Dell deChant, *The Sacred Santa: Religious Dimensions of Consumer Culture* (Cleveland: Pilgrim, 2002).

29. For an expanded conversation on these points, see Quentin J. Schulze, *High-Tech Worship? Using Presentational Technologies Wisely* (Grand Rapids: Baker Books, 2004).

30. For a survey of church designs emphasizing the gathered community as the body of Christ, see Mark A. Torgerson, *An Architecture of Immanence: Architecture for Worship and Ministry Today* (Grand Rapids: Eerdmans, 2007), 11–24.

31. For a more-detailed analysis of this phenomenon, see Todd E. Johnson, "Video Monstrance," *Prism* 9 (2002): 17–19.

32. Felicia Hughes-Freeland, "Introduction," in *Ritual, Performance, Media*, ed. Felicia Hughes-Freeland, (New York: Routledge, 1998), 4.

33. For a very insightful evaluation of early television and its affects, see Donald Horton and Anselm Strauss, "Interaction in Audience-Participation Shows," *American Journal of Sociology* 62 (1957): 579–87, esp. 584.

34. Michael Hammet, *Touring Theatre in the Age of Mass Media* (Eastbourne, England: John Offord, 1980), 5.

35. Birringer, *Media and Performance*, 19.

36. Sarah Beckwith, *Signifying God: Social Relation and Symbolic Act in the York Corpus Christi Plays* (Chicago: University of Chicago Press, 2001).

37. Michael Aune, "Liturgy and Theology: Rethinking the Relationship," *Worship* 81 (2007): 65–67.

38. For a fascinating and graphic depiction of the rota of these plays in York, go to http://jerz.setonhill.edu/resources/PSim/.

39. The Middle Ages saw a decline in the level of education of the average Christian and what is known as a "loss of symbolic competence." The Platonic understanding of presence over time became more literally understood by both clergy and laity. A defining moment in this second, transformational epoch occurred at the church council known as the Synod of Rome (1059–79), where the thought of one brilliant but wholly intolerable character, Berengar, came under scrutiny. Berengar was concerned by the growing literalism surrounding the sacraments and the loss of the Platonic understanding of sacraments. Although Berengar promoted the teaching that was certainly the most widely accepted understanding of the Eucharist in the church's first millennium, his personality made him a desirable target of church officials. For this reason Berengar was forced to sign statements in 1059 and again in 1079 that he believed that Jesus of Nazareth was present in the Eucharistic elements, not only sacramentally but also truly or physically. The physical body of the earthly Jesus was now understood to be present within the bread and cup of the Eucharistic species. This synod serves as the mile marker for transformative sacramental thought. The Synod of Rome defined sacraments and worship in ways that excluded the participation of the laity and increased the authority of the church, not to mention that it distanced God from the ordinary and reduced the presence of God to "hocus pocus." In fact, the term

"hocus pocus" comes from a misunderstanding of the Latin phrase *Hoc est meus corpus*, which are the words said to mark the consecration /transformation of the elements—"This is my Body."

40. For a detailed description of the impact of the Synod of Rome on the Lord's Supper and the veneration of the consecrated elements outside the Mass, see Nathan Mitchell, *Cult and Controversy* (Collegeville, MN: Liturgical Press, 1982).

41. For more details concerning the origins and practice of the Feast of Corpus Christi, see Mitchell, *Cult and Controversy*, 163–200.

42. Beckwith, *Signifying God*, xv. Note how Beckwith also employs the distinction between "present" (incarnation) and "present to" (sacrament) introduced in the previous chapter.

43. Ibid., xvi.

44. Ibid., 41.

45. Ibid., 70.

46. Ibid., 23–25.

47. Ibid., 89.

48. Stanley Cavell, "The Avoidance of Love: A Reading of King Lear," in *Must We Mean What We Say?* (Cambridge: Cambridge University Press, 1976), 346; quoted in Beckwith, *Signifying God*, xviii.

49. Søren Kierkegaard, *Purity of Heart Is to Will One Thing*, trans. Douglas Steere (New York: Harper and Row, 1956), 180–81.

50. "Full, conscious and active participation" was the goal of the reforms made by the Roman Catholic Church at the Second Vatican Council. Since then, this principle has been almost universally accepted by other Christian denominations. Constitution on the Sacred Liturgy, II.14., Documents of the Second Vatican Council, December 4, 1963, http://www.adoremus.org/SacrosanctumConcilium.html.

51. Steven Guthrie, "Temples of the Spirit: Worship as Embodied Performance," in *Faithful Performances: Enacting Christian Tradition*, ed. Trevor Hart and Steven Guthrie (Burlington, VT: Ashgate, 2007), 97–100.

52. Nicholas Wolterstorff, *Divine Discourse: Philosophical Reflections on the Claim That God Speaks* (Cambridge: Cambridge University Press, 1995).

53. Ibid., 175–79.

54. Ibid., 180–82.

55. Shannon Craigo-Snell, "Command Performance: Rethinking Performance Interpretation in the Context of *Divine Discourse*," *Modern Theology* 16, no. 4 (2000): 475–94.

56. Ibid., 478–80.

57. Ibid., 480.

58. For a survey of emerging churches and their practices, see Eddie Gibbs and Ryan Bolger, *Emerging Churches: Creating Christian Communities in Post-Modern Cultures* (Grand Rapids: Baker Academic, 2005); for an introduction to the house church movement, see David Haldane, "There's No Place Like Home, These Christians Say," *Los Angeles Times*, July 23, 2007, http://www.latimes.com/news/local/la-me-housechurch23jul23,0,6712444.story?coll=la-home-local.

59. For detailed descriptions of projects such as these, see Mary Marshall Clark, "Oral History: Art and Praxis," in *Community, Culture and Globalization*, ed. D. Adams and A. Goldbard (New York: Rockefeller Foundation, 2002), 88–105; and Barbara Santos, "Theatre of the Oppressed and Community Cultural Development," in Adams and Goldbard, *Community, Culture and Globalization*, 226–43.

60. The reversal of this trend is not an indication that sketches are becoming an endangered liturgical species, but instead that these pieces are increasingly being recorded and played in worship as video dramas. This trend is no small irony in the context of this chapter.

61. For information about CITE, visit: http://www.ohr.cornell.edu/cite/index.html. For an example of CITE's work, see http://www.news.cornell.edu/stories/Sept07/cu.advance.mr.html.

62. deChant, *The Sacred Santa*, 5, 12–13. Though deChant develops this thesis throughout this work, in these pages he explicitly connects his understanding of the religious dimension of consumerism to Tillich's theology of culture, identifying consumption as the "ultimate concern" of capitalism, which makes it religious according to Tillich's definition.

63. Trevor Hart, "The Sense of an Ending: Finitude and the Authentic Performance of Life," in Hart and Guthrie, *Faithful Performances*, 167–88.

Chapter 4 The Christian at Work: Being an Artist in the Theatre

1. H. Richard Niebuhr, *Christ and Culture* (New York: Harper and Brothers, 1951). This book has come under scrutiny by free-church scholars, and their critique of Niebuhr is important to note. See especially Craig A. Carter, *Rethinking Christ and Culture* (Grand Rapids: Brazos, 2006); and Glen H. Stassen, D. M. Yeager, and John Howard Yoder, *Authentic Transformation: A New Vision of Christ and Culture* (Nashville: Abingdon, 1996).

2. J. Gresham Machen, *Christianity and Culture* (Charlottesville, VA: Mars Hill Monograph, n.d.), 3.

3. Ibid.

4. Ibid., 4.

5. Carter, *Rethinking Christ and Culture*.

6. Cited in Carter, *Rethinking Christ and Culture*, 146.

7. Jacques Maritain, *Art and Scholasticism, with Other Essays*, trans. J. F. Scanlan (Freeport, NY: Books for Libraries Press, 1971), 66.

8. Michael Linton, "Moses at the Met," *First Things*, no. 98 (December 1999): 15.

9. Ibid.

10. T. S. Eliot, "Tradition and the Individual Talent," in *Selected Prose of T. S. Eliot* (New York: Harcourt Brace Jovanovich, 1975), 37–44. The entire essays demands attention; here are a few samples:

Not only the best, but the most individual parts of [the poet's] work may be those in which the dead poets, his ancestors, assert their immortality most vigorously. (38)

No poet, no artist of any art, has his complete meaning alone. (38)

[The poet] must inevitably be judged by the standards of the past. (39)

The progress of an artist is a continual self-sacrifice, a continual extinction of personality. (40)

Poetry is not a turning loose of emotion, but an escape from emotion; it is not the expression of personality, but an escape from personality. (43)

11. See Hans Rookmaaker, *Art Needs No Justification* (Downers Grove, IL: InterVarsity, 1978).

12. Dorothy Sayers, *The Mind of the Maker* (New York: Meridian, 1956), 15.

13. Ibid., 34.

14. Ibid., 47.

15. Ibid., 49–50.

16. Ibid., 50.

17. Francis Hodge, *Play Directing: Analysis, Communication, and Style*, 4th ed. (Englewood Cliffs, NJ: Prentice Hall, 1994), 8.

18. E. Martin Brown, "Drama's Return to Religion," *Theatre Arts* 41 (August 1957): 18–19, 92–93, quote from p. 93.

19. Maritain, *Art and Scholasticism*, 51.

20. Ibid., 52.

21. Dorothy Sayers, "Playwrights Are Not Evangelists," *World Theater* 5 (Winter 1955/56): 61–66. Samples from this important work follow:

If he [the playwright] writes with his eye on a kind of spiritual box-office, he will at once cease to be a dramatist, and decline into a manufacturer of propagandist tracts. (61)

A bad play is a bad play, and though, like some bad statuary and abominable stained glass, it *may* assist the prayers of the faithful, it will do nothing to convince the world at large that the Christian religion is worthy of intelligent consideration. And I am not altogether sure even about the faithful: does bad art really do for them anything that good art would not do better? But today, the chief danger threatens from the opposite direction—a general failure to grasp that no good poetic work can come except from the enkindled imagination. (62)

Evangelism is not the proper concern of the playwright. (63)

A drama (or any other work of art) will not by itself make anybody a Christian. (64)

An unsound play by a good dramatist will always be far more effective than an impeccably orthodox play by a bad dramatist. . . . Sound theology must be in the dramatist before he begins. (65)

22. *Christianity and Theatre* is published by Christians in Theatre Arts (http://www.cita.org). In 2008 CITA produced an anthology of five plays called *Faith on Stage* (Greenville, SC: Christians in Theatre Arts, 2007).

23. Murray Watts, *Christianity and the Theatre* (Edinburgh: Handsel, 1986), 21.

24. See Dale Savidge, "Acting and (the) Incarnation," in *It Was Good: Making Art to the Glory of God*, ed. Ned Bustard, 2nd ed. (Baltimore: Square Halo, 2006), 173–86.

25. Frank Burch Brown, *Good Taste, Bad Taste, and Christian Taste* (New York: Oxford University Press, 2000), 110–11.

26. See Nancy Murphey, *Bodies and Souls, or Spirited Bodies?* (Cambridge: Cambridge University Press, 2006).

27. Meister Eckhart, quoted in Charles Davis, *The Body as Spirit: The Nature of Religious Feeling* (New York: Seabury, 1976), 35.

28. Ibid., 39.

29. Jeff Barker, "Enacted Prayer: A Workshop," presented at the Christians in Theatre Arts Conference, summer 2004. See http://www.nwciowa.edu/worshipdrama/

30. Davis, *Body as Spirit*, 56.

31. Ibid., 49.

32. Brown, *Good Taste*, 110.

33. Maritain, *Art and Scholasticism*, 42.

34. Ibid., 91.

35. See http://chesterton.org/acs/quotes.htm.

Chapter 5 The Christian at Play: Being an Audience in the Theatre

1. See Robert K. Johnston, *The Christian at Play* (Grand Rapids: Eerdmans, 1983).

2. Thomas Aquinas, cited in Jacques Maritain, *Art and Scholasticism, with Other Essays*, trans. J. F. Scanlan (Freeport, NY: Books for Libraries Press, 1971), 62.

3. G. Campbell Morgan, "The Disciple at Play," in *Discipleship* (Grand Rapids: Baker Academic, 1973), 59.

4. Ben Brantley, "The Eternal Vaudeville of the Spiritual Mind," *New York Times*, June 6, 2007, http://theater2.nytimes.com/2007/06/06/theater/reviews/06bran.html.

5. Erik Piepenburg, "Faith Confronted, and Defended, Downtown," *New York Times*, May 6, 2007, http://www.nytimes.com/2007/05/06/theater/06piep.html?n=Top/Reference/Times%20Topics/Subjects/R/Religion%20and%20Belief.

6. See http://www.amazinggracethetruestory.com.

7. Jack O'Brien, "The Road Ahead," *Time*, November 29, 2004.

8. Ibid.

9. Cited in Arthur Holmberg, "Waning of Spirituality Perplexes Artists Today," *American Theatre*, June 1991, 45.

10. Cited in ibid.

11. Cited in ibid.

12. Maritain, *Art and Scholasticism*, 93.

13. Victor Turner, *From Ritual to Theatre* (New York: PAJ, 1982), 115.

14. Frank Burch Brown, *Good Taste, Bad Taste, and Christian Taste*, (New York: Oxford University Press, 2000), 13.

15. David Hume, "Of the Standard of Taste," http://www.mnstate.edu/gracyk/courses/phil%20 of%20art/hume%20on%20taste.htm.

16. Dorothy Sayers, "Playwrights Are Not Evangelists," *World Theatre* 5 (Winter 1955/56): 66.

17. Morris Ertman and Ron Reed's musical, *Tent Meeting*, has been performed around Canada since 1982 and is planned for an American premiere at Theatrical Outfit in Atlanta in the spring of 2009.

18. See http://www.calebgroup.org.

19. Maritain, *Art and Scholasticism*, 58.

20. Ibid., 59.

21. Ibid., 88.

22. Brown, *Good Taste*, 119.

23. For a fuller explanation of the Christian year, see Lawrence Hull Stookey, *Calendar: Christ's Time in the Church* (Nashville: Abingdon, 1996). For an encyclopedic resource detailing each season and holy day, see Mary Ellen Hynes, *Companion to the Calendar* (Chicago: Liturgical Training Publications, 1993).

24. For those unfamiliar with the Easter Vigil or interested in considering its use in the worship of their own community, a good introduction is found in Robert Webber, ed., *The Complete Library of Christian Worship*, vol. 5, *The Services of the Christian Year* (Peabody, MA: Hendrickson, 1993), 381–96.

25. Lester Ruth, "A Rose by Any Other Name," in *The Conviction of Things Not Seen*, ed. Todd E. Johnson (Grand Rapids: Brazos, 2002), 33–51.

26. See http://www.cita.org.

27. Bernard Beckerman, *Theatrical Representation* (New York: Routledge, 1990), 82.

28. Bruce Chilton, *Redeeming Time: The Wisdom of Ancient Jewish and Christian Festal Calendars* (Peabody, MA: Hendrickson, 2002), 29.

29. Francis A. Schaeffer, *Art and the Bible* (Downers Grove, IL: InterVarsity, 1973), 5.

30. Paul Claudel, cited in Maritain, *Art and Scholasticism*, 160.

Conclusion: Dale and Todd Return to the Theatre

1. The goals and purpose of the Unknown Theatre name this explicitly. The following information is from its Web site: http://www.unknowntheatre.com/publicsite/aboutus_abouttheunknown_mani festo.asp.

MISSION STATEMENT
Unknown Theatre is dedicated to making theatre an integrated and necessary part of people's lives—providing regular opportunities for the members of our diverse Los Angeles community to come together, appreciate one another, and search for meaning together.

2. This oft-quoted phrase is from the Constitution of the Sacred Liturgy, the first document released by the Catholic Church in the wake of the Second Vatican Council. See par. II.14, http://www .vatican.va/archive/hist_councils/ii_vatican_council/documents/vat-ii_const_19631204_sacrosanctum- concilium_en.html.

bibliography

Artaud, Antonin. *The Theatre and Its Double*. New York: Grove, 1958.

Aston, Elaine, and George Savona. *Theatre as Sign-System: A Semiotics of Text and Performance*. London: Routledge, 1991.

Augustine. "Sermon 272." In Patrologiae cursus completus: Series latina (PL), vol. 38, edited by J.-P. Migne, 1246–48. Paris: Migne, 1844–64.

———. *The Trinity*. Translated by Edmund Hill. Brooklyn, NY: New City Press, 1991.

Aune, Michael. "Liturgy and Theology: Rethinking the Relationship." *Worship* 81 (2007): 46–68.

Baldovin, John Francis. "*Accepit Panem*: The Gestures of the Priest at the Institution Narrative at the Eucharist." In *Rule of Prayer, Rule of Faith*, edited by Nathan Mitchell and John Baldovin, 123–39. Collegeville, MN: Liturgical Press, 1996.

Balthasar, Hans Urs von. *Theo-Drama: Theological Dramatic Theory*. Vols. 1–5. San Francisco: Ignatius, 1988–98.

Barba, Eugenio, and Nicola Savarese. *Beyond the Floating Islands*. New York: PAJ, 1986.

———. *A Dictionary of Theatre Anthropology: The Secret Art of the Performer*. London: Routledge, 1991.

Barish, Jonas. *The Antitheatrical Prejudice*. Berkeley: University of California Press, 1981.

Barna, George. *Marketing the Church*. Colorado Springs: NavPress, 1988.

Barrager, Pam. *Spiritual Growth through Creative Dramatics*. Valley Forge, PA: Judson, 1981.

Basil the Great. *On the Holy Spirit*. Translated by David Anderson. Crestwood, NY: St. Vladimir's Seminary Press, 1997.

Baxter, Kay M. *Contemporary Theatre and the Christian Faith*. New York: Abingdon, 1964.

Becker, Ernst. *The Denial of Death*. New York: Free Press, 1973.

Beckerman, Bernard. *Theatrical Representation*. New York: Routledge, 1990.

Beckwith, Sarah. *Signifying God: Social Relation and Symbolic Act in the York Corpus Christi Plays.* Chicago: University of Chicago Press, 2001.

Bellah, Robert, et al. *Habits of the Heart: Individualism and Commitment in American Life.* Berkeley: University of California Press, 1985.

Bennett, Gordon C. *Acting Out Faith.* St. Louis: CBP, 1986.

Berger, Peter. *The Sacred Canopy: Elements of a Sociological Theory of Religion.* New York: Doubleday, 1967.

Bert, Norman A. "Theatre Is Religion." *Journal of Religion and Theatre* 1, no. 1 (Fall 2002), http://www.rtjournal.org/vol_1/no_1/bert.html.

Berthold, Margot. *World Theater.* New York: Frederick Unger, n.d.

Betti, Ugo. "Religion and Theater." In *Theatre in the Twentieth Century*, edited by Robert Corrigan, 114–24. New York: Grove, 1963.

Birringer, Johannes. *Media and Performance: Along the Border.* Baltimore: Johns Hopkins University Press, 1998.

Blevens, James. *Revelation as Drama.* Nashville: Broadman, 1984.

Bond, Fiona. *The Arts in Your Church: A Practical Guide.* Carlisle, England: Piquant, 2001.

Brantley, Ben. "As a Nun Stands Firm, the Ground Shifts Below." *New York Times*, April 1, 2005, online edition, http://query.nytimes.com/gst/fullpage.html?res=9801E4D8123CF 932A35757C0A9639C8B63&scp=4&sq=as%20a20nun20&st=cse.

———. "The Eternal Vaudeville of the Spiritual Mind." *New York Times*, June 6, 2007, online edition, http://theater2.nytimes.com/2007/06/06/theater/reviews/06bran.html.

Brockett, Oscar. *History of the Theatre.* 9th ed. Boston: Allyn and Bacon, 2003.

Brook, Peter. *The Empty Space.* New York: Avon/Discus, 1968.

Brown, Frank Burch. *Good Taste, Bad Taste, and Christian Taste.* New York: Oxford University Press, 2000.

Buch, Arthur T. *The Bible on Broadway: A Source Book for Ministers, Educators, Librarians, and General Readers.* Hamden, CT: Archon, 1968.

Burbridge, Paul, and Murray Watts. *Time to Act.* London: Hodder and Stoughton, 1987.

Butcher, S. H. *Aristotle's Theory of Poetry and Fine Art.* New York: Dover, 1951.

Cameron, Michael. "Sign." In *Augustine through the Ages: An Encyclopedia*, edited by Allan Fitzgerald, 793–98. Grand Rapids: Eerdmans, 1999.

Campbell, Thomas P. "Liturgy and Drama: Recent Approaches to Medieval Theatre." *Theatre Journal* 33, no. 3 (October 1981): 289–301.

Carter, Craig A. *Rethinking Christ and Culture.* Grand Rapids: Brazos, 2006.

Casel, Odo. *The Mystery of Christian Worship and Other Writings.* Edited by Burkhard Neunheuser. Westminster, MD: Newman, 1963.

Catholic Church. *Pontificale Romanum.* Paris: Petrum DeBats, 1683.

Cavell, Stanley. "The Avoidance of Love: A Reading of King Lear." In *Must We Mean What We Say?* Cambridge: Cambridge University Press, 1976.

Chaikin, Joseph. *The Presence of the Actor.* New York: Atheneum, 1972.

Chambers, E. K. *The Medieval Stage.* 2 vols. New York: Oxford University Press, 1933.

Clark, Mary Marshall. "Oral History: Art and Praxis." In *Community, Culture and Globalization*, edited by D. Adams and A. Goldbard, 88–105. New York: Rockefeller Foundation, 2002.

Cole, David. *Acting as Reading: The Place of the Reading Process in the Actor's Work*. Ann Arbor: University of Michigan Press, 1992.

———. *The Theatrical Event*. Middletown, CT: Wesleyan University Press, 1977.

Constitution on the Sacred Liturgy. Documents of the Second Vatican Council, December 4, 1963, http://www.adoremus.org/SacrosanctumConcilium.html.

Cooke, Bernard. *The Distancing of God: The Ambiguity of Symbol in History and Theology*. Minneapolis: Augsburg/Fortress, 1990.

———. *Sacraments and Sacramentality*. Rev. ed. Mystic, CT: Twenty-third Publications, 1994.

Craigo-Snell, Shannon. "Command Performance: Rethinking Performance Interpretation in the Context of *Divine Discourse*." *Modern Theology* 16, no. 4 (2000): 475–94.

Davidson, Charles. *Studies in the English Mystery Plays*. New York: Haskell House, 1965.

Davies, David. *Art as Performance*. Malden, MA: Blackwell, 2004.

Davis, Charles. *The Body as Spirit: The Nature of Religious Feeling*. New York: Seabury, 1976.

Debord, Guy. *The Society of the Spectacle*. Translated by Ken Knabb. Oakland: AK Press, 2006.

deChant, Dell. *The Sacred Santa: Religious Dimensions of Consumer Culture*. Cleveland: Pilgrim, 2002.

Dox, Donnalee. *The Idea of the Theater in Latin Christian Thought: Augustine to the Fourteenth Century*. Ann Arbor: University of Michigan Press, 2004.

Dukore, Bernard F. *Dramatic Theory and Criticism*. New York: Holt Rinehart and Winston, 1974.

Edelman, Joshua. "'Can an Act Be True?' The Possibilities of the Dramatic Metaphor for Theology within a Post-Stanislavskian Theatre." In *Faithful Performances: Enacting Christian Tradition*, edited by Trevor A. Hart and Steven R. Guthrie, 51–74. Burlington, VT: Ashgate, 2007.

Eggebrecht, David W. *Spirit in Drama*. St. Louis: Concordia, 2004.

Ehrensperger, Harold. *Religious Drama: Ends and Means*. New York: Abingdon, 1962.

Eliot. T. S. *Christianity and Culture*. New York: Harcourt Brace and World, 1949.

———. *Selected Essays*. New York: Harcourt Brace Jovanovich, 1978.

Ellison, Jerome. *God on Broadway*. Richmond: John Knox, 1971.

Forde, Nigel. *Theatrecraft*. Wheaton: H. Shaw, 1990.

Freedman, David Noel, ed. *The Leningrad Codex*. Grand Rapids: Eerdmans, 1998.

Friesen, Duane K. *Artists, Citizens, Philosophers: Seeking the Peace of the City*. Scottdale, PA: Herald, 2000.

Fry, Christopher. "How Lost, How Amazed, How Miraculous We Are." *Theatre Arts* 36 (August 1952): 27.

Gibbs, Eddie, and Ryan Bolger. *Emerging Churches: Creating Christian Communities in Post-Modern Cultures*. Grand Rapids: Baker Academic, 2005.

Gillespie, Patti P., and Kenneth M. Cameron. *Western Theatre: Revolution and Revival*. New York: Macmillan, 1984.

Grotowski, Jerzy. *Towards a Poor Theatre*. New York: Simon and Schuster, 1968.

Haight, Roger. "The Future of Christology." In *Christology: Memory, Inquiry, Practice*, edited by Anne M. Clifford and Anthony J. Godzieba, 47–61. Maryknoll, NY: Orbis, 2003.

Haldane, David. "There's No Place like Home, These Christians Say." *Los Angeles Times*, July 23, 2007, online edition, http://www.latimes.com/news/local/la-me-house church23jul23,0,6712444.story?coll=la-home-local.

Hammet, Michael. *Touring Theatre in the Age of Mass Media*. Eastbourne, England: John Offord, 1980.

Hardison, O. B., Jr. *Christian Rite and Christian Drama in the Middle Ages: Essays in the Origin and Early History of Modern Drama*. 1965. Reprint, Westport, CT: Greenwood, 1983.

Harris, Max. *Theatre and Incarnation*. Grand Rapids: Eerdmans, 2005.

Hart, Trevor, and Steven Guthrie, eds. *Faithful Performances: Enacting Christian Tradition*. Burlington, VT: Ashgate, 2007.

Hatfield, Louis Duane. *As the Twig Is Bent: Therapeutic Values in the Use of Drama and the Dramatic in the Church*. New York: Vantage, 1975.

Hodge, Francis. *Play Directing: Analysis, Communication, and Style*. 4th ed. Englewood Cliffs, NJ: Prentice Hall, 1994.

Holmberg, Arthur. "Waning of Spirituality Perplexes Artists Today." *American Theatre*, June 1991, 45.

Horton, Donald, and Anselm Strauss. "Interaction in Audience-Participation Shows." *American Journal of Sociology* 62 (1957): 579–87.

Hughes-Freeland, Felicia. "Introduction." In *Ritual, Performance, Media,* edited by Felicia Hughes-Freeland, 1–28. New York: Routledge, 1998.

Hume, David. "Of the Standard of Taste." In *Aesthetics: The Classic Readings*, edited by D. E. Cooper, 76–93. Oxford: Blackwell, 1997.

Hunningher, Benjamin. *The Origin of the Theater*. New York: Hill and Wang, 1955.

Hynes, Mary Ellen. *Companion to the Calendar*. Chicago: Liturgical Training Publications, 1993.

Innes, Christopher. *Holy Theatre*. London: Cambridge University Press, 1981.

Irwin, Kevin W. *Context and Text Method in Liturgical Theology*. Collegeville, MN: Liturgical Press, 1994.

Johnson, Elizabeth. *She Who Is*. New York: Crossroad, 1994.

Johnson, Todd E. "Recent American Protestant Sacramental Theology: Two Decades On." In *In Spirit and Truth*, edited by Philip Anderson and Michelle Clifton Soderstrom, 121–43. Chicago: Covenant Publications, 2006.

———. "Video Monstrance." *Prism* 9 (2002): 17–19.

Johnston, Robert K. *Reel Spirituality: Theology and Film in Dialogue*. 2nd ed. Grand Rapids: Baker Academic, 2006.

Kallestad, Walther. *Entertainment Evangelism: Taking the Church Public*. Nashville: Abingdon, 1996.

Kavanagh, Aidan. *On Liturgical Theology*. New York: Pueblo, 1984.

Kierkegaard, Søren. *Purity of Heart Is to Will One Thing*. Translated by Douglas Steere. New York: Harper and Row, 1956.

King, Peter. "Augustine on the Impossibility of Teaching." *Metaphilosophy* 29 (1988): 179–95.

Kirby, E. T. *Ur-Drama: The Origins of Theatre*. New York: New York University Press, 1975.

Krieg, Robert. "Who Do You Say That I Am? Christology: What It Is and Why It Matters." *Commonweal* 129, no. 6 (March 22, 2002): 12–17.

LaCugna, Catherine. *God for Us*. San Francisco: HarperSanFrancisco, 1991.

———. "God in Communion with Us." In *Freeing Theology*, edited by Catherine LaCugna, 83–114. San Francisco: HarperSanFrancisco, 1993.

Laporte, Jean, and Finian Taylor. *Understanding Our Biblical and Early Christian Tradition*. Lewiston, NY: Edwin Mellon, 1991.

Latham-Jones, Angela. "The Anti-theatrical Prejudice and the Church of the Nazarene: A Late Twentieth-Century Perspective." Paper presented at the Association for Theatre in Higher Education National Conference, August 7, 1991, Seattle, WA.

Linton, Michael. "Moses at the Met." *First Things*, no. 98 (December 1999): 15.

Louth, Andrew. *Origins of the Christian Mystical Tradition*. New York: Oxford University Press, 1981.

Machen, J. Gresham. *Christianity and Culture*. Charlottesville, VA: Mars Hill Monograph, n.d.

Magorrian, Brian G. "For What It's Worth: Theatre and the Church." *Quodlibet Journal* 3, no. 2 (Spring 2001), http://www.quodlibet.net/magorrian-theater.shtml.

Maritain, Jacques. *Art and Scholasticism, with Other Essays*. Translated by J. F. Scanlan. Freeport, NY: Books for Libraries Press, 1971.

McCall, Richard D. *Do This: The Liturgy as Performance*. Notre Dame, IN: University of Notre Dame Press, 2007.

McClain, Carl S. *Morals and the Movies*. Kansas City, MO: Beacon Hill, 1970.

McConachie, Bruce. *Interpreting the Theatrical Past*. Iowa City: University of Iowa Press, 1989.

McGrath, Alister. *Christian Theology: An Introduction*. 3rd ed. Malden, MA: Blackwell, 2001.

McGuire, Meredith. "Mapping Contemporary American Spirituality: A Sociological Perspective." *Christian Spirituality Bulletin* 5 (1997): 1–8.

Merchant, Moelwyn. *Creed and Drama: An Essay in Religious Drama*. London: SPCK, 1965.

Miller, Paul M., and Dan Dunlop. *Create a Drama Ministry*. Kansas City, MO: Lillenas, 1984.

Mitchell, Nathan. *Cult and Controversy*. Collegeville, MN: Liturgical Press, 1982.

Morgan, G. Campbell. *Discipleship*. Grand Rapids: Baker Book House, 1973.

Myers, Gail E., and Michele Tolela Myers. *The Dynamics of Human Communication: A Laboratory Approach*. New York: McGraw-Hill, 1985.

Nagler, A. M. *Sourcebook in Theatrical History*. New York: Dover, 1952.

Nichols, Bridget. *Liturgical Hermeneutics: Interpreting Liturgical Rites in Performance*. Frankfurt am Main: P. Lang, 1996.

Niebuhr, H. Richard. *Christ and Culture*. New York: Harper and Row, 1951.

O'Regan, James. "The Grammar of Symbol." *Modern Liturgy* 14 (January 1987): 13–15.

———. "Making Image Theatre." *Canadian Theatre Review* 50 (Spring 1987): 10–13.

Pederson, Steven. *Developing a Drama Ministry*. Grand Rapids: Zondervan, 1999.

Perry, Michael, ed. *The Dramatized Bible*. 2 vols. Grand Rapids: Baker Academic, 1994.

Piepenburg, Erik. "Faith Confronted, and Defended, Downtown." *New York Times*, May 6, 2007, http://www.nytimes.com/2007/05/06/theater/06piep.html?n=Top/Reference/Times%20Topics/Subjects/R/Religion%20and%20Belief.

Postlewait, Thomas. "Criteria for Periodization in Theatre History." *Theatre Journal* 40, no. 3 (October 1988): 299–318.

Postman, Neil. *Amusing Ourselves to Death: Public Discourse in the Age of Show Business*. New York: Penguin, 1985.

———. *Technopoly: The Surrender of Culture to Technology*. New York: Alfred A. Knopf, 1992.

Powell, Matthew Donald, OP. "The Blackfriars Guild of New York, 1940–1972: An Experiment in Catholic Theatre." PhD diss., University of Wisconsin–Madison, 1984.

Putnam, Robert. *Bowling Alone: The Collapse and Revival of American Community*. New York: Simon and Schuster, 2000.

Rahner, Karl. *The Church and the Sacraments*. New York: Herder and Herder, 1963.

———. "The Theology of the Symbol." In *Theological Investigations*, vol. 4, 221–52. Baltimore: Helicon, 1966.

Redmond, James, ed. *Drama and Religion*. Cambridge: Cambridge University Press, 1983.

Rookmaaker, Hans. *Art Needs No Justification*. Downers Grove, IL: InterVarsity, 1978.

Roston, Murray. *Biblical Drama in England from the Middle Ages to the Present Day*. Evanston, IL: Northwestern University Press, 1968.

Rozik, Eli. "The Ritual Origin of Theatre—A Scientific Theory or Theatrical Ideology?" *Journal of Religion and Theatre* 2, no. 1, http://www.rtjournal.org/vol_2/no_1/rozik.html.

———. *The Roots of Theatre: Rethinking Ritual and Other Theories of Origin*. Iowa City: University of Iowa Press, 2002.

Ruth, Lester. "A Rose by Any Other Name." In *The Conviction of Things Not Seen*, edited by Todd E. Johnson, 33–51. Grand Rapids: Brazos, 2002.

Santos, Barbara. "Theatre of the Oppressed and Community Cultural Development." In *Community, Culture and Globalization*, edited by D. Adams and A. Goldbard, 226–43. New York: Rockefeller Foundation, 2002.

Sayers, Dorothy. *The Mind of the Maker*. New York: Meridian, 1956.

———. "Playwrights Are Not Evangelists." *World Theater* 5 (Winter 1955/56): 61–66.

Schechner, Richard. *Between Theater and Anthropology*. Philadelphia: University of Pennsylvania Press, 1985.

———. *Performance Theory*. New York: Routledge, 1988.

Schillebeeckx, Edward. *Christ, the Sacrament of the Encounter with God*. New York: Sheed and Ward, 1963.

———. *The Eucharist*. London: Sheed and Ward, 1968.

———. "Transubstantiation, Transfinalization, Transignification." In *Living Bread, Saving Cup*, edited by Kevin Seasoltz, 175–89. Collegeville, MN: Liturgical Press, 1982.

Schleiermacher, Friedrich. *On Religion: Speeches to Its Cultured Despisers*. New York: Harper and Row, 1968.

Schulze, Quentin J. *High-Tech Worship? Using Presentational Technologies Wisely*. Grand Rapids: Baker Academic, 2004.

Senkbeil, Peter. "Faith in Theatre." PhD diss., Northwestern University, 1995.

Skelly, Michael. *The Liturgy of the World: Karl Rahner's Theology of Worship*. Collegeville, MN: Liturgical Press, 1991.

Smyth, Robert. *Lamb's Players Presents: Developing a Drama Group*. Minneapolis: World Wide, 1989.

Southern, Richard. *The Seven Ages of the Theatre*. New York: Hill and Wang, 1961.

Stanislavsky, Konstantin. *An Actor Prepares*. Translated by Elizabeth Reynolds Hapgood. New York: Theatre Arts Books, 1948.

Stassen, Glen H., D. M. Yeager, and John Howard Yoder. *Authentic Transformation: A New Vision of Christ and Culture*. Nashville: Abingdon, 1996.

Steiner, George. *Real Presences*. Chicago: University of Chicago Press, 1989.

Stookey, Lawrence Hull. *Calendar: Christ's Time in the Church*. Nashville: Abingdon, 1996.

Tillich, Paul. "Dynamics of Faith." In *Main Works*, vol. 5, edited by Robert P. Scharlemann, 231–90. New York: De Gruyter, 1988.

———. "Religion and Secular Culture." In *Main Works*, vol. 2, edited by Michael Palmer, 197–207. New York: De Gruyter, 1990.

Torgerson, Mark A. *An Architecture of Immanence: Architecture for Worship and Ministry Today*. Grand Rapids: Eerdmans, 2007.

Turner, Victor. *The Anthropology of Performance*. New York: PAJ, 1987.

———. *From Ritual to Theatre*. New York: PAJ, 1982.

Underhill, Evelyn. "A Defence of Magic." In *Evelyn Underhill: Modern Guide to the Ancient Quest for the Holy*, edited by Dana Greene, 31–46. Albany: State University of New York Press, 1988.

Vanhoozer, Kevin. *The Drama of Doctrine: A Canonical-Linguistic Approach to Christian Theology*. Louisville: Westminster/John Knox, 2005.

Vogel, Dwight. *Primary Sources of Liturgical Theology: A Reader*. Collegeville, MN: Liturgical Press, 2000.

Waddy, Lawrence. *The Bible as Drama*. New York: Paulist Press, 1975.

Watts, Murray. *Christianity and the Theatre*. Edinburgh: Handsel, 1986.

Weales, Gerald. *Religion in Modern English Drama*. Philadelphia: University of Pennsylvania Press, 1961.

Webber, Robert, ed. *The Complete Library of Christian Worship*. Vol. 5, *The Services of the Christian Year.* Peabody, MA: Hendrickson, 1993.

Wellworth, George E. "From Ritual to Drama: The Social Background of the Early English Theatre." *Journal of General Education* 19:297–320.

White, Susan J. *Christian Worship and Technological Change*. Nashville: Abingdon, 1994.

Wickham, Glynne. *A History of the Theatre*. Cambridge: Cambridge University Press, 1985.

———. *The Medieval Theatre*. 3rd ed. Cambridge: Cambridge University Press, 1974.

Wilder, Thornton. *Our Town*. In *Three Plays*. New York: Bantam, 1958.

Wilson, Edwin, and Alvin Goldfarb. *Living Theatre: A History*. 4th ed. Boston: McGraw Hill, 2004.

Wolterstorff, Nicholas. *Art in Action: Toward a Christian Aesthetic*. Grand Rapids: Eerdmans, 1980.

———. *Divine Discourse: Philosophical Reflections on the Claim That God Speaks*. Cambridge: Cambridge University Press, 1995.

Young, Karl. *The Drama of the Medieval Church*. 2 vols. Oxford: Clarendon, 1933.

Zizioulas, John. *Being as Communion*. Crestwood, NY: St. Vladimir's Seminary Press, 1997.

index